PERFORMANCE AND PRACTICE: ORAL NARRATIVE TRADITIONS
AMONG TEENAGERS IN BRITAIN AND IRELAND

For all my family, but especially my dad.

Performance and Practice: Oral Narrative Traditions Among Teenagers in Britain and Ireland

MICHAEL WILSON

Ashgate

Aldershot • Brookfield USA • Singapore • Sydney

© Michael Wilson 1997

Published by
Ashgate Publishing Limited
Gower House
Croft Road
Aldershot
Hants GU11 3HR
England

Ashgate Publishing Company
Old Post Road
Brookfield
Vermont 05036
USA

British Library Cataloguing in Publication Data

Wilson, Michael
    Performance and practice : oral narrative traditions
    among teenagers in Britain and Ireland
    1. Oral tradition - Great Britain 2. Teenagers - Great
    Britain - Social life and customs
    I. Title
    808.5 '43' 0835' 0941

Library of Congress Catalog Card Number: 97-74450

ISBN 1 84014 112 3

Printed and bound by Athenaeum Press, Ltd.,
Gateshead, Tyne & Wear.

Contents

Acknowledgements

During the preparation of this book I have received help and advice from many friends and colleagues. Some have read parts of the draft and commented upon it, some have helped with proof-reading and word processing, and others have simply been prepared to engage in debate and discussion with me on the subject or offer support and encouragement. I, therefore, owe a debt of gratitude to the following:

Béaloideas (University College Cork), Dr. Julia Bishop, Dr. Clodagh Brennan Harvey, Centre for English Cultural Tradition and Language (University of Sheffield), Department of Drama (University of Exeter), Dr. Oliver Double, Professor Bill Ellis, Dr. Ger Fitzgibbon, The Folklore Society, Geoff Fox, Iona Opie, Jon Primrose, Les Read, Betty Rosen, Professor Harold Rosen, Professor Peter Thomson, Jayne Tucker, Ulster Folk and Transport Museum, Professor John Widdowson, Professor Jack Zipes.

And, of course, all the libraries, schools and youth clubs, who invited me to work with them and all the individuals who told me their stories.

I am also grateful to Routledge for permission to reprint 'The Story of Grandmother' from *The Trails and Tribulations of Little Red Riding Hood* by Jack Zipes.

Preface

It is now over forty years since Peter and Iona Opie began collecting the folklore of children aged six to fourteen, which resulted in *The Lore and Language of Schoolchildren* (1959), followed by *Children's Games in Street and Playground* (1969) and *The Singing Game* (1985). What this present study is not intended to be is an update or replica of the work the Opies began in the 1950s, yet there are inevitably areas where the two studies overlap.

The Opies collected games, rhymes, songs, jokes, riddles, ignoring the more complex narratives which form the main body of the present study (although riddles and jocular tales take their rightful place), and they defined their informants as aged six to fourteen, whereas I have identified a specific narrative tradition belonging to the top end of their age range and beyond.

However, the most important similarity between the two studies lies in the motivation behind them and the perceptions of both the general public and sections of academia, of the subject matter. In the 'Preface' to *The Lore and Language of Schoolchildren*, the Opies tell of their experiences when embarking on their project.

.....we had first to find out what there was to find out, before we knew whether there existed a subject to study. The generally held opinion, both inside and outside academic circles, was that children no longer cherished their traditional lore. We were told that the young had lost the power of entertaining themselves; that first cinema, and now T.V. had become the focus of their attention, and that we had started our investigation fifty years too late (Opie and Opie, 1959, p.v).

The children who shared their lore with Peter and Iona Opie are now parents (and in some cases possibly the grandparents) of the teenagers who told me their stories, and yet in talking with adults (including other storytellers) about storytelling amongst teenagers, my experience is very similar to that of forty years ago. Nowadays, Sega and Nintendo computers can be added to the list of evils that focus young people's attentions away from their narrative traditions. Young people, I am told, no longer have the ability to concentrate for long enough to enjoy oral stories. They are eager, insatiable consumers of a mass, populist culture which appeals to their worst instincts. In the 1950s the Opies found that contrary to adult popular opinion, there was a huge wealth of oral culture being transmitted amongst young people on an everyday basis, and from my own work as a professional storyteller working with ideas of narrative with young people in schools, libraries and youth clubs, I was acutely aware that teenagers were continuing an oral narrative tradition in a very exciting manner, totally oblivious to whatever the adult population thought. Nevertheless, even when this was pointed out, the inclination amongst adults was to deride teenagers' stories as 'small, but amusing expressions of contemporary neurosis' (as one person described contemporary legends, which make up a significant part of the teenage narrative repertoire), and even when I mentioned this study to a fellow storyteller it was met with the comment, 'But it's not really folklore, is it?'

Such is the way that the older generation dismisses the oral culture of the younger one, and it is certainly probable that in another forty years time, those teenagers who talk to me today will be saying similar things about their own children and grandchildren. I suspect that such attitudes are more due to the inherent conservatism of older generations and their fear of change than anything else. The evidence suggests that it takes a lot more than a bit of technology and elder generation cynicism to undermine an oral tradition.

However it was partly due to the poor status (and even denial) of a teenage narrative tradition that I began to make albeit somewhat haphazardly, an archive of the short and extended narratives which I was being told by young people almost every working day. Steadily this archive grew. As the young people with whom I was working learned of my interest in their stories, the more they seemed to want to tell me.

At the same time there was a general renaissance of interest in storytelling and traditional arts and the number of professional storytellers began to grow rapidly. Nevertheless, I became aware that with this renaissance there was a resistance to any academic analysis of the art from a section of those involved in it. It was as if there was an anti-intellectualism at work within the new wave of interest.

Therefore, I hope this study will achieve two things on a practical level. Firstly, I hope it will give academic depth and wider breadth to the storytelling renaissance in this country and beyond, and secondly, I hope it will give the wealth of narrative amongst teenagers the status it deserves, and earn it its rightful place in an ongoing oral narrative tradition which stretches back many, many generations.

The organisation of the book

This book is divided into five sections. The first section is intended to set out the purposes, perameters and definitions of the study, to explain my approach to it and to validate the rôle of teenagers in an oral storytelling tradition.

The second section seeks to examine issues of relevance to folklore and performance studies but within the context of teenage narrative traditions. To this end the section begins by looking at storytelling as a communicative process in a performance-centred discipline. Other issues examined in this section include how stories circulate, why certain stories come in and out of fashion and the effect of performance on narrative believability, in addition to the rôle of violence and the supernatural within teenage stories and how the mass media and developments in communications technology both feed on and nourish a lively oral tradition.

The third section is a narrative-centred analysis in which I will turn my attention to specific stories and types of story. Firstly, there is an examination of how a variety of analytical approaches can show how a modern teenage story has drawn on a range of much older traditional tales during the course of its evolution. The second chapter in this section approaches from the opposite direction and shows how a well-documented traditional narrative has been modernised and adapted for a contemporary context. I will then turn my attention to two types of story which are not often thought of as being part of the teenage repertoire, and yet play a significant rôle in it. The first is the personal narrative and the second is the riddle, which is not always considered even as part of a narrative tradition. This section concludes with an attempt to draw together the various conclusions of the study and give coherence to the ideas that may be drawn from the work so far undertaken. It also looks towards the future and where further research in the field of teenage storytelling may concentrate.

The fourth section is an archive, a selection of texts that I have collected during the course of the study and is intended to illuminate and inform the main part of the book. (Texts within the archive that are referred to within the main text are marked with an asterisk and cited in the main text by

'Wilson' followed by the text number, e.g. 'Wilson 45'). This in turn is followed by a final section of further appendices and bibliographies.

I would finally like to clarify my own position in relation to this work. I come to this unashamedly from the discipline of drama and theatre studies, yet with a specific interest in popular and vernacular performance culture. It was this that originally led to my interest in folklore. It has always struck me as interesting that, considering our shared concerns about performative action, there is often a limited understanding by theatre and folklore scholars of each other's disciplines. In some ways this book attempts to straddle both those disciplines and indeed often encroaches on other disciplines, such as linguistics, education and sociology, and readers will no doubt recognise that this study adopts a broadly folkloristic methodology and framework of reference.

Nevertheless, it is primarily a book about *performance* and emanates essentially from a theatre studies viewpoint. I would hope, therefore, that my folklorist colleagues may forgive my occasionally explaining in some detail key folklore concepts which they may take for granted, yet may be unfamiliar to drama scholars - and, of course, vice versa. Any faults of this book in this respect are done purely in the spirit of interdisciplinary scholarship.

Part One
INTRODUCTION

1 Definitions, parameters and methodologies

As already stated in the 'Preface', my collecting of teenage oral narratives began in a somewhat haphazard way alongside my work as a professional storyteller. As a result the working methodologies evolved during the process and were adapted as the study progressed. I would, therefore, by way of introduction to the material, like to spend some little time setting the definitions and limitations of this study, specifically to define the terms 'teenage', 'oral', and 'narrative', and also look at some of the general problems of collection, transcription and classification.

Defining 'teenage'

When titling her latest book Iona Opie decided on *The People in the Playground* (Opie, 1993), because this was how the very people whom she was interviewing would describe themselves (Opie, 1993, p.vii). The seven to eleven year-olds whose games, songs, riddles and jokes she was collecting would, she found, always refer to their contemporaries as 'people'. Since she was writing a book about the oral culture of a specific group, then it seemed only right that this should also be reflected in the title, even though the term 'people' is so non-specific as to be of little use in defining the group. A similar process has gone into deciding on the term 'teenagers'.

In strictest terms teenagers are, of course, those aged between thirteen and nineteen, and yet this is not the exact range of my informants. I have collected material essentially from those people aged eleven to seventeen, in other words those people of secondary school age. This is partly because of the way in which the British education system generally divides children into pre- and post-eleven categories and the transition from one to the other is a major and significant one. Very often at the age of eleven, children are moved from a small, friendly, informal classroom situation, relatively free of timetable restrictions and where cross-curriculum teaching allows a close relationship to develop between pupil and teacher, to a secondary school, often ten or twelve times the size of their primary school, which is formal, regimented and impersonal. Such is the impact of this change that it is hardly surprising that it has a strong effect on social behaviour and is reflected in children's folklore. Therefore, there is something which is different between the stories told by secondary school pupils and those told by primary age children and that has not only something to do with age and onset of puberty and adolescence, but also is linked to environment.

However, although such a dividing line is significant and provides a convenient categorisation tool for the folklore collector, it must be exercised with a degree of caution. Although the transition into a secondary school environment is a major sea change in the lives of children and exposes them to regular contact with older, post-pubescent students, it would be wrong to assume that all contact with their pre-eleven world is lost. This is particularly the case in more rural areas where a higher degree of social intercourse between different age groups exists and where more often multi year classes exist in the village primary school. It is not unusual for a Year 5 pupil and year 6 pupil who were friends in the same class at primary school to continue their friendship after the older child has moved up.

I have, therefore, included a number of stories from children who are in their final year of primary education (Year 6). This seems appropriate not only for the reasons given above, but also because very often older siblings will retell stories which they have picked up at secondary school and these will then circulate for a while amongst the older pupils in the primary school playground. The issue is further complicated in areas which have middle schools (eight to thirteen year olds). It is not until Year 9 that pupils move on to upper schools for the final three years of their compulsory education. Middle schools are a mixture of the formality and informality of the two systems. This is not the place to discuss the merits of the Middle School, but it is clear that there are problems in drawing strict definitions. Additionally, pupils in the Republic of Ireland move up at twelve, rather than eleven. It is very difficult to draw clear lines as to when 'teenage' narratives begin to be told and there is an inevitable degree of overlap.

Nevertheless, the majority of stories I have collected seem to emanate from the eleven to fourteen age group (Years 7 to 9). This is partly due to the fact that it is these people with whom I am most often asked to work, but it is also interesting to note that in schools and youth clubs where I run open sessions, the greatest response comes from this same age group. It could be concluded that either the eleven to fourteen year olds are the most active storytellers, or they are the ones most willing to share their stories with me! I strongly suspect the latter.

I am, therefore, using the term 'teenage', not in the strictest sense of the word, but to mean those people from whom I have collected stories, primarily in the eleven to fourteen age range, but possibly as young as ten and as old as eighteen, because this, like Iona Opie's 'people', is a term with which they would most readily identify. It is their social behaviour and the stories they tell which define them as a group much better that any age limitations.

Defining 'oral'

Until relatively recently defining and identifying folklore was a reasonably simple matter on account of the fact that it was generally accepted that one of the most important criteria (if not the most important) for folklore was that it was orally transmitted. Francis Lee Utley emphasises that folklore is always orally transmitted and that it has ideally survived through at least three generations (Utley, 1965). Likewise the anthropologist William R Bascom also sees folklore as essentially dependent on oral transmission. All folklore, it is claimed, is transmitted orally, and yet all that is transmitted orally is not folklore (Bascom, 1965).

This is the traditional definition of folklore and for many years was adequate. However, the folk narrative is, like any other artistic construct, a product of its society, and the technological advances of recent years, which have made the world a smaller place, have meant that folklore can be transmitted via any number of media, including television, radio, film, literature, fax machine, and even the Internet. Therefore, over the past thirty years or so folklorists have had to redraw their definitions to include modern modes of transmission.

In his first book on contemporary legends, *The Vanishing Hitchhiker* (Brunvand, 1981), Jan Harold Brunvand recognises this development when he says, 'the important difference (is) that today's legends are also disseminated by the mass media' (Brunvand, 1981, p.5). Nevertheless, Professor Brunvand also recognises the importance of the oral element: 'Folklore, in short, consists of oral tradition in variants' (Brunvand, 1981, p.3).

In collecting teenage oral narratives I am concerned with any narrative that is told and retold in an oral (and often social) context and, indeed, that is the context in which the stories which are the subject of this study have been collected. The notion of 'purity' of the orally told story, however, becomes increasingly irrelevant, in that the stories may well have originated from a non-oral source, or been influenced as such along the road of its development.

An example of this is the famous ghost story, 'The Monkey's Paw', written by W W Jacobs (1863-1943), which is now well-established in a number of variants within the teenage oral tradition (see Wilson 48-49). They may be stories which have taken a circuitous route. The contemporary legend about alligators living in the sewers, the earliest recorded version of which Brunvand dates as 1935 (Brunvand, 1981, p.188), is also known among teenage storytellers in the 1990s, but they will often cite the source of the story as being a film or television show that use the same motif. Of course, film, television and literature often borrow heavily from folklore and then the stories re-emerge in a new oral variant. There are also stories such as 'The Mad Axeman' or 'The Boyfriend's Death' (Wilson 13-22) and 'The Golden Leg' (Wilson 1-3), which, despite having been published many times in written form, have continued to exist orally impervious to the literary versions of the tales.

It is, therefore, not so important where the stories come from in terms of their validity as folklore (although this may, undoubtedly, be of interest), but more important is what happens once that story enters into oral circulation. The oral tradition has a knack of imposing its own standards of quality and decency. Some stories may be told only once and be met with such a lack of enthusiasm that they will be consigned by the teller to the proverbial dustbin and never told again. However, the best stories will be absorbed into the oral tradition and be retold in any number of appropriate situations. It is a condition of the narratives I have collected that they have been told and retold more than once. It is only then that they can be considered to be in oral circulation and it is, of course, through continued retelling that new variants of the narratives emerge.

These stories generally fall into two categories. There are those stories which circulate freely amongst teenagers and are told by any number of people as a kind of communal social currency. Secondly, there are those stories which are told by only one teller, but told and retold by that teller on many different occasions. These stories tend to be either personal anecdotes and family lore which have found their way into a larger audience and are considered good enough to exist in a wider context, or they are very long and complex narratives, such as 'Tom Tit Tot' (Wilson 93) or 'The Golden Hairs of Knowledge' (Wilson 94). In the latter case these stories are often highly practised and told so expertly that any casual listener will not feel confident or capable of matching the teller's performance. In any case, these stories are often kinds of 'party pieces' and it is generally considered 'bad form' to appropriate one of those stories which is deemed to belong to someone else.

Once, whilst collecting stories at Falmouth Youth Club in Cornwall, I was told by a girl, albeit rather inexpertly and in a stumbling manner, a local ghost story. It was not until the end of the session that another girl approached me, 'That story,' she explained, 'is one of K–'s, and she tells it much better. And it happened to her!' Clearly some kind of social code had been broken.

One of the greatest problems in collecting stories is to decide whether the story you are being told is one that is genuinely in oral circulation (in either of the two ways previously outlined), or one that is being told purely for your benefit as a story collector and will never be told again. The best indicator here, I find, is the reaction of those other teenagers who will inevitably gather round to listen to a story being told. A reaction of 'Oh, this is a good one' or 'I've heard this one before!' is a sure sign that the story is in general circulation. Of course, even if the attendant audience has not heard that particular story before, I may be able to recognise it as a variant of another tale told elsewhere, or at least familiar motifs and structures which may suggest a folkloric dimension. In some rare cases, however, I may simply have to follow my instinct. This is occasionally the case when there is no attendant audience (apart from myself) to listen to the story. Through my experience of collecting stories from teenagers, I have had to follow my nose for a good story and try to sense whether a particular story has the right qualities for it to be worthy of a place in the oral tradition. Very often a hunch is borne out some weeks later when another variant of the same tale is heard in a different location.

In constructing my working definition of 'oral', therefore, I have recognised the fact that folklore may not solely be transmitted orally, yet the oral process has a vital rôle to play. In addition the criterion of repetition (by one or more tellers) is crucial, since it is through repetition that variants evolve, although verification of this can sometimes be problematic.

Defining 'narrative'

In drawing up these definitions I have taken a relatively wide view of narrative, albeit with some specific exclusions. Narrative is simply a series of linked ideas placed within a structure for the purpose of communicating an idea or series of ideas to another individual or group of individuals. In this sense a narrative can be as long and as complex as a novel, or it can be as short and as simple as a question and answer joke. Although these extremes could hardly be more different, they are both linked by virtue of being narratives.

Clearly there is a problem here. By this definition almost all human conversation could be classified as narrative, which in a sense is true, but it is a definition that is too wide for the purposes of this study. I have not concerned myself with the everyday exchanges of teenagers, except where those exchanges and anecdotes have been repeated and acquired a narrative structure and become part of folklore. It is, of course, just as easy for anecdotes to become folklore as it is for folklore to become anecdotes.

I have already explained that the criterion of repetition is important for the story to come under the term of this study, yet whilst trying to keep as wide a definition as possible there are some types of story which are also excluded. For example, I have not included jokes within this study, except when those jokes are of such a length and complexity that they could be classified as 'jocular tales'. Therefore, you will not find any 'knock-knock' jokes, but there are 'shaggy dog stories'. Whilst not denying that jokes are indeed valid folk narratives and play an important rôle in the teenager's narrative repertoire, there are two clear reasons why they are beyond the scope of this study.

Firstly, the field of the joke is so large and complex, not only in the amount of material in this area, which is constantly being added to, but also in terms of its types and functions, that for reasons of sheer manageability the joke deserves a study all of its own, and so falls outside the remit of this present work. Secondly, there is a conflict of interest here between my rôles of collector and storyteller. Most of the stories in the archive have been collected whilst on professional engagements in schools, libraries and youth clubs. Whilst it is always within my brief to encourage young people to tell stories for themselves, jokes can be a more sensitive issue.

As well as displaying inventiveness and wit, jokes can often be a vehicle for the most obnoxious and undisguised displays of racism and sexism. There may be a case for the folklorist to objectively collect such material for research purposes, but it is not acceptable for the professional storyteller to encourage such attitudes and even let such jokes go by without comment, since the performer must always have a relationship with the material. Therefore, I have felt it best to leave the joke alone, except as already stated, in cases where the joke is part of a longer, more complex narrative, and often defined by the teller as a 'funny story'.

Also excluded from this study are the songs and rhymes which constitute a large percentage of the Opies' work. These are undeniably folklore and often have narratives as well and yet they tend to play little part in the teenage lore. Perhaps it is because these rhymes and songs are often attached to certain games or rituals which are no longer performed beyond primary school, or perhaps it is because teenagers consider them too childish, but either way these things seem to be the domain of the younger child. Also, verse narrative is different from prose narrative in the sense that it is more tightly structured and therefore, prone to different pressures and factors of variation and transmission.

However there is an overlap with the work of the Opies in that I have also collected riddles, although I have limited them to true riddles (Opie and Opie, 1959, p.74) and logic riddles, which are particularly popular with teenagers and have a clearer and more definite narrative to them. I have not, however, included wellerisms - e.g. 'What did the big chimney say to the little chimney?' 'You're too young to smoke' (Opie and Opie, 1959, p.82) - which I have tended to think of more as jokes than riddles, although the line of definition is, admittedly, very fine.

I have also included superstitions within the scope of this study, but only those where a specific narrative is suggested. Therefore, I have not included superstitions of the type, 'walking under a ladder will bring bad luck', but I have included,

> Right, this is what my friend told me. He said that if you've got a post and you've got your partner the other side and you just link onto them and you just turn round and you say 'Black Jack' forty times, they say after you come home from school you've got a spirit called Black Jack following you and they say that he goes like that (storyteller squeezes shoulder), and then they say you look back and there's nothing there. (Wilson 80)

Also if someone were to tell me of an incident where, for example, a friend walked under a ladder and met with a catalogue of disasters, thus proving the old superstition, then this would also be included.

The main body of the archive is made up of ghost stories, family lore, local legends (both old and modern), riddles, jocular tales, anecdotal lore and even long traditional narratives. Indeed ghost stories are very prominent within the teenage narrative repertoire. Whilst it is true that ghost stories are very popular and, indeed, the supernatural and macabre are widespread throughout teenage lore, it would also be wise to exercise extreme caution if condemning teenage repertoire as being narrow. Such themes and motifs are also prominent in traditional folklore and teenagers will commonly classify a story as a ghost story, when in fact they are talking about something completely different. There have been numerous occasions when I have been promised a ghost story only to be told an urban legend, a superstition, or even a fairy tale. The problem is, of course, that stories can belong to more than one category. As I often say to classes of teenagers: fairy tales can be ghost stories too.

I have, therefore, in defining the parameters of the types of narrative to be included in this study, tried to be as open as possible, whilst at the same time keeping the material in manageable proportions. This study is intended to cover a wealth of developed narratives of varying length and complexity which are in oral circulation amongst those children of top primary and secondary school age.

Techniques and problems of collecting

When I first began collecting stories from teenagers I was doing it passively rather than actively. That is to say that I was not specifically encouraging teenagers to tell me their stories, but simply giving some space to those who wanted to share their stories within the context of my work as a storyteller. If, at the end of a session with a class of adolescents, nobody wanted to tell a story, then all very well, but if a group or an individual approached me, eager to tell, then I felt it was consistent with my rôle in encouraging a storytelling culture to allow that opportunity and to record their efforts. However, as I became more aware of the vein of untapped material that existed and I began to take my rôle as collector more seriously, then I began more actively encouraging teenagers to tell me their stories and would specifically ask them to tell me the stories they knew, so that I could record them. In addition, as my rôle as collector developed, then so did my techniques and my awareness of the issues involved. I began to allow more time within sessions for the collecting of stories and I would make more careful selections as to the stories I would tell myself. I began telling 'primer' stories, stories which I knew would begin to spark off other narratives from my teenage audience.

The material was, therefore, largely collected by myself when on engagements as a professional storyteller in schools, libraries and youth clubs after priming the audience with a couple of stories of my own. Where possible all stories were collected on audio cassette, which, of course, presented its own specific problems.

To some degree, however, these very problems also determined the techniques of collecting. For example, a classroom situation is a more threatening one to a teenage storyteller than, say, the youth club. Therefore, the classroom storyteller may need constant encouragement to tell a story in anything more than fragmentary form, whereas the youth club storyteller may well be in continual danger of being drowned out by an excitable and excited audience. While such audience participation and interruption may well be 'authentic' and an important part of the storytelling event, it does not make the job of the collector and, inevitably, the transcriber, any the easier.

I remember collecting stories from teenagers once at a youth club in Okehampton. The only place we were allocated for the storytelling was the sports changing rooms, whose acoustics had such an echo that when I later came to transcribe the material, the recording was largely useless, since not only did the echo render speech at a normal speed incomprehensible, but also any interruptions were so intrusive that it became impossible to decipher what was being said. Therefore, when I made a return visit to the club, we had to ensure that stories were told at an abnormally slow pace and that total silence from the audience was maintained throughout. The result was decipherable texts presented totally artificially. The quality of the storytelling event was sacrificed for the technical quality of the recording.

This intrusion of the collector and his/her equipment and requirements is the biggest issue for anyone involved in collecting folklore in the field. My own policy has been to minimise that intrusion, even if it means sacrificing the quality of the recording made. This is no simple matter, since it is quite natural for the collector to be the centre of attention. However, I have always tried, as much as is possible, to blend into the background even in a one-to-one situation, let the storyteller do all the talking and draw attention away from the tape recorder. To this end I have (nearly) always opted for a small hand-held recorder with a built-in microphone. These machines are about the size of a personal stereo, and take standard-size cassettes. Unfortunately, the quality of recording is very poor, especially when trying to record a group of people, and information is often lost because of it. The machines, however, are very compact and 'low-tech' and are easily forgotten when placed discreetly on a table. Although the quantity of information gained from a 'low-tech' recording is less, that information may be more useful as the equipment has been less intrusive.

Of course, even here, there is always some level of intrusion. The storyteller is always aware that s/he is being recorded - indeed it would be both morally and legally doubtful if s/he were not made aware of the fact - and the collector's presence is always a factor, no matter how invisible one tries to make oneself. No collector can ever remain neutral to the material being collected as the collector is always a constituent part (and often the most important part) of the context that determines the performance. As Lee Haring says in his study of the influence on performance of the interview situation; 'The interview itself becomes the present of the informant; content is determined by the present situation and the presence of the investigator' (Haring, 1972, p.383), and later the items the interviewer receives and decodes are selected by the performer on the basis of their appropriateness to that audience at that moment. Such a process of selection, being one of the circumstances making the storytelling event unique, determines what the interviewer records; thus the presence of the 'observer' determines the phenomenon observed (Haring, 1972, p.387).

This is made doubly so when, as in the case of my own collecting, the informants are told primer stories by myself. The stories I tell are always carefully selected to act as a catalyst for the telling of stories from their own repertoires, and those choices are always informed by my own knowledge and expectations of those repertoires. Therefore, the primer stories will inevitably influence the stories the teenagers tell, at least initially, and this must not be forgotten.

Of course, ideally there would be no need to tell any such primer stories, but the fact remains that adolescents are intensely private in their storytelling, and a level of trust needs to be established between collector and informant and the stories gently coaxed out of the latter. Primer stories are an effective way of doing this and probably the least intrusive, as the collector is then able to withdraw, if the primer stories have been effective, as the storytelling session gathers its own momentum and takes control of its own progress.

Edward Ives describes the collecting of material as a 'trialogue', saying that 'the informant will be performing for both you and the tape recorder' (Ives, 1980, p.53), and this is indeed the case. No field collector can totally eliminate his/her presence nor that of the recording equipment. All that can be done is to limit the intrusion as much as possible whilst recognising the extent of that intrusion and the influence it exerts over the collected material.

It is also important to remember that there is an innate desire on the part of the storyteller to please and do themselves justice. Therefore, any signs of approval or disapproval on the part of the interviewer will have a profound effect on what the performer chooses to disclose. I always try to maintain a low-key attitude of approval, irrespective of what is being told and how it is being told. Whilst a display of approval can serve to encourage and support the timid storyteller, it is also important to avoid placing value judgements on informants and their offerings.

Much also depends on how the interviewer is perceived by the interviewee. For example, whilst teenagers will quite liberally swear in each other's company, they will be far more guarded about their language in the presence of an adult for fear of reprimand. In spite of efforts to reduce my own status when collecting amongst teenagers, I cannot hide the fact that I am an adult, and this, I suspect, is a major contributory factor to the lack of swearing in the texts I have collected.[1]

The performer's relationship to the recording equipment is a further factor in determining what is actually collected. In my own experience, the presence of recording equipment with teenagers can have one of three possible effects. In an ideal situation, the informant is able to 'block out' the equipment and perform as 'naturally' as possible. This obviously requires a certain confidence, maturity and presence of mind, and also a recognition that a 'natural' performance is the one that is most desired by the collector. Some storytellers are better at doing this than others.

For some teenage storytellers, however, the presence of recording equipment is extremely intimidating. I have known the most eloquent storytellers clam up completely when confronted by a microphone of any sort, which is, of course, extremely frustrating for the collector.

I can remember collecting stories from a group of teenagers in the Forest of Dean, Gloucestershire, using a mini-disc recorder, which although compact and unobtrusive in itself and giving excellent recording quality, required the use of a microphone about three times the size of the actual machine. The resulting effect of this was that one gifted storyteller with a fund of stories to tell, refused to utter a word while the microphone was pointed at her. As soon as my attention was diverted she would begin telling stories in hushed tones to a small group of friends. During the course of three two-hour sessions that I spent with the group, I was only able to collect one short fragment from her.

On the other hand the presence of the 'high-tech' equipment captured the interest of some of the group and encouraged them to tell stories when otherwise they might not have done so. The very act of recording their efforts raised their status and esteem (and likewise the risks) in a way that encouraged some and discouraged others. Indeed some storytellers take the presence of recording equipment as an invitation to over-exaggerate their performances to sometimes pantomimical proportions. The use of video equipment, whilst providing the collector with additional information through the visual dimension, only seems to exaggerate these problems.

Indeed, since performance relies on the developing relationship between performer and audience, it seems that the collector and his/her equipment are often the most significant shaping element in that audience, so greatly influencing the performance, and this must always be borne in mind.

Limitations of the collection

It has never been my purpose to produce a definitive collection of stories from the teenage oral repertoire, but merely to collect enough material to provide a general overview of the situation and starting point for further study. In doing this it is, of course, important to recognise the limitations of the body of collected material, since the stories that I have gathered have been to some degree controlled by a number of factors.

As already mentioned, my own presence and the use of primer stories will have an influence on the material collected. Likewise, the fact that I was, whenever possible, making permanent recordings of the performance, inevitably influenced the choice of material. Time is a further significant factor, especially in school situations where much of the collecting was crammed into the short changeover period between lessons. Clearly these situations are not conducive to the collecting of long, complex narratives, and the storytellers are undoubtedly fully aware of this.

There is, in addition, an equally significant way in which I have unwittingly shaped the collection. It must be remembered that nearly all the stories have been collected during the course of my work as a professional storyteller. In other words the stories have been collected from those children at schools and youth clubs to which I have been invited. That is to say that, for example, I have collected a significant amount of material from Gillingham School in Dorset not because the pupils there are particularly prolific storytellers, although this may be the case, but rather because the school itself saw fit to ask me to visit on a number of occasions. The identity of those schools relies on a number of factors, such as the motivation of the staff and their prioritising of outside visits within their programmes. In my experience it is the children at schools and clubs run by well-motivated and interested staff that also have a greater self-confidence and willingness to tell stories. Of course, money is also a determining factor in whether I am asked to visit a particular institution. There is, therefore, a heavy weighting towards well-resourced schools in relatively affluent, middle-class areas. Visits to working-class schools and clubs tend to be concentrated more locally to myself, as travelling expenses can also be a costly burden to schools.

The third important element to be added to this equation is my own personal network of contacts, which largely determines the geographical areas in which I work. Understandably, I have a strong network of contacts in South-West England, but have also been able to develop work in both parts of Ireland. On the other hand, I have not as yet worked in Scotland, and so there is no material gathered from there (except, of course, where families have moved south of the border to areas I have visited). Appendix 4 shows the geographical distribution of schools, libraries and youth clubs where I have collected material with a county by county analysis of my visits.

As can be seen, although there is a wide geographical spread, there are significant omissions. This is not to say that my sample is unrepresentative, because I believe it is widespread enough for it not to be so, and there is also ample evidence to suggest that much of the material is universal but with local and individual embellishments. However, the lack of material from Scotland and Wales, is important to note, likewise the fact that the material from Ireland has been collected almost exclusively from the cities of Dublin, Cork and Derry, with little attention paid to more rural areas, particularly the Irish-speaking areas of the *Gaeltacht* in Western Ireland. There is also no material collected from inner city schools in London and particularly those with large multi-ethnic populations. Betty Rosen's account of working with storytelling in such a school (B. Rosen, 1988) is an indication of the exciting work still waiting to be done. Indeed none of these omissions negates the collection I have made, as such omissions are inevitable, but they rather point towards areas where future study might be directed. In fact, as a more integrated Europe looms on the horizon, this may offer further possibilities for comparative research.

Therefore, although there are discernible limitations to the material so far collected, and it is imperative that these be recognised, we must also accept that the net could be widened ad infinitum, and that remains the task of further research projects.

Methods of transcription

It may be rather obvious, but nonetheless significant for that, to note that none of the texts in this volume is in the original recorded form. They have all been through an additional dilutory process, namely that of transcription. The problem of representing oral speech in written form is one that has preoccupied folklorists and oral historians for many a long year. It seems that once again we are faced with another continuum of possibilities. On one end of the scale we have the approach best exemplified by the eighteenth and early nineteenth century collectors. Here, no attempt at all was made to represent the original oral versions, but instead the aim was to transform the material into well-crafted literary pieces for a largely bourgeois readership. To this end the material was ruthlessly edited and rewritten over numerous editions, different variants merged to make a single tale and so forth. The result was the modern literary fairy tale, far removed from the original oral folktale (see Zipes, 1992, p.7).

On the other end of the scale we have the sort of verbatim transcripts which attempt to capture every single nuance of the original oral version, employing phonetic script to capture variation of dialect and a series of signs and symbols to denote rhythm, pause, cadence, pitch etc. This is all backed up by comprehensive contextual notes and a visual record of the performance. Both extremes have their advantages as well as their disadvantages, and each fulfils quite opposite functions.

The literary text will be accessible and readable and ideal for the general reading public wanting to acquaint itself with folktales. However, this is of little use to the modern folklorist who requires as full and accurate a record of a single storytelling performance as possible, in order to provide a correct analysis of the performative dynamics and consequent textual meanings. On the other hand the verbatim text so cherished by the scholar can be impenetrable and of little value to the lay reader.

It would appear that with the passage of time folklorists have gradually moved towards the verbatim text. Already by the end of the nineteenth century, although many folklorists were still rewriting the stories into literary pieces, some effort was at least being made to reflect the dialect and oral speech patterns of their informants. Over the last twenty or thirty years, as folklore studies have moved towards performance theory, the verbatim text with full contextual notes has been increasingly favoured.

Bill Ellis puts forward a powerful argument for the full text, showing how texts can easily be misinterpreted through lack of contextual information (Ellis, 1987). Ellis's argument is that

> it makes little sense to consider the legend a text apart from its performance. The interaction that precedes, follows, and often interrupts the telling is as central to the event's meaning as the plot alone (Ellis, 1987, p.34).

There is no argument to be had with this, and this study of teenage narratives has served to emphasise the validity of Ellis's case. Ellis also notes that, although verbatim texts are often espoused by scholars, a certain amount of editing would appear to be standard. Ellis criticises both Brunvand for his extensive use of summaries, in spite of his claim that 'verbatim oral texts from their natural contexts, along with background information about storytellers and listeners, are the basis for reliable interpretations of folk stories, meanings and functions in the societies in which they are found' (Brunvand, 1981, p.23), and Ives for proposing that verbatim texts are unnecessary, since folklorists requiring detailed information about a particular performance should always return to the original recording as the best available source of reference.

Ives, however, has a point. The performance is, of course, the ideal, and a recording is not the performance itself, but merely a representation of it. Furthermore the recording only contains a fraction of the information associated with that performance, namely that which is spoken. It contains no visual information, no background information on the performers and audience, very little contextual information etc.. The transcription is yet a further distillation of this. Therefore, Ives concludes, even the most accurate transcription can only ever be third best to the original performance and second best to the recording and thus a waste of time and effort.

The debate between Ellis and Ives on this matter must, nevertheless, be qualified. Ives, it must be remembered, is primarily concerned with the interview as a means of gathering information, whereas Ellis is interested in the storytelling performance and surrounding event. That is to say that Ives is concerned, not with the performance, audience interaction and social context that generates it, but rather with the information that can be gleaned from the shared material. The intricacies of performance are important to Ives only in order to clarify the information being presented by the informant. Ellis, on the other hand, focuses his efforts on the social construct of the storytelling act. For him it is not the material that is important (he is presumably collecting stories that he has heard on many previous occasions), but the way it is presented and the dynamics of performance that influence the entire process. It can, therefore, be understood why, for Ives, the transcript is merely a rough guide to the primary source of the recorded interview and unnecessary in a verbatim form, whilst for Ellis it is a way of recording and interpreting vital contextual information not always present on the tape.

Ellis's own definition of verbatim includes the non-linguistic features of performance, but he is essentially working towards an ideal, envied by us all, but in practice rarely realised. To produce the sort of texts that Ellis encourages us to would require at least two video recorders (one for the performer and one for the audience), and such a level of technology is neither practical nor possible. It is also very often not even desirable. As Ellis readily agrees 'the act of recording inevitably influences the performance itself' (Ellis, 1987, p.36).

If, during a session at a busy youth club, a teenager were to approach me and begin spontaneously telling a story, would I stop him/her, try to silence the background noise from the table tennis players and the record player, set up complicated equipment and ask for a repeat performance, or would I simply reach for my small recorder, whilst maintaining eye contact and try to get the clearest sound with all the background activity still going on? Of course, I could try the former approach, but the verbatim text I might then be able to produce would not necessarily be more useful or more accurate, because the authenticity of performance would be lost. In our quest for maximum information, we must exercise extreme caution that the information we are receiving is the information we want. For my part, I would tend towards the latter approach, preferring to struggle with a poor quality recording made in 'natural' circumstances. Ellis freely admits that 'the performance recorded in so limited a form may be far more spontaneous and natural than that captured by videotape recorder' (Ellis, 1987, p.36).

The same is true of summaries. In my experience it is not uncommon for a teenager to rush up at the end of a session, quickly tell a story and then disappear, all before I have even had a chance to reach for my tape recorder. It is the bane of the folklorist's life that much of the most interesting material is communicated when the tape recorder has been switched off. This, however, should not be an excuse for discarding that material, but, instead, of trying to make the best of it in far from ideal circumstances. I would jot down a summary as soon after the event as possible, noting any figures of speech and turns of phrase that had stuck in my mind from the performance.

It is not that summaries are of no use to the folklorist, but that they are of limited use. Whilst they offer us no information at all (or very little) on the performance itself, they do provide us with information on plot, character, setting and narrative sequence, which is of some value. I would argue that this is far better than simply discarding otherwise important material, simply because it does not measure up to the exacting standards of the fully verbatim transcription.

The problem occurs when we try to pretend that a particular text is something which it is not, for example, drawing conclusions about a performance from a summary. As long as we recognise our information for what it is, it is the lot of the folklorist to make the best analysis from limited resources. As Brunvand says, 'it should be the goal of all present and future collectors to secure the fullest possible data in stories and the human sources' (Brunvand, 1981, p.23), and yet 'with incomplete data, some worthwhile conclusions......are possible when existing information is evaluated and compared' (Brunvand, 1981. p.23).

There is a further, totally practical, argument around the verbatim text, and that is the question of time taken to produce such transcripts. It is extremely time-consuming to note down every small detail of a particular telling and, when dealing with a large volume of texts, as is the case with this study, it is impractical to produce fully verbatim transcriptions. Since one of my declared aims here is to provide a sizeable range of material to give a general overview of a situation relatively neglected by folklorists, it became a practical

18

consideration to keep the task of transcription in manageable proportions. It may well be appropriate for future research to concentrate in more detail on a much more restricted number of texts, and then the use of verbatim texts would be not only desirable but essential. However, in the meantime, in this volume, will be found two types of text.

The summary

This is where a story has been told and for whatever reason, a recording has not been possible. Instead I have tried to write down as accurate a rendition of the telling as possible, including any special linguistic features that were noteworthy. Of course, this is based entirely on my own memory and the accuracy depends both on how soon after the telling I was able to construct the summary and also how many other stories were told me at the same time. If it was told in isolation, then there is a much greater chance of my remembering the details of the narrative. Therefore, some summaries are more detailed and of greater use than others. They do not claim to give much, if any, information on the performative aspects of the text, but merely comment on plot, structure, character and narrative sequence.

The edited transcription

The edited transcription is not a verbatim text, as Ellis would define it, but it probably is more faithful to the recording than that which Ives would propose. There has been no paraphrasing, and indecipherable phrases and words have been left out in favour of a series of full stops superscripted by a question mark. Occasionally I have added my own suggestions for missing words in brackets. Certain linguistic devices and strategies such as 'you know' and 'like' have not been removed; likewise, repetition and corrections also remain in the texts. All that has been removed are unintentional stumbles and hesitations ('er', 'um' etc..). There is also no indication as to length of pauses, although where there has been an intentional pause for dramatic reasons, this has been noted by a series of dots. I have also not employed a scheme to denote variations in pitch, slides and slurs. However, words which are uttered intentionally loudly, such as 'jumps' at the end of ghost stories, appear in capital letters.

It is also important to note that oral speech does not follow the same paragraphing as written text. Therefore, in transcribing texts, I have begun new paragraphs wherever there has been an ellipsis in the narrative. That is to say that, whenever the storyteller has included an intentional pause with the purpose of denoting a progression of the narrative in either time or place, then I have begun a new paragraph. Thus, paragraphs often begin with 'well' or 'so' to indicate such a narrative progression. This is, of course, a performance strategy, and it can be seen from the texts that some storytellers make greater use of it than others.

For both summaries and edited transcriptions I have tried to indicate all other contextual notes within the annotations accompanying each text.

Concluding remarks

My intention is that this brief introduction has laid bare the problems encountered and methodologies adopted in collecting, transcribing and organising the stories which are the subject of this study, and made clear the limitations of the collection as a whole. However, I also hope that they are seen as an accurate survey of the situation, at the time of writing, of teenage oral narrative traditions and practices in Britain and Ireland. Nevertheless, it is both a reward and a frustration that, as I have been recording in the field, I have become increasingly aware of the vast quantity of work that remains to be done. It seems that the more you find out, the more there is to be found out! My intention is that debate around teenage storytelling will continue and other scholars may feel able to fill in the many gaps in scholarship that still exist. However, I hope that this study represents a valuable contribution to that debate, especially in terms of the interdisciplinary connections between folklore, popular culture and performance theory and teenage and adolescent culture in general.

With the accompanying texts I have attempted to maintain the highest possible standards of accuracy in the circumstances. I have tried to tread the fine line between textual accuracy and contextual authenticity and I hope that I have succeeded more often than I have failed. Of course, everybody has their own idea of where the balance should be struck, and while most decisions have been made on the spur of the moment in complex fieldwork situations, taking into account a whole range of different and opposing factors, we are all striving towards the same ideal. I have merely tried to recognise the context of each individual telling and recording and attempted to work with it.

Note

[1] I am reminded of this by a personal experience. Let me quote from my own fieldwork notebook.

After one lad had told me a story, he said, 'I've got another one.'
'Great!' I said.
'But it's rude.'
'That's all right,' I said. 'I don't mind.'
But after a moment's thought he shook his head.
'No,' he said with a sheepish grin, and disappeared.

Part Two
ISSUES

2 Aspects of performance in teenage storytelling

It is perhaps not our first instinct to think of storytelling as a performance art, but rather as a literary one. In our late twentieth-century environment we are engaged in a constant drive to organise, label and compartmentalise. Even in terms of oral storytelling we can listen to the text, collect it, edit it and publish it. Until relatively recently the study of folklore has been essentially a text-based discipline, hence the numerous publications of texts, which bear little or no reference to the collector's informants and the circumstances under which they were gathered. We can, of course, by means of the text understand the story as a piece of literature. However, over the last twenty years or so progress has been made in folkloristics towards a more performance-centred approach (see Ben-Amos and Goldstein eds., 1975, pp.1-7), and more recently, with the renaissance of interest in storytelling and the rise of the professional storyteller, we have begun to appreciate his/her art in its performative mode. We can now go to our local arts centre or theatre and enjoy a concert from a professional storyteller, and this fits in nicely with our own understanding and expectations of what performance actually is; we purchase our ticket, sit in our seat and wait for the lights to dim and the show to begin. The event is the performance itself and the storyteller will employ all the devices and techniques any solo performer could be expected to employ. We can, therefore, easily come to an understanding that the (professional) storyteller is engaged in both a literary and a performance-based discipline.

This is all very well, but this simply begs another question. Storytelling is the art form of social interaction and we are all commonly engaged in such activity, because it is through the creation and re-creation of narratives that we give meaning to our experiences, hopes, fears, desires and expectations. In the words of Terry Eagleton, 'We cannot act or desire except in narrative' (Eagleton, 1981). Likewise Jerome Bruner proposes that humankind possesses 'a readiness or predisposition to organise experience into a narrative form' (Bruner, 1990, p.45). This is indeed Harold Rosen's 'impulse to narrative' (H. Rosen, 1988, p.168). To what degree then can we consider such social and conversational storytelling as a performance art?

Let us take the example of two people exchanging personal experience stories on a bus. Storytelling it certainly is, and yet if such storytelling is performance, then a) it does not correspond to any of our other notions, experiences and expectations of performance, as generally defined by a visit to the performance site, and b) the participants (both alternating rôles of teller and listener) are probably blissfully unaware of it. Is performance, therefore, always a conscious mode of expression, or can a performance still take place without either the performer or audience being actively aware that a performance is taking place? To answer this we must return to the beginning and consider what it is we actually mean by performance.

If there is one thing which connects the professional storyteller in the provincial arts centre with the conversational storyteller on the bus, it must be orality; the very fact that their stories are being told. They are both communicating a narrative to an audience through oral language and accompanying gesture (where necessary) in a manner that by its very nature is ephemeral and shaped by a number of factors which are external to the text of the story itself. That story may well be told again, but no matter how many times it is told, it will never be told in exactly the same way, because the circumstances under which the story is being told will never be repeated.

When Peter Brook talks of performance he defines it as a man[1] walking 'across (this) empty space whilst someone else is watching him, and this is all that is needed for an act of theatre to be engaged' (Brook, 1972, p.11). For Brook, who is busy assembling an argument for us to consider theatre in its basic state, stripped bare of all its contemporary trappings (set, lights, costume, etc), this definition may serve very well, but unfortunately as a definition of performance, it is somewhat lacking.

Let us again take our example of the two people on the bus. To give Brook his due, he has identified one very important aspect of performance, namely that two of its essential ingredients are performer and audience. Without either of these, performance cannot happen. This is because performance is first and foremost about communication, communication between (at least) two persons. It is not, as Brook would have it, about entering empty spaces. In our bus example, the storyteller does not need to enter the space before the story can begin; both storyteller and audience share the same space and may well indeed have been occupying that space for some time before one began telling a story to the other. Admittedly, entering the space may be a part of a performance, but it is not integral to it, because performance is a communicative mode and 'the entire network of cultural communications has its rules of appropriateness' (Ben-Amos and Goldstein eds., 1975, p.4).

This is much more in line with theories of folklore developed along socio-linguistic lines by, among others, Richard Bauman (cf. Bauman, 1977) and Dell Hymes, who notes, 'The notion of performance is central to the study of folklore as communication' (Hymes, 1975, p.11). What this means in practical terms is that whenever a communication enters its performative mode then certain rules and conventions which govern that mode will come into play, irrespective of whether the performer and audience are aware that they have entered that particular mode. In this sense, therefore, it is not vital that participants are conscious of the performative mode in operation for a performance to take place (although awareness may conceivably result in a better quality of performance). For the performer these conventions will mean that s/he will take control of the conversation, take responsibility for shaping it, telling the story well and, of course, entertaining the audience, for it is at least partly through the enjoyment factor that the audience will evaluate the performance. In order to do this, the storyteller will employ any number of techniques, including a heightening or formalisation of language or gesture, voice variation, maintaining of eye contact and a careful management of information. For their part the audience will afford the performer their attention, resist interruptions, allow themselves to be led by the storyteller, surrendering control to him/her and, upon conclusion, making an evaluation of that performance in terms of its competence and the enjoyment factor.

This is true of all performance, as much of our bus-storytellers as of a professional storyteller in a recognised arts venue or even a night at the National Theatre. Admittedly, a performer is far more likely to be interrupted if they are engaged in conversational performance than is an actor at the National, but interruptions will only occur in order to add to the performance, or when it is deemed necessary, because it is merely the intensity at which the performative mode of communication is operating that controls the extent to which the conventions of the mode may be broken. At this point the following model of the performative mode may be useful.

The performance continuum

CONVERSATION------------------CULTURAL PERFORMANCE[2]
<-teenage narrative-> <-professional storytellers->
The Cloakroom   Halloween Party   Theatres
School Bus   Camp Fire Session   Arts Centres

e.g. at the bus-stop   e.g. at the theatre

LOW INTENSITY-------------------------HIGH INTENSITY
informal   formal

By using the above model we can see that our bus storytellers would be engaged in informal, low-intensity performance, where the conventions of the mode are weaker, whilst the professional storyteller at the arts centre is engaged in formal, high-intensity cultural performance, where the conventions are strong and strictly adhered to. Nevertheless, we can see that all storytelling is, in fact, performance and that it is this very thread which binds together narration in its many forms.

Furthermore, Bauman draws our attention to another peculiarity of the performance mode of communication, and that is its invitation to the audience to discover a sub-text in the performance. When we see a play, we are not only being told the story of that play, but we are also being invited to read other, subliminal messages into it. For example, *King Lear* is not just a story about a king who goes mad and falls out with his daughters, but also contains messages about trust, family and sanity/wisdom, and we are invited to read those messages and interpret with reference to our own experience.

Likewise, when we are told a story, be it at high- or low-intensity, the message is communicated that there is more to this tale than meets the eye. There is a purpose behind its telling; the story is being told because it strikes some chord of truth within us; it is, after a fashion, a comment on some (possibly insignificant) aspect of contemporary life. In some way it speaks to our inner psyche. It is what may be called the *latent truth* of a story.

We must now ask ourselves the question: at what point does conversation, or indeed any communication, enter its performative mode? It is clear that not all conversation is performance, for example exchanging pleasantries about the weather does not in itself constitute performance, although telling a story of being stranded in a blizzard does, and yet certain things happen in the relationships between performer, audience and language/narrative when the performative mode is in operation. At some point a signal is sent to the audience by the performer that changes the mode of communication. This is, of course, metacommunication, a piece of communication which communicates about communication. In other words, a communication which tells us that the following communication will be operating in the performative mode, and thus, as outlined above, certain rules are going to apply, certain things will be expected of us as an audience, and in return, we may expect certain things of the performer.

This argument becomes much clearer if we begin by looking at those metacommunicative signals which are associated with cultural performance. If we go to see our professional storyteller at the arts centre, the audience will enter and take their seats. It is clear that the performance has not yet begun, no signal has been given, and the audience are free to engage in conversation, read their programmes, buy a drink, etc. However, at some point a signal, or series of signals will key the performance. The house lights may dim, the stage lights may brighten, the stage curtains may open, the performer may be introduced by a compère. In the (bad) old days the orchestra at the theatre would even have played the national anthem. The chatting immediately stops and all attention is focused on the performer, because all these signals are communicating one thing; we are just about to enter the performative mode of communication and we must all behave according to the conventions!

The communication between performer(s) and audience will continue to operate in its performative mode until a further metacommunicative signal is given which ends it. In terms of the theatrical cultural performance this may be the dimming of the stage lights, the raising of the house lights, the closing of the stage curtain and so on (in fact the reversal of the conventions which have signalled the start of the performance; a neat symmetry). At this point the rules which have been governing the communication are abandoned and it reverts to its previous mode.

At the other end of the scale there are also metacommunicative signals which key an informal, conversational performance. These are not so stylised and are less so the more informal and conversational the performance. For example, at its most informal, the story may be keyed by something as simple as 'well...' or 'Now then...'.

As insignificant and inoffensive as this may seem, it is still, within the terms of the communication, a signal that the speaker is about to begin telling a story, a performance, and once again the same set of rules and conventions come into play. Of course, as explained earlier, the lower the intensity of the performance, the less strictly these rules will be enforced by performer and audience.

As a storytelling performance becomes more formal and more conscious of itself, the keying formula will become more stylised. A little further up the scale, the story may be introduced with 'I know one like that...' or 'That reminds me of the time...' and so on. If we move yet further up the scale towards the cultural performance, where storytelling is formalised, this is where the more recognisably traditional keying formulae may be used, such as 'Once upon a time...'.

In the same way the performance will be concluded with another metacommunicative signal ranging from, for example, '...and there you go!' to '...and they lived happily ever after', depending on the intensity at which the performance has been operating.

We can see, therefore, that it is the thread of performance that links the everyday, informal storytelling of conversation to the highly stylised, formal storytelling of the theatre and the professional storyteller, and moreover it is the context in which these performances take place that very much influences the way in which the story is told, the intensity at which the performance mode operates.

Paraperformance: a definition

If we are to accept that storytelling, even as a means of social discourse, is performance, in the sense that when a person begins to tell a story the performance is keyed by one or more metacommunicative means, and this in turn imposes a performative frame (and all its implications) upon that discourse, then we must also consider the various elements which together constitute the notion of performance.

According to Richard Bauman (cf. Bauman, 1977) performance consists of both artistic action and artistic event, in other words it is a combination of what the performer actually does and the context in which it is done. In order to clarify our terms I shall henceforth refer to artistic action as performance and the combination of action and event as total performance.

Furthermore, in terms of storytelling, we can, with a little help from Harold Rosen (H. Rosen, 1985, p.34) break down performance into three distinctive elements, namely story (the sequence of events and actions about to be narrated), narrative discourse (the framework or text into which the story is fitted) and narrating (the process by which the narrative discourse is communicated). The relationships of these three elements is shaped and influenced by artistic event, which, for reasons outlined below, I shall henceforth refer to as *paraperformance*.

Paraperformance is essentially all those elements which together constitute the context in which a performance takes place. John McGrath is quite right when he points out that total theatrical language does not only include the various ingredients of performance, set, properties, lighting, music, etc., but also

> the nature of the audience, the nature, social, geographical and physical, of the venue, the price of tickets, the availability of tickets, the nature and placing of the pre-publicity, where the nearest pub is, and the relationships between all these considerations themselves and of each with what is happening on stage (McGrath, 1981, p.5).

This is, of course, also the case with a storytelling performance and precisely that to which Bauman alludes. However, I have shied away from the term event to mean paraperformance because event is an element of paraperformance rather than paraperformance itself. Event can be used to label the social structure in which performance takes place, for example, at a sleep-over party, at a past-lights-out storytelling session on school camp, etc. Storytelling may in fact only be one of a number of sub-events at such an event, along with, for example, eating, putting more wood on the fire, etc. In addition to this we must also take into account the further elements of paraperformance, such as those outlined by McGrath.

Bauman's use of the term 'event' is also inappropriate because it suggests a certain grandeur, or at least a clear consciousness on the part of performer and audience that a performance is actually taking place. Since we have already established that storytelling can often happen in a social and conversational way, when the performative frame is operating at its lowest intensity, it is also reasonable to suppose that the participants in a storytelling performance may not actually be consciously aware that, beyond the imparting of information, an event is indeed taking place.

Let us take the example of somebody telling a personal experience story to an acquaintance at a bus-stop. Whilst we can, as outsiders, recognise the performative frame in operation and identify its components, the teller and listener may not be aware of it, as it would only be subconsciously influencing and controlling their physical and linguistic behaviour. Moreover, in this example we must also take into account a further element of paraperformance; the weather. Whether it is pouring with rain or blowing a gale is, of course, likely to have a profound effect on all elements of performance.

Paraperformance is, therefore, all those elements which are not part of the performance itself, but surround the performance, shaping and influencing it; event, venue, nature of audience, time of day, time of year, weather, to name a few. When paraperformance is combined with performance the result is total performance.

31

A brief contextual study

I would now like to analyse two versions of 'The Vanishing Hitchhiker' bearing in mind the aforementioned theories of performance and how texts can be shaped by the various elements of paraperformance. I have chosen this particular story partly because it is so widespread - Brunvand calls it 'the classic automobile legend' (Brunvand, 1981, p.24) - and partly because, if my memory serves me correctly, it was the first contemporary legend that I heard as a teenager in the mid-seventies. It is also a story which has been widely documented and analysed and thus, in our analysis of it in performance, we need not be distracted by the need to establish its pedigree as an old traditional tale[3].

Both versions I shall quote here were collected by myself from teenage storytellers at different times under different circumstances and conditions. The first telling (Wilson 7) was collected on 11 November 1992 from Alex Cossley, a twelve-year old boy from Gillingham School in Dorset. At this time I was visiting the school in my rôle as a professional storyteller, working with the children on stories and telling them a wide range of tales from a variety of traditions. In the morning I had spent an hour with Alex's class and, as I always do with secondary school students, at the end of the session I issued an invitation for anybody who had a story to tell me to find me during the lunch hour, when I would be delighted to record their story. Alex was one of a number of students who joined me in the school library that lunchtime to swap stories. During the session, about twelve storytellers came forward to tell their tales, although there were probably no more than four people, along with myself, present at any one time.

The context of the second telling (Wilson 8) was very different. This was collected from Catherine Wriggle, aged about fourteen, at Falmouth Youth Club, Cornwall, on 9 March 1993 in the presence of three or four of her female friends, myself and Sally Tonge, Literature Development Worker for Cornwall. This was my second visit to the club and was the first of two sessions I did there as part of a mini-project aimed at collecting the club members' oral stories and working with them on producing a modest booklet of those stories for sale and distribution amongst the wider community in Falmouth. It was a project which was a joint initiative between the Literature Development Worker Project and Falmouth Youth Services and followed on the heels of a successful session in December 1992. The telling took place in a relaxed atmosphere in a room furnished with bean bags and, apart from the appearance of the occasional boy, seemed to be an exclusively female (apart from myself) affair.

Here are the two versions:

Story A

> One day there was this man and this woman, married, and driving down
> the road in their car and they seen this girl on the side of the pavement
> and she looked like she needed help, so they picked her up and asked her
> where she wanted to go and she said, 'Can I go home?' So they asked
> her where her home was and she told them, so they took her there. They
> didn't actually go in, but the girl knocked at the door and she walked
> indoors.
>
> But that night they wondered what had happened to her, so they
> decided to go back the next morning and they went back, knocked on
> the door and this old lady came out and said, 'Come in.' And the man
> and the woman go, 'We sent a girl in here last night, we picked her up
> off the side of the road.' And she showed them this photo and it's a
> picture of the girl and she said, 'She's been dead for thirteen years!'

Story B

> There was this man and he was going out in his car and there was this
> really pretty girl, blonde hair and everything, y'know - all the works!
> And she's hitchhiking, and so he decides to give her a lift.
>
> And they were talking and he dropped her off and she must have left
> her wallet or something.
>
> Anyway, he was going along again and he gave this man a lift.
>
> So he handed it in to the police - the wallet - and said, 'Oh, I gave this
> young lady a hitch-hike and she left her wallet.' And he goes, 'Oh,
> thanks,' or something like that.
>
> And so they phoned the parents and they said, 'Our daughter's been
> dead for seven years!'

Let us first consider Alex's story (Story A). The situation immediately prior
to Alex's telling is that somebody else has just finished telling another story.
It may well be that the previous story has reminded Alex of 'The Vanishing
Hitchhiker', but in any case there will have been some brief discussion of the
previous story, (an evaluation by the other listeners, for instance and/or an
attempt by myself to ascertain the source of the narrative), and certainly Alex
will have been identified as the next storyteller. The audience are already
waiting for Alex to begin, and so it might be expected that he needs to do

very little in terms of signalling the beginning of his story and the departure into the performative mode of communication.

Nevertheless, Alex must give some signal to his audience, he must use 'a structured set of distinctive communicative means... in culturally conventionalised and culture-specific ways to key the performance frame' (Bauman, 1977, p.16). In this case, because his audience is already waiting, Alex can do this quickly, yet he still does it formally with the words, 'One day...'. Although at first sight this may seem to have more to do with the setting of the scene within which the story takes place, it is, in fact, first and foremost, a piece of metacommunication. It is one of Bauman's 'special formulae' (Bauman, 1977, p.21) which serve to key the performance. It is a phrase which belongs to the same group of conventional story openings any professional storyteller might employ, such as, 'Once upon a time...', 'There was and there was not...' and 'Not in my time, nor your time, but in somebody else's time...', and yet it does not have the same implications. By saying 'One day...' Alex gives a clear signal to his listeners that his performance has begun, yet he does not place his story within the realm of the traditional tale, as indeed 'Once upon a time...' would, but also there is enough formality in the opening to raise his narrative above the merely anecdotal. Thus, by formally placing his narrative in the recent past he gives it a certain status and weight, whilst arguably sacrificing some of the authentication which an anecdotal angle may give it. We can see, therefore, that even by the first two monosyllabic words, Alex has set the tone and his audience's expectations for the rest of the story.

This is indeed how the story progresses, with a certain air of formality, authority and propriety. The story tells us that the car is occupied by a couple, a man and a woman (it is, incidentally, more usual for the car to be driven by a lone male traveller), and yet this is not the usual couple to be found in teenage narratives, the boyfriend and girlfriend, out driving in search of sexual adventure. Alex goes to some length to impress on us that in this story the couple are married, everything is above board. The positioning of the word 'married' in the text simply serves to emphasise this fact. Alex then goes on to give us further proof, if any were needed, of the altruistic and selfless world these people inhabit. In Alex's story there is in fact no hitchhiker (undeserving poor), but a girl who appears to be injured and in need of help (deserving poor). In true Christian style the Samaritans stop to offer help and so take the injured girl back to her home.

Once again the story differs from the usual in that their passenger is safely delivered home; there is no disappearance, no possession left behind in the vehicle, in fact nothing to prompt the travellers to visit the house the following day, nothing except their altruistic concern for their passenger's well-being. It is only then that the girl's identity as a ghost is authenticated through the photograph.

None of this is at all surprising, given the paraperformative details of the story. Gillingham is a relatively middle-class, wealthy market town in the heart of conservative, southern England. It is, in fact, a place which is inhabited, as is Alex's story, by 'decent' people. The characters in this story reflect the same morals to which the people in Alex's community would subscribe in an ideal world; Christian, middle-class and free of crooks, scroungers and unmarried lovers. In addition to this, the story was told at school on a day when I was a visitor to that school. Not only does the context of school dictate a certain code of behaviour, but also I was there as a figure of authority, a member of the teaching establishment, however much I might try to behave otherwise. Alex would, therefore, be sensitive to the idea of not overstepping the mark with me - there are things which he would not say or allude to in my presence which would be perfectly acceptable in the company of his friends. This is further reinforced by the fact that the performance took place in the school library, a setting which also demands a certain element of restraint and control on behaviour. In some ways we were more on my home ground than his.

It is also worth mentioning my own rôle in all this as a professional storyteller. As I have said, I had already told stories to Alex and his friends that morning in class and so he was very much aware that, in telling a story to somebody who made his living from such activity, he would not only be laying open his narrative for assessment, but also his narrating. Therefore, Alex is concerned with turning out a high standard of performance, and one way he does this is by formalising the telling of his story and increasing the intensity of the performance mode. It is a performance that is conscious of itself and is trying to raise the performer's own status with the 'guest' and within his own peer group through it. In this way it can be seen clearly how the text and the telling of a story (performance) can be shaped by the circumstances and context of that performance (paraperformance) to result in total performance.

Let us now compare Alex's story to Catherine's story, which was told under markedly different conditions. The circumstances immediately preceding Catherine's telling (Story B), however, would have been similar to those preceding Alex's. Once again Catherine's story may well have been triggered by the previous story and certainly she had already volunteered to tell the story before she actually began - she did not simply interrupt the conversation with her story. The audience were already listening to and focusing on the storyteller and so Catherine needed only a very limited, low-profile keying for her performance. This is done with the phrase 'There was…' which is again a formula in the tradition of 'Once upon a time…' and in its subtle way signals the start of the performative mode. There is, of course, a purpose for this subtlety, because it is in line with the very conversational style of the storytelling, the low-intensity of the performative mode, as we shall see later on in this analysis.

However, let us first look at the major protagonists in Catherine's story, because there are fundamental differences from those in Story A. This time the story follows the usual pattern of a lone male traveller, which of course introduces a whole new dimension to his stopping for the hitchhiker, namely that of the possibility of procuring sexual favour. Furthermore, the girl is no helpless victim as in Story A but she is dressed up to the nines. In fact the implication in the story is that she is dressed in such a manner in order to provoke the sexual urges of passing motorists and so increase her chances of getting a lift; she is using her sexuality to manipulate the situation. At this point it is worth remembering that the story was being told to a predominantly female audience. Under these circumstances we can understand why the characters take on such rôles, because a specific message is being conveyed to that audience. On the one hand, at this point in the story there seems to be a certain amount of gender back-biting against girls who put on 'all the works' in order to provoke the opposite sex, whilst at the same time there seems to be the much stronger cautionary message warning against the predatory nature of the male. Indeed it is implied in the story that it is precisely because of her appearance that the driver decides to give the hitchhiker a lift. Either way there are different energies and motivations at play in Catherine's story from those in Alex's.

Nevertheless, this is as far as it goes: there is no further development in their relationship beyond that of driver and hitchhiker, because that is not what the story is about. The sexual messages are ones that have simply been emphasised for the benefit of the audience. Instead they simply strike up a conversation as any fellow travellers might do and he drops her off at her chosen destination. However, it transpires that she has accidentally left her wallet behind. This serves two purposes for the narrative. Firstly, it gives the driver an (innocent) reason for trying to re-establish contact with the girl, in the same way that the Christian, charitable concerns of the couple in Alex's story do. Without this there could be no revelation of the girl's identity as a ghost. Secondly, in Catherine's story the girl is, unusually, not dropped off at her home, but at some unspecified location. Given that most people carry some form of personal identification in their wallet, this provides the link between the girl and her home where her parents are able to confirm the girl's death. In many variants where the ghost leaves behind a token to affirm her identity as a ghost, the token in question is a jacket or other garment, left on the back seat of the car once the girl has been delivered home. Of course, in this story it has to be a wallet (confirming article) to enable the parents (confirming characters) to be traced.

After the discovery of the girl's wallet on the car seat, there now follows a brief, but rather out-of-place interlude when the driver picks up another hitchhiker, this time male. There seems to be no purpose for this episode as it plays no important part in the narrative. Indeed, no sooner has the second passenger been mentioned, than he promptly disappears for the remainder of the story. However, in terms of the performance, this episode has a very important rôle as a filler. What has happened here is that the storyteller has momentarily lost the thread of the story, forgotten what happens next. There is nothing particularly serious or unusual in this, it happens to us all in conversation from time to time, but Catherine now needs a filler, a piece of unimportant narrative, which does not have a substantial effect on the plot and so can be discarded again as soon as she has picked up the thread of the story. This brief episode (which, incidentally, could easily have been extended without affecting the story, if it had been necessary to do so) buys her a little time, and then all that is required is to insert a brief ellipsis and remind us of the wallet when the driver visits the police station. What is particularly interesting is that Catherine is able to get away with this momentary lapse of concentration in her telling, partly because of her skill in using a filler, keeping the narrative flowing, but also because of the conversational manner of her narrating. Because the performative mode is operating at a low intensity, there is not as much risk for the performer.

Catherine's style of storytelling throughout is in complete contrast to Alex's. Whereas Alex's is formal, carefully structured and highly conscious, Catherine's is far more relaxed, informal and, although she offers no authentication for the story, such as it having happened to a *foaf*[4], there is an almost anecdotal quality to her performance which gives it a certain authenticity. It is almost as if she is reporting a true set of events. From very early on in the story this conversational style is self-evident. When she describes the hitchhiker, she tells us that in addition to her blonde hair she has 'everything, y'know.' This type of direct address to the audience is a piece of metanarration which is typical of conversational speech patterns.

Further evidence of Catherine's conversational style can be seen in her constant understatement and undermining of her own authority as a storyteller. After the hitchhiker has been dropped off she tells us that 'she must have left her wallet or something.' Catherine does not pretend to be the expert, the authority here. She thinks that this is the way the events happened and presumes it to be so, but is not promising anything, because, of course, she was not there. Whilst this honesty adds to the believability of the story, it diminishes its authority and status, something which a storyteller working at performative high intensity could not afford to let happen. She uses the same device towards the end of the story when reporting the words of the police officer. First of all there is the understatement ('Oh, thanks.') followed by the undermining of authority ('or something like that.').

However, Catherine's performance is completely consistent with the context in which it took place. The setting was essentially a social one, in the informal atmosphere of the youth club. This was definitely their space and my position was not one of authority, but one of equality. Furthermore, Catherine's audience was primarily made up of her closest friends - they had all chosen to come to the session as a social group.

Geographical location is also important, since Falmouth is not Gillingham. Falmouth has a sizeable working-class population employed in the docks and the fishing and tourist industries, and it is children from these working-class families who tend to frequent the youth club. Within the district the club has a perhaps unfair reputation for being 'a bit rough'. It is reasonable to suppose that Catherine would not be affected by middle-class sensibilities towards sexuality in the same way as Alex, and this, coupled with the fact that she is two years older than he and the other elements of paraperformance already stated, means that she is able to feel comfortable about accentuating the overtones of sexuality within the story.

Bearing in mind all of this, a formal style such as Alex's would have been totally inappropriate to the situation. Furthermore, unlike Alex, Catherine was not trying to impress me or anybody else with her storytelling skills. Her prime concern was simply to pass on the details of the story for the purposes of the project in which we were engaged, and so she was far less conscious of her performance. Once again we can see how the various elements of paraperformance are able to exert a remarkable effect on the elements of performance.

There is, in addition, one aspect of performance shared by both Story A and Story B. This is the question of length, and it would be worth commenting on it here. Both stories are very economical in their telling and are much shorter than the numerous examples quoted by Brunvand (Brunvand, 1981, pp.24-40) or Bennett (Bennett, 1984, p.45). It is worth noting that on both the occasions on which the stories were collected, there were several storytellers waiting eagerly with stories to tell. Richard Bauman talks of the ground rules which govern social events (Bauman, 1977 pp.28-9). In this sense 'event' means the greater circumstances that surround the storytelling, such as a party or, in these cases, a storytelling project in a youth club or a lunchtime session in the school library. One of the ground rules operating at both these events was that, in consideration of other storytellers, one person must not hog the floor for too long. Everyone must have a chance to tell the stories they want. Therefore, the stories were both kept short in accordance with the given set of circumstances.

Finally, in our analysis of these two stories, it is interesting to see how both stories are brought to a conclusion:

'She's been dead for thirteen years!'
'Our daughter's been dead for seven years!'

As well as the remarkable similarity in sentence structure in which the endings are formally framed, it is interesting that both tellers quote folkloric numbers. Although not as common as the use of number three, seven and thirteen can be found as motifs in many traditional stories, and so, once again, teenage oral narrative can be placed firmly within the greater oral narrative tradition.

Conclusions

Every story is unique in the sense that every storytelling performance is unique; a story is never told in exactly the same way twice. Whilst this has been accepted for a long time, it is only recently that the importance of the performative context, which frames and shapes each individual telling, has been fully realised. Earlier folklorists concentrated solely upon the similarities of texts in a quest to discover a definitive and 'correct' version, rather than investigating the differences between texts and attempting to explain them in anything other than purely ethnocentric terms.

However, the development of performance-centred theories of storytelling has gone a long way to refine the way in which we look at extant folklore, in socio-cultural terms, and to bring an awareness of the extent to which paraperformative considerations can influence, and indeed define, any particular story and, hence, the meaning with which it is endowed. Our analysis of 'Vanishing Hitchhiker' variants has merely vindicated this approach as we can see how the same story, told by different tellers, under different circumstances, can be radically changed in form, content and meaning.

Notes

[1]   Brooke's word, not mine!

[2] Bauman uses this term to describe an event that is centred around a performance. The audience, probably after having bought tickets, arrive at a venue predetermined as one for performance, with the prime intention of witnessing that performance, and all attendant activity is built around it. It is conscious performance at its most extreme.

[3] This is not only done adequately by Brunvand, who dates the story back to the middle of the nineteenth century, but also more thoroughly in Gillian Bennett, 1984, where she firmly places the story within a long tradition of ghostlore.

[4] *Foaf* is an acronym invented by folklorist Rodney Dale and stands for 'friend of a friend', an authentication often offered in the telling of contemporary legends. For example, legends are often described by storytellers as having happened not to someone they personally know, but somebody one step removed from that.

3 'The Hook', 'The Mad Axeman' and 'The Licked Hand': studies in believability, fashionability and popular circulation

It has long been accepted that what are often called contemporary or urban legends - the debate on the exact terminology to be used still rages - are a significant part of the teenage repertoire. Folklorists who have studied the genre (Brunvand, Dégh, Ellis, Smith, Dundes to name but a few) all make reference to the teenage or adolescent horror legend or scare story. One of the problems with this is, of course, that in coming from the genre (the contemporary legend) rather than the constituency (teenagers/adolescents), it falsely elevates the importance of this type of story in the teenage repertoire. Whilst it is clearly true that the horrific, the macabre, the bizarre and the distasteful are all very important and recurring images within the teenage oral narrative tradition, it would be wrong to place all such stories under the contemporary legend heading. The teenage repertoire is clearly far more complex than that. However, previous studies of the contemporary legend genre give us the impression that teenagers tell nothing but these stories.

Moreover, it has been widely accepted that the story usually referred to by folklorists as 'The Hook' is the most popular and widespread of all teenage horror stories. Brunvand calls it 'one of the most popular adolescent scare stories' (Brunvand, 1981, p.50), even suggesting that it is a story that is adolescent specific; 'Eventually most people outgrow their youthful fascination with legends the likes of 'The Hook' or 'The Roommate's Death'. They either forget the stories entirely in later years, or they come to regard them with a sophistication gained from age and experience as mere foolish whims of their schooldays' (Brunvand, 1986, p.70).

To his credit Bill Ellis challenges the notion of 'The Hook' as 'the classic contemporary legend' (Ellis, 1994, p.63) and also its status as a popular teenage story. According to Ellis our perception of the perennial popularity of 'The Hook' grows out of its prominence in the collections of contemporary legends in the 1960s and 1970s when the genre first became fashionable. However, recent investigation tends to indicate that the story is now most often quoted by adults remembering stories that were told during their own adolescence. He notes that 'texts collected recently do not record recent traditions, but memories of texts heard up to three decades ago' (Ellis, 1994, p.65). Ellis concludes that the story has been in decline since the seventies and indeed by the early eighties had virtually sunk into obscurity, and that its 'continued citation as a currently popular legend may be thus naive' (Ellis, 1994, p.66). This, of course, has further implications for a consideration of how certain stories go in and out of fashion.

For me the continued belief in this story's enduring popularity amongst teenagers is evidence of the failure of folklorists to take seriously teenagers as transmitters of a strong narrative tradition, since my own fieldwork seems to support Ellis's conclusions. Out of all the texts I have collected from teenagers since 1989, I have only one version of 'The Hook'; furthermore this story having been obtained by the informant, not from an oral adolescent source, but from a published version which appeared in *Readers' Digest*, no less, thus seemingly supports the claim that it is now more often told by adults as a story from their own teenage years.

Here it is:

> This boy and girl were out somewhere and they were listening to the radio and there was an urgent newsflash come on. It said, 'This man has just escaped from this loony bin,' and he had a hook instead of a hand and they said, 'Be careful!' 'cos he's very near where they were.
>
> So the girl got a bit worried and said, 'Take me home.' So the boy sort of said, 'Yes, OK.' and when they got home, he got out of the car, he went to open her door and the hook was on the door. (Wilson 12)
> (Karen Young, age 13, Gillingham School, Dorset, 11.11.92)

The performance of this particular story is interesting since it suggests a very matter-of-fact, economical rendition of the story, lacking detail and excitement. It is, in fact, told very much as a newspaper report. Whilst this adds to the story's authenticity it does not have the vitality that might be expected from the telling of the story strictly from within the teenage tradition. It bears all the hallmarks of a story which has come from outside the culture, but has attracted the teller sufficiently for her to adopt it and introduce it into her own repertoire. It is possible perhaps that the story has become obsolete within the teenage tradition, only to re-emerge (from outside it) at a later date.

At first sight it is certainly a little surprising that 'The Hook' is not more popular amongst teenagers than it currently is. It certainly contains many of the elements and motifs seemingly so important to many of the most popular stories, namely, the car, the courting couple, the radio warning, the threat (of the unpredictable criminally insane), the fear, the deformity, the (threat of) gruesome murder, etc., etc. In fact, the claim that this story is a 'classic' adolescent horror story could indeed be justified in that it is a near-perfect construction of an example of the genre. However, this simply invites the question: why then has it not retained its popularity? To answer this we must consider the reasons why the story became so popular in the first place and, in addition, why the story was superceded in popularity by two other well-documented contemporary legends, 'The Boyfriend's Death' and 'The Licked Hand',as is indeed the case.

Let us first consider the case of 'The Boyfriend's Death' (Wilson 13-22). This again is a story about which Brunvand claims 'the usual tellers of the story are adolescents' (Brunvand, 1981, p.5), and quotes the earliest recorded version as being collected by Daniel Barnes in 1964. As the following analysis will show, it is one of the most, if not the most, popular oral stories told today, not, incidentally, purely by teenagers, but probably predominantly so.

However, before proceeding I should like to challenge the title of the story. 'The Boyfriend's Death' is a fine example of folklorists attaching a semi-descriptive title to a story for classification and identification purposes, based on what may be considered as a 'typical version of a well-known urban legend' (Brunvand, 1981, p.5).

Bill Ellis (1994) has already shown the limitations of describing oral texts as typical. Variants are, of course, created through performance, which in turn is determined by the constituents of paraperformance. Typicality implies conformity, standard and normality. There can be no such thing as normality in terms of the fluid, oral text , as each performance provides a unique text moulded by a unique set of circumstances. Ellis puts the point effectively:

> Bluntly, what is 'typical' in the corpus is variability, and by rigging criteria we could rearrange these texts into 'ideal', 'typical' and 'atypical' in virtually any configuration. Any effort to privilege any particular motif or any 'typical' version of the story as a repository of 'hidden meaning' is futile. (Ellis, 1994, p.67)

The fact remains that in many variants it is a husband or father, rather than a boyfriend, who is killed and this has a significant effect on the sexual meanings implicit in any performance of the story, as will be seen later. In some versions it is not only the male protagonist who is killed but sometimes also the female and occasionally the whole family. Again these variants have implications for the meaning of the text.

In *Urban Myths* (Healy and Glanvill 1992) the authors title the story 'The Maniac on the Roof' (Healy and Glanvill, 1992, pp.8-9), which is by far a more satisfactory title and more appropriate to the story, particularly the teenage variants, as it draws attention to the killer rather than the victim. However, I propose to give the story another title and one which I shall use henceforth, namely 'The Mad Axeman'.

On the surface of it there seems to be little justification for adopting this title. It is rare for the killer in the story to be referred to directly as The Mad Axeman. Indeed there is often no reference to his insanity (except his obvious criminal insanity as exposed by his actions) and there is not always a reference to an axe, except by implication - how else could a head be severed? In fact, the only weapon commonly mentioned is a stick on which the victim's severed head has been placed. Nevertheless my justification for this title lies in the fact that, whilst the majority of stories in the teenage repertoire are not given titles by their tellers (certain local legends usually being the exception), this particular story does indeed often (but not always) circulate amongst teenagers under a title, and where it does that title is neither 'The Boyfriend's Death' nor 'The Maniac on the Roof', but 'The Mad Axeman'.

If I am running a storytelling session in a secondary school with, let's say, a group of Year 8 (12-13 year olds) pupils and I ask them whether they know a story called 'The Boyfriend's Death', I would expect only a small proportion to put up their hands; maybe about the ten per cent who do so, rather than having recognised the title as a title, have recognised it as a motif of 'The Mad Axeman' and made the connection. If I were then to ask the same group if they had heard of a story called 'The Mad Axeman', I would expect anything from thirty to seventy (or even eighty) per cent to respond positively. If I then told them a common variant of the story I would expect from sixty to one hundred per cent to recognise it, or at least recognise it as a variant of another story they know.

We must now, of course, ask ourselves the very pertinent question of why, given the usual lack of madness and axes in the story, it should have assumed this title amongst adolescent storytellers. I should like to advance the following theory.

In talking about the emergent popularity of 'The Hook' during the 1950s, Bill Ellis suggests the likely influence of the 'persistent publicity given the Caryl Chessman case during this period' (Ellis, 1994, p.63). Chessman was a known criminal who was arrested in 1948 following a number of robberies upon courting couples in Los Angeles. The robber would pull up in a car with a red light, masquerading as a police officer. He would then commit an act of armed robbery. Furthermore, on two occasions the female victim was forced to leave the car and perform oral sex. Apparently, a wave of hysteria swept Los Angeles up to Chessman's arrest, and when he was finally executed in 1960 his image among the public was still one of a perverted sadist. Most interestingly, Chessman's nickname was Hooknose, due to a facial deformity he had suffered after an accident as a child. As Ellis rightly asserts, 'the "Hookman" image predates Chessman, but it seems likely that the rise in popularity of such narratives was tied to the increasing interest in his case' (Ellis, 1994, p.63). In other words, the popularity of the story was enhanced by a set of widely-publicised real-life incidents which seemed to echo a folkloric truth. This is interesting because it seems that something similar may have happened to 'The Mad Axeman'.

On 12 December 1966 Frank Mitchell absconded from Dartmoor Prison[1] in an escape orchestrated by the infamous East End gangsters, the Kray Twins. Mitchell was a physically huge man who had originally been jailed for robbery with violence and had spent eighteen of his thirty-two years in secure establishments. He had never been a murderer (although he was once acquitted of attempted murder) nor a rapist, but his reputation for violence was well-known. He had been birched several times in prison for violent behaviour. He was also of very limited intelligence and had acquired the nickname of 'The Mad Axe-Man'[2] after an incident when he threatened 'an elderly couple with a felling axe while on the run from a hospital for the criminally insane' (Pearson, 1984, p.219).

Whilst in Wandsworth Prison he befriended Ronnie Kray, and after Kray was released and Mitchell transferred to Princetown, the two remained in close contact. It is Mitchell's time at Dartmoor that is particularly interesting, because the Governor at the time, realising that continual birching and punishment simply served to toughen Mitchell up, make him more resentful of authority and indeed to nurture his violence, decided to introduce a more liberal regime. Mitchell was treated as a trusted prisoner, was allowed to work outside the prison on the open moorland, where he showed an extraordinary ability to train wild ponies. In the meantime the Governor promised to press for his early release.

Whilst it seems that the Governor's policy had impressive results in transforming Mitchell's behaviour, it also appears that, especially considering that he was rated as a dangerous prisoner, he was allowed extraordinary privileges, enjoyed by no other inmate. It appears that he was practically allowed to come and go as he liked, presumably so as not to antagonise him, and was a regular visitor to some of the remote pubs on the Moor and even had an affair with a local schoolmistress. Indeed stories about Mitchell visiting the pub before returning to prison for the night are still told around

Dartmoor. Apparently it was not uncommon to see him walking back from the pub across the Moor of an evening.

However, the Governor's attempts seemed not to bear fruit and the Krays were in need of boosting their image in the criminal underworld and so Mitchell's escape was planned.

In preparation, Mitchell, for some reason, made himself a black nylon mask out of his girlfriend's nightdress. In his book *The Profession of Violence: The Rise and Fall of the Kray Twins*, John Pearson describes the escape:

> Mitchell was wearing his black nylon mask as he came lumbering through the moorland mist towards the green Vauxhall parked on the Princetown road. (Pearson, 1984, p.226)

From there Mitchell was driven to London and had already been installed in a safe house by the time the authorities had realised he was missing. A massive hunt was launched as Mitchell briefly became Britain's most wanted man and the Moor was combed for the fugitive.

However, Mitchell, the Mad Axe-Man, was never seen again. The story goes that he became restless and unpredictable whilst lying low and in the end the Krays had him murdered, although no body was ever found and nothing could be proved. The Krays were eventually accused of his murder, but they were acquitted for lack of evidence. In the meantime, there were sightings of Mitchell as far away as Melbourne and Casablanca, but the trail always went cold. As Pearson says, 'to this day the Axe-Man is still officially on the run, one of the few men in history to have made a successful getaway from Dartmoor' (Pearson, 1984, p.237).

At the time of the escape there was, understandably enough considering Mitchell's history, a great wave of hysteria which spread through the country, but particularly around the towns and villages of Dartmoor and Devon. The story hit local and national headlines on Tuesday 13 December 1966 and remained a prominent news story right through the Christmas period and into the New Year. Although the story was to some extent superceded in the national press by the Rhodesia Crisis, the story of Mitchell's escape, other escapes it seemed to precipitate[3], and the resultant Mountbatten Report on prison security enjoyed unbroken front page status in the *Exeter Express and Echo* and the *Western Morning News* throughout the holiday period.

This extraordinary press attention can be seen to reflect the wide public concern and local hysteria caused by the escape, but it seems equally likely that the press stories, having little to report in terms of police progress in recapturing Mitchell, resorted to giving unprecedented prominence to the mythological qualities of Mitchell and uncorroborated stories from local residents about him, and so simply fanned the flames of hysteria with their reporting.

When the story broke on 13 December the *Express and Echo* led with the headline, ' "Axe Man" believed still on Dartmoor' and the *Western Morning News* with the equally sensational, 'Dartmoor Hunt for Axe Man. "Lock your doors" warning from police'. Even the national press joined in as *The Times* declared, 'Dartmoor Axe-Man Free Again'. Indeed in those early reports all the press seemed to concentrate on two aspects not directly relevant to the escape. Firstly there was the matter of Mitchell's size and strength. The *Express and Echo* reported that Mitchell, who was 'known as the most violent criminal in Britain' (13.12.1966), was a man of 'enormous strength' (13.12.1966). The *Western Morning News* said that he had 'immense strength and is known as the most violent criminal in Britain' (13.12.1966). Both these newspapers quoted a story of how Mitchell had recently shown off his superhuman strength to prison officers by lifting up the front end of a car whilst two of them sat in the front seats. In fact, the image of Mitchell as being superhuman or non-human was one that was constantly portrayed by the press. In a front page article on 14 December 1966, *The Times* described Mitchell as 'strong as an ox, but charming too......and could chop through prison chairs with his bare hands and bend railings.'

The second aspect of the early press reports which deserves our attention is the prominence given to Mitchell's Axe-Man image and the history behind it. Mitchell had escaped from secure institutions on two previous occasions. The *Express and Echo* informs us that during 'both his previous escapes he kept couples hostage by threatening them with an axe or hatchet' (13.12.1966). In the *Western Morning News* the story has already begun to bear resemblances to the contemporary legend. Here, it is claimed, 'he kept *young*[4] couples hostage by threatening them with an axe' (13.12.1966). Likewise *The Times* picked up on the incidents: 'On that occasion (1957 escape from Rampton) he had attacked *several*[5] people with a hatchet' (13.12.1966), and, on his 1958 escape from Broadmoor; 'he attacked a man with an axe and tried to strangle him and his wife before escaping in their car' (13.12.1966). These stories as sensationalised by the press differ significantly from the version of events previously quoted from John Pearson. This can only be seen as part of the twin processes of demonising Mitchell and the blurring of distinction between the reality of the escape and the contemporary legend of 'The Mad Axeman'.

In fact, the press reporting of the case caused the by now former Governor of Dartmoor Prison, who had been responsible for the liberal policy on Mitchell, to make a statement explaining that the nickname 'The Mad Axe-man' was an unfair one, as Mitchell had never actually attacked anyone with an axe, but only threatened to do so *(Western Morning News,* 19.12.1966). Nevertheless, the dehumanisation of Mitchell is very important to us in comparing the case to the story of 'The Mad Axeman'.[6]

It is also worth noting that in their initial reports on 13 December, both of the local papers made prominent reference to the warnings broadcast by the police, the *Western Morning News* even alluding to it in their headline. The fact that the police issued a warning through the television that no-one should try and tackle Mitchell is interesting enough, since it can only have added to the public panic, but what is more interesting is again the prominence given to this by the local press. Indeed *The Times* did not even see fit to mention it in their rôle as national press, and yet the broadcast of the warning is also a very significant part of the contemporary legend, both in terms of the plot (without the warning the young woman may not have been left alone in the presumed 'safety' of the car) and also the dramatic tension.

With reporting of this nature it is hardly surprising that the fears of a nervous local community were fuelled towards hysteria. Local police stations in Devon were bombarded with supposed sightings of Mitchell and prominence was given in the press the following days to stories of how Mitchell had been a regular customer at the Peter Tavy Inn and the Elephant's Nest pub on Dartmoor. This in turn raised national concerns about prison security in general and further played on the fears of the local community.

On 21 December 1966 the *Western Morning News* printed a front page story with the headline, '"Axe Man" Escape Rumours Harmful, says M.P.' The M.P. for Tavistock at that time was one Michael Heseltine who raised concerns in the House of Commons that stories concerning the Mitchell escape were fanning the flames of hysteria within his constituency. He told of one of his farming constituents;

> Milking times had been adjusted to enable the work to be finished before dark, and even when inside the house, with all the doors locked and bolted, his wife felt unable to move from one room to another without being accompanied by her son carrying a loaded gun.

Likewise on 30 December 1966 in an article about the Boxing Day jailbreak at Dartmoor, the *Western Morning News* told of Mr Ball, a resident of Tavistock, who 'had slept with a gun under his bed since Mitchell had escaped.'

It seems that the Mitchell escape captured the imagination of the British public and the residents of Dartmoor in particular. It seems reasonable to suppose that the panic which followed the escape was heightened by the press coverage and especially the way in which it concentrated on the legendary features of the case, but there has to be more to it than that.

We know that 'The Mad Axeman' was in existence prior to 1966, albeit perhaps not quite as commonly as it is today, and yet it seems plausible that at least part of the reason for the wave of panic following the events of 12 December 1966 was the coincidental folkloric similarities of the real life case of Frank Mitchell, The Mad Axe-Man. Of course I am not suggesting that the contemporary legend is based upon the real-life events, but I am proposing that this was one of those moments that captured the imaginative subconscious of a community because life imitated existing folkloric belief. In fact, the story of 'The Mad Axeman' underwent exactly the same sort of process as Ellis claims happened to 'The Hook' (and so resulted in an increase in popularity of the story) following the press reporting of the Caryl Chessman case in the States. The story of Mitchell touched a subconscious nerve within the community which was aggravated, either consciously or subconsciously, by the reporting of the media, which concentrated precisely on those folkloric coincidences.

If this is the case and Mitchell himself has been absorbed into folklore, then the case could have heralded a modification in the legend and also account for its rise in popularity and its replacement of 'The Hook' as the classic adolescent horror tale. Certainly, as will be discussed later, the two stories share very similar motifs and images, express the same fears and concerns of society as each other, and are often even told for similar effect, and so a surge in popularity of one of the stories may well render the other practically redundant. Furthermore, the continued popularity of 'The Mad Axeman' could at least be partly due to the fact that Frank Mitchell was never found. For all we know, he could still be out there!

Further evidence of the emergent popularity of 'The Mad Axeman' following the Mitchell escape comes from interviews with acquaintances who were living in and around Dartmoor at the time. A colleague from Exeter University who was at Dartington in South Devon in December 1966 has vague recollections of the case and the wave of public interest in it that followed. He also has a clear memory of people consciously making themselves secure in their homes at night to guard against Mitchell as an intruder. In addition, he categorically remembers the first time he was told the story of 'The Mad Axeman' , which was in 1969, shortly after moving to Exeter. Here the story was told as true and having happened on Dartmoor in the recent past to a male and a female student from the University. At the time, he told me, he believed it.

Jayne Tucker has lived all her life in the same village on the north edge of Dartmoor and attended local schools. She was nine years old when Frank

49

Mitchell escaped and has a very clear memory of returning from Exeter and the bus being searched by the police. In an interview with me (Appendix 2) she also told me that she first heard 'The Mad Axeman' as a story when she was a young adolescent 'in the early years of my secondary school', which would incidentally have been about the same time as my Exeter colleague also heard the story for the first time. She recalls the story as being very popular amongst her peer group at this time, 'because that's when you're getting into all the horror stories and stuff'. Interestingly enough, she relates the story specifically to the time of her own adolescence and that the story was fashionable at the time; 'It's like a period of jokes that go round, like knock-knock jokes would be trendy for a while and then they fade off, and I suppose this story at that time was going around'.

Because Jayne's adolescence coincides with the seeming emergence of 'The Mad Axeman' as a popular story, it is difficult to establish whether she heard the story because she was an adolescent or because the story was becoming popular. I suspect that it is actually a bit of both. If the story was equally popular before 1966/7, then even though she was only nine at the time and the story may not have circulated much amongst her own peer group, it is probable that she would at least have been aware of the story before, especially considering that she had two elder sisters, both teenagers at the time, and that there is greater intergenerational mixing amongst children in small rural communities, such as the one in which she lived. Jayne is certainly sure that she never heard the story prior to Mitchell's escape.

What is most interesting, however, is that there is no doubt whatsoever in Jayne's mind that the story was linked to Frank Mitchell. It was, in fact, my own telling of the story one evening in the pub that initially reminded her of her own experiences.

The story was definitely being told as 'The Mad Axeman' and, moreover, this was the central image in the story. As Jayne says, 'all the newspapers called him a Mad Axeman anyway. I couldn't even remember his name, it was always the Mad Axeman. You never talked about Frank Mitchell, you talked about The Mad Axeman. So the Mad Axeman "joke" would, therefore, stick in my mind as about Frank Mitchell'. Although she admits that the Mad Axeman in the story was not necessarily Mitchell, the story was inextricably linked to him. The poignancy of the story was increased by the fear that this could have been Mitchell. Jayne says that, 'when you heard stories about the Mad Axeman you tended to believe them because you knew this man had escaped from Dartmoor Prison and, I suppose, the implication was that it could be him'.

This issue of 'believability' is crucial to the argument. 'The Mad Axeman' , as with many contemporary legends, is even today often (but not always) told as a true story and is also very often accepted as true by the audience. As Georgina Boyes says, '....they express in a succinct and entertaining form what narrators wish to present as a truth about contemporary life and behaviour' (Boyes, 1984, p.64). Also David Buchan recognises that the issue of truth is central to the study of modern legends:

> The legend proper used to be defined as a traditional story 'told as true', but this definition has had to be altered to accommodate change in attitude within tradition, for nowadays many legends proper are told in at least partial disbelief, told in inverted commas, and involve a more complex kind of response (Buchan, 1981, p.3).

As far as 'The Mad Axeman' is concerned, Jayne Tucker is quite sure that the Mitchell incident was crucial to the believability of the story. I would go perhaps one step further in suggesting that the story became popular at least partly because of its increased believability, the fact that the Mitchell escape served to validate it.

Whether or not a particular story is told as true has a pivotal effect upon the meaning of the individual text. In a horror story, for example, such as 'Johnny, I Want My Liver Back' (Wilson 32-35), the story is rarely, if ever, told as true. Perhaps it is simply too far-fetched for this. It is also told for different reasons. In David Buchan's words, it is a 'gruesome-funny tale' (Buchan, 1981, p.10) and is told primarily for its entertainment value. This is not always the case with 'The Mad Axeman'.

In fact 'The Mad Axeman' is a useful example with which to investigate this phenomenon, precisely because it is sometimes told as true, and sometimes as untrue. According to Boyes, 'these legends articulate, and to a great extent validate wishes and fears' (Boyes, 1984, p.64) and to Brunvand, 'the story reveals society's broader fears of people, especially women and the young, being alone and among strangers in the darkened world outside the security of their own home or car' (Brunvand, 1981, p.11). This is certainly the case and when the story is told and believed as true, then the articulation of those fears transforms them into cautionary messages; Brunvand says that '...a story like "The Boyfriend's Death" simply warns young people to avoid situations in which they may be endangered' (Brunvand, 1981, p.11). When Jayne Tucker heard the story in the late 1960s she also interpreted the story as being loaded with an implicit warning about 'this man up on the Moor as this threat to good clean girls'.

On the other hand the story is often told as not true, or rather the truth element is not given any great weighting, and in these cases when the story is told for entertainment purposes, it is the violence and the gruesomeness

51

which is exaggerated beyond the realms of credibility and into the grotesque and at this point the story begins to become humorous.

In her essay 'Legend: Performance and Truth', Gillian Bennett tackles exactly this issue. In her analysis of two different legends (one told as true and one as untrue), she concludes that in the case of the non-belief tale, 'the aim of the storytelling seems to be to arrive at the punchline and get a quick laugh' (Bennett, 1988, p.22) and that 'likelihood and local colour are both sacrificed for dramatic effect' (Bennett, 1988, p.22). Furthermore, recognising that a storyteller's attitude towards the believability of a story can be seen in the text and the performance strategies employed, she is able to identify major differences in strategies for 'true' and 'untrue' stories.

According to Bennett, the 'true' story is more likely to contain specific references to character, location and time. It is more often personalised. In addition the text is likely to be structured and broken down into clear paragraphs. The storyteller will deliver the story with a certain degree of care and deliberation, and will invest an increased degree of performative energy in that delivery.[7] Furthermore, the story told as true is more likely to be structured after the Labovian model.[8]

On the other hand, the story told as untrue may employ greater use of opening formulae and the delivery may sound rehearsed and scripted. Bennett sees this as being essentially non-conversational in tone (Bennett, 1988, p.31). In other words, she assigns truth to the informal end of 'the performance continuum' and untruth to the formal end. In showing that 'legend is a genre capable of straddling the divide between fact and fiction' (Bennett, 1988, p.32), she quite rightly challenges Herbert Halpert's assertion that legend and truth (as opposed to untruth) are inextricably linked (cf. Halpert, 1971).

An application of these theories to my own archive will often bear out the truth of Bennett's assertions, and yet what may be additionally significant here is that on the evidence of my own fieldwork, it would seem that male storytellers have a greater propensity to exaggerate and tell the story for entertainment (i.e. as untrue) than female storytellers (Wilson 14-16 & 20). This is not to say that females are more gullible than males, or that males are not capable of telling or accepting the story as true, but it may be that there is a gender difference in the priorities of meanings with which the storytellers wish to endow their stories. Male storytellers seem more prone to tell the story for laughs or to disgust, whereas female storytellers seem to prefer to warn and scare. In fact it could be that male storytellers tend to focus upon the central male character (the killer), whilst female storytellers concentrate upon the central female character (the girlfriend/wife). Of course, we must tread carefully here because we are dealing with incomplete data - how the story is told and the meaning of the text depends equally on the identity of the audience and other paraperformative influences as on the identity of the storyteller - but this again ties in with Jayne Tucker's experience.

She gives great importance to the single gender identity of her own social grouping: '...at that age I didn't mix with boys, you know, it was a peer group of girls and there was all this sort of giggly, girly talk about a mad axeman up on the Moor'.

This phenomenon could, of course, be put down, at least partly, to the gender rôles within many of the texts. Although it is the boyfriend/husband who is usually decapitated and thus the primary victim of the killer, it is the girlfriend/wife who is perceived as being under the greatest threat. The boyfriend/husband is simply a less important character in the story, fullfilling the rôle of traditional protector, and when he is removed, the girlfriend/wife becomes more vulnerable.

If we are to interpret the story on the basis of a male to female threat (it is interesting that Jayne Tucker remembers the story as being 'a woman in a car on Dartmoor near Princetown'. The woman is the central character and no mention is made of the boyfriend/husband), then this again has implications for the meaning of any particular text. Where we are able to identify in a text that the main threat is to the girlfriend/wife figure, then the story acquires a much stronger sexual aspect.

Freudian theorists have made much of the phallic imagery and symbolism within adolescent horror legends. For example, in his analysis of 'The Hook' (Dundes, 1971, pp.21-36), Alan Dundes interprets the actual hook as a phallic symbol and the hook being ripped off as an act of castration which defuses the girl's sexual vulnerability. Moreover, Dundes concludes that the hook symbolises not an outside threat, but the sexual alter ego of the boyfriend/husband. It is a kind of Dr Jekyll and Mr Hyde, where the maniac with the hook represents the uncontrollable beast within the male. Likewise, the same analysis could be applied to 'The Mad Axeman'. The axe or pole can be seen as a phallic symbol on which is impaled the head (symbolising self-will and self-control) of the Jekyll-male, as it has been totally overpowered by the sexual, animalistic, Hyde-male. At this level the story becomes purely about female vulnerability when alone with a male friend.

It is of course extremely difficult to disprove such analysis, and I am not for one minute supposing that there is no sexual content, nor even that the sexual symbolism in the story is not important, since clearly it is. It is simply a question of emphasis. We must remember that in some texts the threatened people are a family (Wilson 14) or father and son (Wilson 21) and the sexual element, whilst it may be present (it could be argued) is very much subdued.

What can be said is that there is very often a strong sexuality prevalent in the story and, in cases where the story is told with a clear cautionary aspect to it, then it is in the interest of the storyteller to emphasise the sexuality. Indeed Jayne Tucker not only implies that the stories she heard in her own adolescence were about a threatened female, but also that 'there were undertones of sexuality developing'. We must simply be wary of endowing the story with an inherently strong sexuality as, once again, the various elements of paraperformance will have a great influence on the intensity of the sexual element in any particular text.

What I feel is most important in trying to explain the rising and sustained popularity of 'The Mad Axeman' are the elements of truth and believability, which, as previously argued, go hand in hand with the cautionary and sexual aspects. It is here that the Frank Mitchell case comes back into play. Brunvand says that 'rumours or news stories about missing persons or violent crimes...can merge with urban legends, helping to support their air of truth, or giving them renewed circulation after a period of less frequent occurrence'[9] (Brunvand, 1981, p.10). It seems reasonable to suppose that because the Mitchell case so closely mirrored the existing legend, thereby giving it validity, the real-life events began to merge with the legend in order to maximise its efficacy as a believable and cautionary story. Therefore, because the story became so effective in this function, it acquired greater popularity and has maintained that to this day, particularly around Dartmoor, where it continues to have particular significance.

Before proceeding any further with this analysis, it is appropriate to consider one particularly important question which has emerged from it, namely the nature of the oral transmission process and the 'size of the world.'

On the one hand we can see from Bill Ellis's analysis of 'The Hook' that this particular story was very popular during the late 50s and early 60s. For his data Ellis has turned to the seventy-six texts and summaries contained in the Folklore Archives of the University of California at Berkeley. Ellis concludes that the popularity of 'The Hook' grew during the time of Chessman's appeals, reaching a first peak around about 1960 (the date of Chessman's execution). There was a second peak around the mid-sixties, which Ellis cautiously proposes may well be unreliable data as this coincides with Alan Dundes's initial interest in contemporary legends and the period of most active text collecting. Quite rightly, however, Ellis draws closer attention to 'its decline in popularity after this initial peak' (Ellis, 1994, p.65). According to the data in the Berkeley Archives, the story declined sharply from the mid-sixties onward and seems to have become obsolete by the end of the seventies, at least amongst adolescents. Ellis's consistent analysis is successful in showing how the popularity of 'The Hook' is linked to the Chessman case.

On the other hand I hope that my own analysis of 'The Mad Axeman' has shown how the popularity of this legend can be linked to the case of Frank Mitchell in 1966. However, we do have a problem in establishing a link between the two analyses.

Ellis is working entirely from American data, and whilst he is convincing about the state of the legend in the United States, we cannot necessarily apply his conclusions to Great Britain. Likewise, my own data comes from Britain and Ireland and equally does not necessarily relate to the American situation.

How can we be sure that 'The Hook' enjoyed the same popularity in Britain in the 50s and early 60s as it did in the States? Perhaps it has always been relatively uncommon? At the same time, can we show that 'The Mad Axeman' rose in popularity post-1966 in the States as it did here in Britain? Does it still remain high in the popularity stakes today and, more importantly, does the story now often exist under the title of 'The Mad Axeman'?

In other words, if we are to attribute the decline of 'The Hook', at least partly, to the rise of 'The Mad Axeman', we must ask ourselves questions such as whether popular trends in narrative are culture-specific, or is the distance across the Atlantic not so great after all? To what extent do we in Britain share a common culture with the United States, and does this cross to other European nations?

Much of the evidence that we do have is inevitably anecdotal. In a recent personal communication, Bill Ellis told me that in his own experience and that of his colleagues, 'The Mad Axeman' has indeed superceded 'The Hook' in the States as a popular story and this has been the case for some years. However, the Mitchell case was practically unknown in the States and the image of the Mad Axeman is noticeably absent from the American tradition. Here the story continues to be known as 'The Boyfriend's Death'.

Therefore, the rise in popularity of the story in the United States cannot necessarily be directly related to those reasons for the escalation of the story's popularity in Britain. The reasons for the story's triumph in the States remain unanswered, but there is, of course, the possibility of a knock-on effect from events in Britain.

There is indeed some evidence that would seem to indicate that movements in contemporary legends are international, at least among countries with developed economies and advanced communications networks. No longer can the folklorist claim certain stories to be culture-specific. Where communication is international, then so, inevitably, is folklore.

In the preface to *The Mexican Pet*, Jan Harold Brunvand admits that in spite of the subtitle of his first book, *(The Vanishing Hitchhiker: American*

Urban Legends and Their Meanings), 'the urban legend as a genre is not an exclusive American phenomenon' (Brunvand, 1986, p.12). We also know, by comparing the collections of contemporary legends published in Britain (not to mention Sweden, Germany, France, Finland, Holland, Italy, Poland and South Africa) to the American collections, that many of those stories popular in one country are also popular in another. This is also borne out by my own research. Indeed, when doing a presentation to one group of secondary school pupils, I told a version of 'The Mad Axeman' as a way of getting them talking about the stories they knew and told. It so happened that one of the students had recently moved to England from South Africa. He told me that 'The Mad Axeman' was a very popular story amongst his friends in South Africa and he proceeded to tell me the version he knew. Interestingly enough, the 'mad axeman' image was present.

Whilst we know that British culture is particularly susceptible to influences from across the Atlantic, it may not be unreasonable to suppose that this is a two-way traffic. Further research may well show that the popularity of 'The Mad Axeman' and its transformation in Britain in the late 1960s predates a similar rise in the States. Perhaps the events in Britain simply acted as a catalyst for 'The Boyfriend's Death' in other parts of the world.

The current international popularity of 'The Mad Axeman' can also be detected in two examples from other media. In the film *Dead Poets' Society*, a group of adolescent students go on a midnight trek to a cave to tell each other ghost stories. One student volunteers to get the ball rolling and begins to tell a variant of 'The Mad Axeman'. He only gets a couple of sentences into the story when his colleagues shout him down, because they all know the story already.

My second example comes from another experience of my own. On Thursday 10 March 1994, I was working in Mill Vale Middle School, Dunstable, Bedfordshire with a class of Year 8 students (12-13 year olds). At one point one of the students volunteered to tell a 'true' story. Needless to say the story was another variant of 'The Mad Axeman', this time set in a lay-by on the nearby M1 motorway. The fact that motorways in Britain do not have lay-bys did not seem to deter the storyteller. When the storyteller had finished, another female student raised her hand. She said that the same story had been told (without references to Dunstable and the M1, presumably) by one of the characters in *Home and Away*[10] on the previous evening's episode. She had also heard the story before and had, up until then, believed it to be true. Although she was loath to totally disbelieve the story, she now had some nagging doubts.

These two examples show not only the way that the modern media are involved in the process of transmission of contemporary folklore, and plunder its resources for their own purposes, but also that 'The Mad Axeman' is a story currently popular at least in the United States and Australia. Out of all the contemporary legends there are, they both chose the same one!

However, although the Mad Axeman image in relation to this particular story seems to be essentially British, the axe man motif itself has a much wider currency in modern folklore. A good example from the United States is Sylvia Grider's 'The Hatchet Man' (Grider, 1980), an analysis of variants of the contemporary legend often known as 'The Roommate's Death' (cf. Brunvand, 1981, pp.57-62) collected at Indiana University.

Here the assailant is once again an escaped convict who attacks unsuspecting victims with an axe. There are other similarities between this story and 'The Mad Axeman', (for example, both stories feature some kind of warning or advice, advice that is, incidentally, always ignored causing the couple to be separated; in both there is a strange noise which serves to increase the tension, and they conclude with the gruesome discovery of their murdered friend), and yet the stories are essentially different.

However, the most interesting analysis of 'The Mad Axeman' story is Mark Glazer's 'The Cultural Adaptation of a Rumour Legend: "The Boyfriend's Death" in South Texas' (Glazer, 1987). Here he inadvertently identifies the main difference between most American and most British variants of the story.

His analysis is based upon collections made amongst Mexican-American communities and he identifies two major types of the story currently in circulation. Type A stories are similar to most of the published American texts, in that the couple are never married and the identity of the murderer is never known. Furthermore, the boyfriend is left hanging (sometimes inverted) from a tree, and the noise is that made by his feet or fingernails scraping along the car roof. Type B stories, on the other hand, seem to conform more closely to the variants that I have collected in Britain and Ireland. Here the couple are often engaged or married. Sometimes it is even a family that is involved. The murderer is also always identified at the end of the story, and the manner of death is decapitation rather than hanging[11].

Although Glazer is right to bestow importance on the manner of death in the stories, his conclusion that the story is essentially a warning to pay 'proper attention to his car' (Glazer, 1987, p.107) is rather doubtful, as he makes the mistake of identifying the boyfriend/husband as the main victim in the story, whereas, as previously argued, the narrative primarily revolves around the female.

However, what is particularly interesting in Glazer's analysis is that he is able to trace the Type A story back to 1949, whereas his earliest text of the Type B variant is 1971, interestingly enough only shortly after the story began to rise in popularity in Britain. From this he concludes that 'it would seem.....that Type A stories were known in the area earlier than those of Type B' (Glazer, 1987, p.94). If Glazer's conclusion is to be believed, then it would appear that the variants most popular in Britain are a modern version of the older type prevalent in the States. This would seem to be consistent with the absence of the axeman motif in current American versions, since the Mitchell case fits so well into Type B versions in Britain, whereas in the States, where Mitchell was unknown, it is simply the older Type A story which rose to be dominant.

What is clear is that, through our studies of 'The Hook' and 'The Mad Axeman' , we can see that current events and the intervention of the mass media can play an important rôle in determining the popularity, development and circulation of any particular legend. However, this alone does not account for the popularity of some stories which appear to have risen in fashionability for no obvious reasons and may well, in the future, decline equally mysteriously. I am thinking in particular of the contemporary legend named by Brunvand as 'The Licked Hand' (Brunvand, 1984, pp.73-7, Healy and Glanvill, 1993, pp.14-15, Wilson 23-30). The story itself has received relatively little attention in the past from folklorists; Brunvand himself devotes a mere four pages to the story in his first four volumes. Perhaps this is partly due to the fact that the story shares many of the motifs, fears and concerns displayed in 'The Hook' and 'The Mad Axeman' (threat from the criminally insane, vulnerable female, false security from ineffective protector figure, etc.) and that the preference for folklorists has been to concentrate on these two stories and thus neglect 'The Licked Hand'.

However, from my own experiences of collecting stories from teenagers and adolescents, I have collected more variants of this story than any other. This, of course, does not necessarily mean that it is currently the most popular story in the teenage repertoire; that place I would still reserve for 'The Mad Axeman'. Often when I am collecting stories, my teenage informants may not wish to tell 'The Mad Axeman' , either because I have previously indicated that I already know the story (as already explained, I often use this story as a way of getting teenagers talking about the stories they know) or that the story is so well-known that they presume that both myself and the group of co-listeners who sometimes gather round, must have already heard it. Either way there is an innate desire amongst storytellers who are telling stories to collectors to tell something special, unique that they think may not have been heard before, because, of course, they wish to make a favourable impression, especially considering the high status rôle of visitor I often enjoy, particularly when collecting stories in schools. Unfortunately, 'The Mad Axeman' is usually considered too commonplace. Nevertheless the high number of 'Licked Hand' variants in my archive does indicate that the story is very popular and widespread.

Furthermore it also seems to be the case that, although the story has certainly been around for a good many years (the earliest version quoted by Brunvand was collected in 1967 and appears in *Hoosier Folk Legends* by Ronald L Baker, Bloomington, Indiana University Press, 1982. cf. Brunvand, 1984, p.75), the rise to its current position of popularity is a relatively recent phenomenon. Evidence for this again comes partly from the lack of attention paid to it by folklorists - if the story had been so popular, surely it would have enjoyed a higher profile amongst contemporary legend scholars than it has. It is also a story which, unlike most other contemporary legends in the teenage repertoire, is relatively unknown amongst the general public. Certainly if 'The Licked Hand' arises in a session with teenagers, then it will produce a murmur of recognition from the adolescents and merely a look of unknowing confusion from the teacher, which is not the case with, for example, 'The Mad Axeman' and 'The Vanishing Hitchhiker', which produce reactions of universal recognition. Indeed, 'The Vanishing Hitchhiker', although relatively common amongst teenagers, is probably better known amongst older generations. This observation seems to refute Brunvand's claim that 'The Licked Hand' 'circulates widely at different age levels' (Brunvand, 1984, p.74). This is not to say that it is purely a teenage story, but it certainly seems that it is by far and away most popular amongst this age group at the present time. It is certainly not a story that I remember from my own adolescence in the mid 1970s.

In fact the first time I heard the story was in Abingdon, Oxfordshire on 21 November 1991, when it was told to me by two girls, Rachel and Katie, both aged twelve. Here is their version:

Rachel:	There was this person and she had a dog and every night when she went to bed, it licked her hand.

Katie:	And then this night she couldn't sleep.

Rachel:	So she put her hand out and the dog licked it and then she heard a dripping noise. It went drip, drip, drip, drip. So she went to find it and she couldn't.

Katie:	And then -she went back to sleep and the dog licked her hand. Then she woke up again and she heard drip, drip, drip drip...

Rachel:	Drip, drip, drip, drip, drip.

Katie:	Yeah, that as well. And then...

Rachel:	So she went in the bathroom and there was her dog and it was...

Katie: It was lying over the shower door with its throat cut and the noise was all its blood dripping and she thought, 'Well, how can that be? It couldn't be my dog....

Both: My dog just licked my hand.'

Rachel: So she went back in the room...

Katie: And turned the light on....

Rachel: And there was a man there that was licking her hand!

(laughter)

(Wilson 23)

There are several issues that arise from this particular performance that warrant further analysis.

Firstly, this particular version of the story was told as a two-hander by Rachel and Katie. It was a set piece that had been rehearsed and, although the actual performance did not go exactly as planned (I was told that it had been originally intended that one of them was going to tell the story, whilst the other did the 'drip-drip' sound effects), they were each aware that they had specific rôles in the performance. Furthermore, although the venue for the storytelling was not at all formal - they dragged me off to a quiet corner of the playground - it was a performance that was very conscious of itself and could, therefore, be rated relatively highly within the range of teenage narrative on the 'performance continuum'.

The formality of the delivery can be detected in the economy of the performance. There are very few unnecessary words and very little in the way of repetitions (except, of course, where this is part of the narrative technique) - the narrative smoothly moves from one episode to another swiftly to the conclusion. Note also the stylised formality of the language employed in the only direct speech in the narrative: 'Well, how can that be? It couldn't be my dog....My dog just licked my hand.'

However, possibly the most interesting aspect of this particular performance is the ending. It is one of only two versions out of all the 'Licked Hand' variants I have collected, that does not conclude with a message written in blood on the wall, mirror or window indicating that something other than the victim's dog has been licking her hand (the 'writing on the wall' is a motif which Brunvand, quite rightly, asserts has biblical allusions. cf. Brunvand, 1990, p.204). This is odd, for the very reason that in the other variants, this is the final pay-off, the punchline, which is very important to a successful performance of the story and the efficacy of the narrative. However, Katie and Rachel omit this ending, understating it rather by a simple explanation of what has happened.

The reason why this should be the case can only be explained by the purpose behind the telling and that is that it was a rehearsed, formal, two-hander, designed for entertainment. In spite of the gruesome nature of the story, the girls play down these elements as their intention is not to entertain through shocking. Certainly, they build up the suspense, but not to frighten, rather to amuse. On the conclusion of the story, both girls burst into laughter, as if they had taken me in. It was as if I had been expecting a shocking or a 'jump' ending, but they had deliberately undermined it and tricked me. When the woman discovers her mutilated dog in the bathroom, she is not shocked, but simply inquisitive, and this inappropriate behaviour adds to the amusement. Although this is the only two-handed version of the story that I have collected, I have often referred to it when discussing the story with teenagers. Invariably their reaction has been to confirm that either they too had heard the story told in this way, or at least that this would be an acceptable and consistent manner in which to perform it.

This dramatic intention (i.e. entertainment) is, however, not always the case and, indeed, is rarely so. This, of course, is not to deny that any storyteller must entertain the audience, but very often 'The Licked Hand' is told as a scare story. It is probably the story most commonly offered whenever I ask a group of teenagers if they know any ghost stories. Of course, it is not actually a ghost story, but the intention to frighten is the same. Furthermore, implicit in 'The Licked Hand' as horror-cum-scare story is the cautionary element - the warning for vulnerable women to be on their guard against the uncontrollable, predatory male. This, I believe, is, at least in performance terms, again linked to that old question of truth and believability. Let us consider the following story from Allan, aged 13, from Plymstock Comprehensive School, Plymouth (Wilson 24).

> Right, it's dark and this lonesome old granny lives up on Dartmoor and it's about half past nine at night and she hears about during the day that people have escaped from Dartmoor Prison and she left her window open during the night because it's hot and she always hangs her hand over the bed for her dog to lick it.
> And then outside her bedroom there's a woodpile and there's an axe in the stump of wood, the person that comes and takes the axe.
> He goes under and kills the dog and licks her hand and she wakes up in the morning and all the dog's splattered everywhere, blood everywhere, and on the wall it says, 'Guess who licked your hand last night?'

This text is particularly interesting because it is told as believable and Allan goes to some considerable length to impress upon us the 'truth' of his story without actually saying so. From the very start, when Allan keys his performance with 'Right, it's dark...', there is a note of solemnity to his narrating. This simple introductory statement indicates to us the end of frivolity and that we are getting down to serious business. A further authentication for the story is offered by the fact that it is given a specific location, namely Dartmoor, where, of course, happenings of this nature are always occurring - at least folkorically. Another clue to the seriousness of Allan's delivery can be seen in the economy of the telling. He dispenses with unnecessary description, simply giving us enough information so that the narrative makes logical sense. The whole story is dispensed with in a matter of three sentences. He avoids melodrama to the point of eliminating the sound of dripping blood from his story and even his description of the mutilated dog is only a relatively minimal four words long and very much understated. His ending the story with the fateful words, 'Guess who licked your hand last night?', is the only piece of text obviously designed to increase the dramatic tension significantly, and this, I feel, is done not so much melodramatically, but to increase the poignancy of the story and, therefore, by implication, its believability.

However, Allan's most effective technique of authentication is the way he relies on images and motifs which will be recognisable to his audience, partly because of their folkloric pedigree, and in particular because of their similarity to 'The Mad Axeman'. Firstly, there is the warning. We are told that she has heard of the danger during the day, which acts as a kind of premonition, a piece of dramatic irony for us, the audience. It is also comparable to the radio warning that is broadcast in 'The Mad Axeman'. Also Allan explains that the supposed danger has come from a jailbreak at Dartmoor Prison. Finally there is the motif of the axe. It is not common in variants of 'The Licked Hand' for an axe to be the assailant's weapon, but once again Allan's use of the image further lends to the believability of his story.

We can see, therefore, that the dramatic intention of Allan's story is not primarily to entertain, but to scare (and, therefore, warn) his audience. This he achieves by increasing the solemnity and seriousness of his text, as well as by drawing upon recognised motifs, and so he makes his story more credible.

Nevertheless, Allan's variant of the story is not typical. In fact, we find ourselves once again returning to Bill Ellis's analysis of 'The Hook', because (as Ellis found) there is no such thing as typicality in an oral text. Whilst we can identify certain aspects of commonality, the only thing that is typical is a degree of variation. There is no 'perfect' text.

As can be seen from the following statistical table, compiled from nineteen collected variants of 'The Licked Hand', a wide range of variation exists and is the norm.

Variability in 'The Licked Hand'

Victim	Woman (18)	Man (1)		
Setting	Specific (5)	Non-Specific (14)		
Threat	Man (3)	Devil (2)	Prisoner (6)	Other* (8)
Drip-Drip	Yes (15)	No (4)		
Site	Bathroom (11)	Bedroom (3)	Other (5)	
Dog	Hanged (11)	Splattered (3)	Other(5)	
Message (site)	Mirror (2)	Wall (7)	Door (1)	Window (3)
	Other (4)	No message (2)		
Message (wording)	Guess who? (3)	Humans/Devils can (11)	Other (3)	
	No message (2)			
Storyteller	Male (14)	Female (5)		

* 'other' also includes non-specified information.

Whilst we can detect some weighting of commonality towards a non-specific setting, the dog being hanged in the bathroom and the exact wording of the message, the only conclusive weightings seem to be towards the macabre dripping sound and the fact that the threatened character is female. Indeed Allan's story shares little in common with other variants.

If we were to construct a 'perfect' text, we would end up with something like:

A woman lives on her own and every night she puts her hand under the bed for her dog to lick. One night she is woken by a dripping sound and she puts her hand under the bed for the dog to lick. In the morning she finds her dog has been killed and a message in blood inviting speculation as to who or what was under the bed licking her hand.

Of course no variant conforms to this model, because it is a text that has been constructed without an audience, and we can only conclude that variants are an essential part of the oral process, determined by the circumstances surrounding the performance, and that any search for a 'typical' or 'ur-' text is pointless.

It is perhaps because the story seems to tell of another male to female threat that Brunvand suggests that the story is told by 'adolescent girls' (Brunvand, 1984, p.76)[12] and yet he offers no evidence to support this. From my own collections there are in fact significantly more male storytellers than female, as far as this story is concerned. Whilst this may in part reflect my own presence as a male storyteller, the figures do seem to indicate that there is no weighting towards any particular gender in terms of the storyteller. It may be possible to identify an inclination on the part of male storytellers to exaggerate the gory details in the story and for the female storytellers to deliver more believable, cautionary variants, yet this too must be treated with extreme care, as the examples from Allan and Rachel and Katie show.

We must, however, acknowledge that there is a sexual element in the story, which is sometimes exaggerated and sometimes diminished, depending on the storyteller, and that this is arguably more pronounced than in either 'The Mad Axeman' or 'The Hook'.

The central character is a woman, who this time has neither boyfriend nor husband, and so, in terms of the narrative, is more vulnerable because of her implied innocence. Furthermore, it is made clear that she is at her most vulnerable when she is in bed at night. Recognising herself that this is the case, she places her hand under the bed for reassurance from her protector, the dog, and so she is lured into a false sense of security. However, once again it is the protector (the protective male) who is killed and the woman who is left increasingly vulnerable and threatened.

In 'The Licked Hand' though, it is not difficult to see the licking of the hand (or foot) as a sexual act, and, therefore, in a sense, the woman is a victim of symbolic rape. This can be interpreted as the folk motif of a woman being duped into making love to an impostor whom she believes to be her husband or lover.[13]

Once again, however, it is important not to get too carried away with the sexual symbolism. Although it undoubtedly exists, for many adolescents the story is told because it is gruesome and scary, not because it is about sex. The prevalent sexuality merely adds to the story's intensity and, therefore, to its efficacy.

After all this analysis we are still left with the question: why is 'The Licked Hand' currently so popular amongst adolescents, especially when its concerns and fears seem to duplicate those in the equally prolific 'Mad Axeman'? The only conclusion I can offer is the following one.

As we approach the end of the twentieth century, we live in an increasingly violent and unpredictable (or so we perceive) world under constant pressures of change. This has served to intensify the fears and concerns expressed in these two stories and, therefore, perhaps there is now room for a number of popular stories reflecting these in the teenage repertoire. It simply shows an increase in the intensity of those fears and concerns.

Also we must remember that the threat to the woman character in 'The Licked Hand' is more sinister and alarming than in 'The Mad Axeman'. In the latter story, the victims break down in a desolate spot, often near a prison and usually on account of a foolish negligence to check the petrol gauge before setting out - a proportion of blame is hence attached to the victims, or at least the male victim. Whereas in the former story the woman is in the presumed security of her own home. The implication is that where once we had to guard against putting ourselves in vulnerable situations, we can now no longer be safe even in our own homes. Perhaps the recent popularity of 'The Licked Hand' merely echoes the common concerns of the 1990s.

Notes

[1] The prison at Princetown on Dartmoor was first built to house French prisoners of war from the Napoleonic Wars. It was later transferred to civilian use. However, its bleak, inhospitable surroundings and its foreboding architecture have earned a stark reputation. Many stories exist of escapees who have returned after a couple of days on the run, begging to be let back in after getting lost in the wilderness of the Moor.

[2] In his book *The Profession of Violence* (1984), John Pearson hyphenates Axe-Man when referring to Mitchell. On the other hand the press reports were inconsistent, sometimes inserting a hyphen, sometimes not. For the sake of clarity I have followed Pearson's example of using a hyphen (Axe-Man) when referring directly to Mitchell, and omitted it (Axeman) when referring to the character in or the title of the contemporary legend. The only exceptions to this are in cases when I am quoting directly from the press, which are, of course, always references to Frank Mitchell.

[3] In the days immediately following Mitchell's escape a number of prisoners in different jails around the country also made a bid for freedom. Prisons at Wandsworth, Birmingham and Eccleshall all experienced escapes and on Boxing Day there was a further escape from Dartmoor when five prisoners went on the run. Whether or not these were copycat escapes, the result was to increase the level of anxiety amongst the general public and to keep the Mitchell Affair in the public eye.

[4] My emphasis.

[5] Again my emphasis.

[6] Mitchell's dehumanisation is interesting in terms of there being a tradition on Dartmoor of the non-human, beastly threat, most commonly

65

exemplified in 'Black Dog' stories. The 'Black Dog' tradition was, of course, the basis of Arthur Conan Doyle's *The Hound of the Baskervilles* and continues to this day in the guise of large cat and 'Dartmoor (sometimes Exmoor or Bodmin) Beast' sightings. Indeed, one variant collected by myself (Wilson 16) unequivocally calls the story 'The Exmoor Beast'. It is almost as if the dehumanisation of Mitchell was part of the process of making him folklorically acceptable.

[7] In my experience it is also possible for a storyteller to increase the believability of a story by undermining their own authority as storyteller, leaving out many specific details. The subtext here is that the storyteller cannot know intimate details of a true event at which s/he was not present. In order for the story to be believable, the storyteller must also be believable and be realistic about the knowledge they claim to have of a supposed happening.

[8] William Labov and Joshua Waletsky in their essay 'Narrative Analysis: Oral Versions of Personal Experience' (in June Helm ed., *Essays on the Visual and Verbal Arts*, pp.12-44. Seattle: University of Washington Press, 1967) propose the following structure for oral narrative:
1 ABSTRACT - a résumé of the story in advance
2 ORIENTATION - setting the scene
3 COMPLICATION - triggers the main narrative action
4 EVALUATION - the 'point' of the story
5 RESOLUTION - the outcome
6 CODA - events brought back to present

[9] A further example of this is covered by Stewart Sanderson in his article 'From Social Regulator to Art Form: Case Study of a Modern Legend' (*ARV*, vol. 31, 1981, pp.161-66) in which he analyses the growth in popularity of the legend 'The Killer in the Backseat' around the Leeds area at the height of the murders committed by Peter Sutcliffe, a.k.a. 'The Yorkshire Ripper'.

[10] *Home and Away* is a popular Australian soap opera aimed primarily at a pre-pubescent and early adolescent (largely female) audience. It is broadcast midday and late afternoon, five days a week on I.T.V.

[11] In Glazer's versions the severed head is usually left in a sack to be discovered in the morning, unlike the British versions where the head is hit upon the roof of the car, terrifying the occupant.

[12] Also in discussing the story in both *The Choking Doberman* and *Curses! Broiled Again!*, he constantly refers to the storytellers as being female.

[13] A famous example of this would be the story of the conception of the boy Arthur in Arthurian legend.

4 The rebellious spirit: subversion through violence and the supernatural

The heavy use of supernatural and violent imagery is probably the most noticeable characteristic of the teenage narrative. From the very outset it is plainly evident that the adolescent repertoire is simply littered with headless corpses, gruesome amputations and dismemberings, vengeful ghosts and killer dolls. Folklorists refer quite openly to the 'adolescent horror legend' (cf. Ellis, 1994) or 'teenage horrors' (Brunvand, 1981, p.47), and adults will often show distaste for teenagers' stories precisely because of the high level of unsavoury imagery; they will occasionally cite such imagery as an argument against teenage narratives, in order to devalue it. Teenage narratives, I have heard argued, are not worthy of study, because they simply incorporate a seemingly never-ending sequence of violent and/or supernatural images. It is, in effect, shallow, lowest-common-denominator folklore. I have even heard tell that the content of teenage narrative is symptomatic of a general decline in moral standards.

Whilst recognising the importance of such imagery, we must endeavour to explain why it should be so prevalent and the function it serves. It is the purpose of this study to show that whilst violent and supernatural images and motifs are essentially different, in that a violent image may not necessarily be supernatural and a supernatural image may not necessarily be violent (although this is often the case), both types of imagery are generally linked within stories and are employed in teenage narratives with the same purpose in mind.

On the one hand it is important for all sorts of reasons to recognise the preponderance of violence and the supernatural. After all, teenagers themselves will freely admit to a fascination with such material. If, in my rôle of professional storyteller, I am running an open storytelling session aimed at a teenage audience, it will often be advertised as a session of ghost or horror stories, not because I will be telling or listening to exclusively ghost stories, but because this is giving a subliminal message to the potential audience. The sub-text is that this is something that is for them, something that addresses their own cultural agenda and speaks their language. Likewise, if you were to ask a teenager what sort of stories they like, they are most likely to request a ghost or a horror story. Again this is not to say that other stories will not be enjoyed. But it is worth noting that a teenager who offers to tell a ghost story, may well proceed to tell a contemporary legend, a joke, a personal experience story, a UFO story, a piece of family lore, a local legend etc., etc.

From this we can conclude that teenagers rarely think of stories in generic terms, at least not in the way that folklorists and academics have to. What a teenager often does, it would seem, is simply to recognise the motifs and images in a story (not necessarily the most prominent ones either) which most appeal to him/her. In this way any type of story can (and often will) be generally classified as a 'ghost story' by a teenager as long as there is some appealing element of the supernatural, macabre, violent or rationally inexplicable. Therefore, when Gary Moore of Lipson Community College, Plymouth offers the following story (Wilson 76), he does so as part of a session in which he and a group of friends are exchanging ghost stories.

> Right, once there was this man and (he) had an argument with his wife and he ran off. And he went to this bridge and jumped off into the water and he tried swimming and that but he couldn't keep up 'cos of the current and he went under and he died.
>
> And then the police were searching for him for three days, then they couldn't find him and then after three days he turned up on one of the river banks and he was all wrinkly and everything. And then that's it.

Here we have a simple piece of reportage - apparently it is a true story of a local incident and Gary's story is incomplete and undeveloped, hinting at a larger and fuller narrative- and contains a small amount of distasteful imagery and a tragic suicide, and yet Gary has no difficulty in claiming it for his own repertoire and telling it in the context of a ghost story session. Indeed it could be argued that in the teenage understanding of the genre, the ghost story is synonymous with the teenage story. This is because, in adolescent terms, the definition of the ghost/horror story may be stretched to include any story with an ironic twist, a story which challenges an accepted order, and the more extreme and violent that challenge then the more effective it is. Ghost stories are stories which are not safe stories, but stories in which the unusual and unexpected will happen, stories to turn the normal world upside-down.

However, before embarking on a more detailed analysis of the rôle of violence and the supernatural within teenage oral narrative, it is worth pointing out that this is not a modern phenomenon. The prominence of violence and the occult in teenage narrative has often been quoted as evidence for an unhealthy obsession amongst adolescents, fuelled by the experience of an increasingly violent society and glamourised by mass media made ever more accessible to the young through economic and technological developments within the home and society in general. So-called video nasties now available over the counter and regulated by ineffective censorship laws, and the recent upsurge in popularity of simulated violence through computer games, all contribute to and are symptomatic of, we are told by moralists and fundamentalists, a general moral decline in society brought about by a lack of discipline in the school and home and an absence of parental guidance and control.

Whilst it may be argued that the more violent a society becomes, or the more it accepts violence as a norm, then the more that moral shift will be reflected culturally, and in particular in popular and populist culture. The relationship between art and society in general is extremely complex and the notion of dismissing cultural trends on the grounds of taste is, at the very least, suspect. It is also quite absurd to presume that the cultural use of violence is specific to the late twentieth century. Violence was just as prevalent, if not more so, in earlier societies and this violence is represented culturally. This is nowhere more obvious than in folklore. Decapitations, cannibalism, dismemberings and violent sadism are just as much part of the folk and fairy tale as they are of the modern teenage narrative.

It has already been shown that the teenage repertoire links in to and is reflective of an older narrative tradition. It modernises traditional stories or borrows heavily from their motifs and structures, and so when a teenager tells of mad axemen and hairy hands, s/he is being totally consistent with traditional narrative imagery, as well as portraying it in a way that reflects the modern violence of a modern society.

The same is true of the supernatural. As has been shown in studies by other folklorists (Bennett et al), hitchhiking ghosts (Wilson 7-11), hairy hands (Wilson 31), ghostly mirrors (Wilson 67-68), clocks stopping at the death of the owner (Wilson 52-53), to name but a few, are the stock-in-trade of the old, traditional narrative as well as of the modern adolescent repertoire. Let us take, for instance, the following story, told by John, a thirteen year old student again from Lipson Community College in Plymouth (Wilson 40).

It's about a story I was told.

There was this lady who lived near this school. She lived up the road, there's this pub that had been boarded up and things like that and she told me a story.

The landlord that lived in it about ten years ago, killed his wife and two children in the front room and took them down into the cellar and buried them in the corner. Then he killed himself and when the police came out they only found his body and blood all over the wall.

So they got rid of all their possessions and things and the next tenants moved in, the landlord. And when they went in they found all this blood and like thing on the wallpaper.

So they stripped it all off and put on their own expensive wallpaper and they didn't know why, but red patches kept on showing where the blood was on the walls.

So they stripped it down again, thinking there was something wrong with the paste, and it was a different paste and the same thing happened again.

So they ended up getting some professional decorators to come in and then decorate it. And they decorated it and the blood was coming through as well.

And then at nights things started moving around, around the pub, bottles and things.

So the landlord and tenant was a bit scared of this and they called in their cousin or auntie who was a ...what d'you call them?...and she stayed in the room where the blood kept on seeping through onto the wallpaper and she was asleep and she imagined herself getting up and walking out of the door and down to the cellar and she was looking at this hump of earth in the corner of the cellar, 'cos it was an old pub and the cellar floor was still out of mud. And she saw this lump and she woke up and ran and got the landlord or whatever and took them down to see and showed them this lump she'd seen in her dream.

So they called the police and the police came down with spades and dug up the lump and found the decayed bodies of the landlord's wife and child.

Here we have many of the elements which may be seen to characterise the teenage narrative. It is a story of murder, but also of extremely violent murder, emphasised by the reappearing blood. It is also a murder of tragic poignancy, as it is a double murder committed by the father of the house, who then kills himself. Added to this is the introduction of an element of mystery; 'When the police came out, they only found his body.' John's insertion of this information early on in the story is an effective piece of dramatic irony. It tells us, the audience, that there is unfinished business, there are still two bodies missing and this can only spell trouble for later on in the story. It is only when new tenants move into the pub that the real horror begins and the blood keeps reappearing on the walls as a ghostly reminder of the past violent tragedy.

Three attempts are made to solve the problem through conventional means (redecorating the haunted room) until they finally call in a spiritual medium who is able to locate the missing bodies and so presumably end the hauntings by bringing the violent episode of the past to its natural conclusion.

In John's story we can identify the following elements which are all, either separately or severally, characteristic of the teenage ghost narrative.

1) Violence - the murder
2) Tragic Poignancy - the family situation
3) The Unfinished Business - the undiscovered corpses
4) Horror - the blood
5) The Haunting - manifestation of blood on walls
6) The triumph of the supernatural over conventional
   wisdom

It may also be significant that the story is told about a specific location, as a local legend. Let us then compare the story with another local legend, this time from County Antrim, Northern Ireland. It is a well-known traditional narrative of the area, collected by myself from a non-teenage source, Billy Teare, a storyteller from Doagh, also in County Antrim.

Well, what's supposed to have happened, well...

One of the previous owners from - you're not interested in dates? 'Cos I don't really know.

Basically, what's supposed to have happened was that, I think one of the previous owner's wives was almost, well she wasn't very often seen about, yer man sort of kept her in the one room and then she disappeared and was meant to have gone to some relatives.

And whether she was murdered or not....I'm not too sure about that either....where you can see from here, that room was supposed to be the room she was kept in and there was some dastardly deed supposedly done in there and ever after that anybody who owned Red Hall,...no matter what they did with the room, whether they painted it or put wallpaper on it, whatever, this blood was supposed to always show through the paper or show through the paintwork and it was usually in the form of a sort of bloody red hand. It showed through on one wall

73

and eventually the doorway to the room was sealed up and the window bricked up and plastered over, and that's the way you see it today.
Right, that's about it.

On the one hand the two narratives are separate, distinguishable from each other in time and location; the first is set in contemporary Plymouth and the second in historical Antrim, and yet we immediately notice that both stories share the central motif of ineradicable blood stains at the site of the past tragedy.[1] However, the similarities go beyond this. We can see that the story of Red Hall follows an identical structural pattern to that proposed for John's story.

1) Violence - the murder or 'dastardly deed'
2) Tragic Poignancy - the family situation
3) The Unfinished Business - undiscovered murder/body,
   'disappearance' of the woman
4) Horror - the blood
5) The Haunting - manifestation of blood (hand) on
   walls
6) The triumph of the supernatural over conventional
   wisdom - defeat is eventually admitted and the room
   sealed off

We can see, therefore, from this example that a concern with violence is not limited to the teenage repertoire and that their 'ghost' stories display patterns that are comparable with those of many adult storytellers and other traditional narrative.

Sex and violence

Much has already been made of the inherent violence in the folktale, especially in terms of Freudian analysis, which seeks to explain the violent imagery as a symbolic physicalisation of latent sexual fantasy. Thus, Alan Dundes explains the maniac's hooked hand in the contemporary legend 'The Hook' as a phallus, attempting (unsuccessfully) to penetrate the female passenger. Likewise the Mad Axeman in the legend of the same name tries to penetrate the vehicle in which the lone woman is waiting. In the Grimms' version of 'Rotkäppchen' ('Little Red Riding Hood') the story concerns itself with rape,[2] and the woodcutter, a character, incidentally, added by the

Grimms to give the story a new moral meaning, carries an axe as a symbol of his masculinity.

In his essay on 'The Castrated Boy' (Carroll, 1987), Michael P. Carroll interprets this particular contemporary legend[3] as one about female fantasies of male castration, reflecting 'the gratification of their (women's) unconscious desire to castrate a male' (Carroll, 1987, p.219).

Furthermore, in terms of the Freudian theory that within folktales lurk our most basic fantasies, the level of violence in teenage stories could be interpreted as either a manifestation of the Oedipus Complex amongst male storytellers - a desire to kill the father expressed in terms of a violent intrusion upon a rational, patriarchal society - or as the logical extension of penis envy amongst female storytellers - a desire to castrate a male as in 'The Castrated Boy', again symbolised by a violent, unfettered attack on a male-dominated world.

Whilst accepting that sexuality has a (sometimes important) rôle in teenage storytelling and that that sexuality is often represented symbolically, it would, I think, be wrong to give it the overinflated importance that forms the basis of Freudian analysis.

It is often assumed that adolescents' stories would be both sexually explicit and heavily sexually symbolic. I am sure that sexual fantasy is extremely common amongst adolescents and plays a large part in shaping their behaviour as a growing sexual awareness influences their social lives, their expectations and, also, what is expected of them. Furthermore, I am also sure that sexually explicit jokes and anecdotes are exchanged amongst teenagers, as this is an important part of the liminal process, a part of the education required to allow transition into the adult world. Unfortunately, I have no way of bearing witness to such exchanges, since as an adult I am excluded (again the curse of the folklorist and his/her inability to remain neutral to the material), and I can only base my assumption on my own (imperfect) memories of adolescence. However, leaving such jokes and brief exchanges aside, it comes as a surprise to many that sexual elements in teenage narratives are largely inexplicit. This is because such sexual explicitness would largely be outside their own experience, and narrative situations are based in reality rather than fantasy, no matter how incredible the actual events within the narrative may appear to be. In discussing the task of interpreting folktales, Jack Zipes tells us that 'a thorough analysis.....must take into account the background of the narrators and their communities' (Zipes, 1992, p.30) and that 'changes (in the tales) depend on the social *realities*[4] of the period in which the tales are told' (Zipes, 1992, p.33).

It will be seen that whilst there is a latent sexuality lurking in the shadow of much teenage storytelling, the stated relationships between the sexes remain firmly within the tellers' own experience. Therefore, whilst there is clearly an implied sexuality in the threat posed by the Mad Axeman to the lone, abandoned female passenger (Wilson 13-22) or to the woman by the potential assailant in 'The Licked Hand' (Wilson 23-30), it remains unstated and firmly in the imagination, whereas the stated relationships between the genders are those of girlfriend/boyfriend or husband/wife and their behaviour never exceeds the limits of public and adult morality.

There is, of course, purpose behind this. In order for the bizarre and incredible events within a story to have maximum effect, they must grow out of a realistic and believable situation. There is little to be gained for the teenage storyteller from gratuitous sexual explicitness. Teenage storytellers will, instead, carefully manage the information of a story as skilfully as an adult teller. To explicitly state sexuality in a story would simply render the other powerful (and violent) images less effective and, whilst there is an implied link between the violence and sexuality within oral narratives, this is not, at least in the teenage experience, their prime purpose.

The supernatural, rites of passage, morbidity and mortality

In his essay 'Legend-Tripping in Ohio: A Behavioral Survey', Bill Ellis asserts that 'the legend-trip....is linked to the coming-of-age crisis among white small-town or suburban adolescents' (Ellis, 1982, p.61). Here Ellis is talking specifically about legend-tripping, an activity closely linked to storytelling, which involves the ritual telling of a ghost story and then a visit to the location where the story is supposed to have taken place. Furthermore, he is dealing primarily with a post-pubescent sixteen to eighteen year-old age group, whereas the majority of material in this study is collected from pre-pubescent and pubescent storytellers. Nevertheless, Ellis is right to make the link between this kind of activity and age. The fascination of adolescents with all things supernatural has long been linked with the varying crises and awakenings of puberty. Brunvand claims that this represents the journey from the safety of childhood into the unknown, potentially dangerous world of the adult; 'Therefore, although the immediate purpose of many of these legends is to produce a good scare, they also serve to deliver a warning' (Brunvand, 1981, p.48). Ellis would seem to agree, arguing that legend-tripping is, at least in part, to do with confronting fears within a safe environment (Ellis, 1982, p.69).

There are certainly no grounds for disagreeing with the substance of these conclusions. The world of the supernatural is a world in which humans have little or no control. Things happen to them, things which are beyond the rules of the controlled and rational world which we normally inhabit; the characters in these ghost stories are generally not in control of events, and their safe world where things happen according to natural laws is invaded by the irrational world of the supernatural. This can be seen to symbolise the transition of the adolescent who is likewise entering a world over which s/he has little or no control. The telling of ghost stories is a way of confronting those fears about the unknown road ahead, and a method of rehearsing the entry into unfamiliar and uncontrollable territory. Likewise, such activity (and especially the more extensive legend-tripping phenomenon) can be seen as part of a complex initiation process, controlled by one's contemporaries, from childhood into post-pubescent society.

In addition we can also interpret this fascination with the supernatural as a reflection of the common concerns of mortality, which are heightened during liminal periods. During any periods of transition in our lives, whether it is the passage into adulthood or the death of a parent or partner (effectively a transition into an older generation), we are reminded of our own mortality and often turn to the supernatural as a way of dealing with fears and realisations. Considering that puberty is a relatively long period of transition, it cannot be surprising that issues of mortality are a major concern amongst adolescents.

However, to explain away the proliferation of supernatural motifs and images in the teenage narrative purely in these terms would be as incomplete as interpreting images of violence purely in terms of sexuality. I believe that such images are so common in teenage stories for one very important reason, a reason which Bill Ellis also recognises when he describes legend-tripping as 'from start to finish a way of "giving the finger" to adult rationality' (Ellis, 1982, p.69), for teenage storytelling is also about 'ritual rebellion' (Ellis, 1982, p.69) and this is signalled by the heavy use of violence, horror and the supernatural.

Bakhtin, the teenage story and the emancipatory potential of the folktale

The eminent American folklorist William R Bascom claimed that folklore 'serves to sanction and validate religious, social, political and economic institutions and to play an important rôle as an educative device in their transmission from one generation to another' (Bascom, 1965). It is true that on occasions folklore can indeed serve the purpose of passing on a set of moral values from one generation to the next, thus preserving the status quo - this is particularly true of stories with a sacred significance, for example - and the notion of folklore as a vehicle for the transmitting of knowledge is indeed important. Nevertheless this is an over-simple view, particularly when we are discussing the folktale, since a story is just as likely to attempt to criticise and undermine the existing social and economic structures as support them. Of course, this all depends very much upon the circumstances under which the story is being told, both in the specific paraperformative terms of the telling and in the wider historical context. The potential for the orally transmitted narrative to be a vehicle for satire and social criticism is surely not in question.

Jack Zipes tackles the issue head on and comes down firmly in opposition to Bascom's views, preferring to recognise the 'emancipatory potential' (Zipes, 1992, p.ix) of the folk tale. The fairy tale, which Zipes defines as being the literary form of the oral folk tale, on the other hand represents the appropriation of the folk tale 'in its entirety by aristocratic and bourgeois writers in the sixteenth, seventeenth and eighteenth centuries' (Zipes 1992: 7), thus endowing it with new meanings. However, Zipes maintains that 'the folk tale is part of a pre-capitalist people's oral tradition which expresses their wishes to attain better living conditions through a depiction of their struggles and contradictions' (Zipes, 1992, p.27), and he concludes, in clear defiance of Bascom; 'No matter what has become of the fairy tale, its main impulse was at first revolutionary and progressive, not escapist, as has too often been suggested' (Zipes, 1992, p.36).

Although Zipes is concentrating his study upon the pre-industrial, agrarian folk tale, his conclusions clearly can be seen to apply to the folk tale in a wider context in the sense that it represents an emancipatory and revolutionary force rather than a reactionary and conformist one, by retaining cultural power in the hands of 'the people'. This notion of the revolutionary and rebellious potential of folklore is one that was developed by Mikhail Bakhtin and is particularly relevant to teenage narratives. It does, I think, hold the key to our understanding of the meaning of violent and supernatural imagery in the adolescent repertoire.

In his study of Rabelais (Bakhtin, 1984), Bakhtin uses folk and popular culture as his starting point, arguing that folk culture is subversive in nature by challenging accepted codes of taste and morality.

> To be understood he (Rabelais) requires an essential reconstruction of our entire artistic and ideological perception, the renunciation of many deeply rooted demands of literary taste, and the revision of many concepts. Above all, he requires an exploration in depth of a sphere as yet little and superficially studied, the tradition of folk humour (Bakhtin, 1984, p.3).

The notion of humour is given prime importance in Bakhtin's analysis. Laughter, he argues, has been often neglected in folklore study and yet it should be at its very centre since laughter is a revolutionary tool. He cites examples of medieval popular culture where carnival pageants, comic verbal compositions and curses, oaths and blasons populaires were used as weapons of parody and satire against officialdom. The same, of course, is true of the early modern commedia dell' arte, which grew out of folk traditions and was well-known for its outspoken criticism of Church and State, leading to the widespread censorship of the form.

This humour was made most effective, Bakhtin suggests, through what he calls 'grotesque realism' (Bakhtin, 1984, p.18), which, amongst other things, is characterised by an exaggeration of the physical. It rejects the 'aesthetics of the beautiful' (Bakhtin, 1984, p.29) as conceived and defined by the Renaissance, but indulges in representations of the extremes of physicality. Images of the physical are, in effect, exaggerated to grotesque proportions.

Bakhtin also identifies the importance of the madness motif which he argues,

> is inherent in all grotesque forms, because madness makes men look at the world with different eyes, not dimmed by 'normal', that is by commonplace ideas and judgements. In folk grotesque, madness is a gay parody of official reason, of the narrow seriousness of official 'truth' (Bakhtin, 1984, p.37).

Bakhtin, like Zipes, also notes how the folk form was adopted by literary movements, notably Romanticism, and given new meaning. Literary Romantic grotesque he sees as fundamentally different from folk grotesque; 'only in Romanticism do we find the peculiar grotesque theme of the tragic doll' (Bakhtin, 1984, p.40). This is interesting because, of course, the theme of the doll with human or superhuman capabilities is one that is important in modern folk narratives and particularly in the teenage tradition. It may well be that this has grown out of literary Romanticism, but it is worth noting that if this is the case, then a further transformation in meaning has taken place as it has been reabsorbed into an oral (or, as Bakhtin would prefer, 'unofficial'[5]) tradition, since in the teenage narrative the doll is not seen as a tragic victim, but as a vicious, unpredictable and murderous threat. The following example is common and widespread (Wilson 36).

> There was a young girl called Mary and she was about to go to bed and she says, 'G'night mum,' and she started walking up the stairs, and she

had this doll and she could hear kids' voices going, 'Mary on the first step, Mary on the second step...' up to, like, the fifth step.

And she was going, 'Oh no!' and she ran back and says, 'Mum, mum, I can hear these voices,' and she says, 'Oh it's just your imagination, go back to sleep. Go on, go back upstairs.'

So she started walking and she could hear these voices going, 'Mary on the sixth step, Mary on the seventh step..' right up to the ninth step.

She said, 'Oh mum, I can still hear these voices, it's really scaring me.'

She said, 'Well, don't worry about it, dear. Go on, go on upstairs.' And she walked to the bottom step and started walking to see what happens, and she started walking up and got to the landing and she could hear, 'Mary on the landing. Mary in the bedroom, Mary in her bed.'

So she'd gone to bed and went to sleep.

And the next morning her mum went up to get her and she'd got a pierrot doll and the little girl had been killed. Mary had been killed and the pierrot doll was smiling and the tear had gone.......There was a knife in her back.

(Catherine Wriggle, age c.14, Falmouth Youth Club, 9.3.93)

To sum up Bakhtin's argument, folk culture is essentially a subversive culture, which undermines authority and the status quo by presenting grotesque images of physical extremes which fly in the face of official perceptions of taste and decency and, furthermore, has the nerve to create humour out of it.

It seems that this analysis is particularly pertinent to a study of teenage storytelling, and I would argue that the preponderance of violent and supernatural imagery in teenage narratives serves the primary purpose of rebelling against authority, cocking a snook at the adult world, of which they will soon (but not yet) be part. In the words of Bill Ellis; 'The legend provides the incentive to rebel against this "stagnant", adult-governed establishment' (Ellis, 1982, p.69).

It is important to note that teenage narratives are not simply littered with horrific images; they are littered with grotesque images which are horrific, because they offend so-called standards of public decency. This is not to say that violent and horrific images are introduced gratuitously. In fact, in the hands of a skilful storyteller such imagery is carefully controlled, as is all other information, to maximise the effect of the grotesque. It is only when the unskilful storyteller is at work that we see violent image piled upon horrific image and so destroying ultimately its effectiveness.

What it is vital to understand is the effect such imagery is designed to produce. It is, of course, structured to elicit a clear reaction amongst the audience; moreover not just a reaction that is internalised, but one that is outwardly and publicly expressed. However, that reaction is not one of shock, but rather of laughter. Of course, laughter can be part of a nervous reaction, but in my experience the laughter produced by teenagers in response to grotesque, violent imagery is laughter born of genuine humour and pleasure.

Let me take one step further. Such imagery is intended to produce laughter amongst its teenage audience and shock amongst its adult audience. In fact, when there are adults present at a teenage storytelling session, especially where those adults are seen as being in a position of authority (e.g. teachers), at least part of the laughter and pleasure of the teenage audience can be put down to the distaste and discomfort of the adults. The one is directly proportional to the other!

In the same way that Bakhtin's folk carnival challenges the structures of authority, so the teenage narrative will often offend our adult sensibilities, because that is exactly what it is meant to do. Let me quote an example from my own experience.

On 8 November 1994 I was conducting some fieldwork at Cheyne Middle School on the Isle of Sheppey, Kent. I was telling a class of Year 7 students (11-12 year olds) 'The Singing Bone', in the hope that it might prompt a variant from the class. Sure enough, a female student came forward with a story about a man who suspected his wife of having an affair. He then strangled her with a length of piano wire and restrung the piano with a string made from the skin of the dead woman. Thenceforth when the piano was played, it sang a song which told of the murder (Wilson 39). Clearly this is a variant of 'The Singing Bone' and, excited as I was to hear the story, the reactions of the class teacher and the storyteller's contemporaries were equally interesting.

The teacher, who had not flinched during my own quite bloody retelling of 'The Singing Bone', showed visible and audible signs of distaste and discomfort as the more gruesome details of the girl's story unfolded, even though the story was being told in summary form as a response to my own telling. On the other hand, the students who had shuddered during my story, found their colleague's version quite hilarious. In fact, as the teacher's disapproval became apparent, the audience began to take even more delight in the story, some even giving vocal support and encouragement to the teller.

David Buchan talks of 'the gruesome-funny' (Buchan, 1981, p.10) tale, and it is quite clear that violent and horrific imagery may be used in teenage storytelling to provoke laughter rather than disgust. This is even, it could be argued, the case with the 'jump' story, where although the prime intention in the telling is to make the audience jump by increasing the tension during the performance and then releasing it with a shout, the ultimate reaction is usually one of laughter, undermining the artificially enhanced fear experienced during the telling. Admittedly this laughter has much to do with the sudden release of tension, but there is also a sense of collusion in the shared laughter between audience and teller that a taboo has been broken in the gruesome sharing of the story.

It is also worth noting that tied up closely with images of horror and violence in the teenage narratives is the theme of madness. As already explained, Bakhtin gives great weight to this in relation to grotesque forms. Of course, Bakhtin sees madness as an ultimately positive force since it defies the restrictive rationality of conformity and the status quo, and yet, whilst representing an irrational and uncontrollable force, in the teenage narrative it is more often than not depicted as a threatening force, specifically out to do harm. As Bill Ellis says, 'the more popular threats are maniacs and escaped mental patients who prowl around "parking" roads, looking for unwary carloads of teenagers to liquidate' (Ellis, 1982, pp.62-3). Likewise, looking through a sample from my own archive, lunatics are just as likely as escaped murderers and the Devil to prey on unsuspecting victims.

If the use of violent and horrific motifs and images is, at least partly, to do with rebellion, challenging and subverting accepted standards of taste and authority, then this is also the case with the supernatural and the occult. Of course, supernatural and violent/horrific images often go hand in hand in teenage narratives, in that supernatural images are often horrific as well, or ghosts have a tendency towards acts of violence. However, this is not always the case, and yet I would still argue that the simple telling of a ghost story, in a teenage context, is to some extent an act of defiance to the adult world.

Firstly, ghost stories are subversive on a symbolic level, in that by telling such a story, the storyteller is describing, and thus giving credence to, a world which is in stark opposition to adult society. Here is a world in which rationality offers little defence against supernatural forces. No amount of reasoned argument will protect the lone female from the Mad Axeman, and no amount of moral decency will prevent an encounter with a determined ghost. It is, in other words, a world without order, an anarchic place where nothing can be taken for granted. It is not that by depicting such a world teenagers are creating a utopian ideal - there is too much danger and threat for that - but they are laying claim to situations which reflect their own concerns and defy the rationale of existing patriarchal power structures.

Ghost stories also offer a secondary, and potentially stronger, level of subversion, and this lies in the uneasy relationship between the supernatural and Christianity. Whilst I shall not examine the contradictions in this relationship between the supernatural and Christian theology in any great detail, it is important to note that things are far from settled in this sphere and the growth over recent years in evangelical fundamentalism in the United States and Europe has brought the issue to the fore.

Of course, most adults have no moral objection to ghost stories as such - we all enjoy a good scare as much as the next person - but many would also have strict views as to how far things should go, for example drawing the line at legend-tripping or more obvious cases of experimentation with the occult. There are also certain movements within the Christian Churches, usually those on the right wing, which are opposed outright to any cultural expression of the supernatural, on the grounds that any such activity fundamentally is anti-Christian. To talk of ghosts, it is argued, is to flirt with witches, Satan and Devil-worshipping. Ghostlore forms part of a pre-Christian (and, therefore, Pagan and anti-Christian) system of folk belief, and perhaps this is why hardly a Hallowe'en goes by without letters in any local press from religious leaders and laypersons (often hysterically) demanding an end to children's participation in any Hallowe'en event. It is a fear, incidentally, which is often fuelled by Hallowe'en scare stories which have been well-documented by contemporary legend scholars (cf. Grider, 1984). Although such opinion is in the minority, it is an active and vocal minority, usually with a strong local power base on schools' boards of governors, community councils, parish councils, etc., and in my professional career, I have heard of many occasions where schools and libraries (even from time to time whole county-wide library services) have abandoned all Hallowe'en activity for fear of the fundamentalist backlash. It is a very real threat and I too have experienced a situation where, whilst I was telling a Devil-as-trickster folktale to a class of primary school children, a young child covered his ears with his hands and declared, 'I don't want to hear about the Devil! I'm a Christian!'

Of course, such extreme reactions are rare and not the norm and, furthermore, it is somewhat heartening to know that, in spite of the rantings of the religious and political right, folk custom is made of sterner stuff. However, rare as it is, it is nonetheless a loud and effective voice which makes itself heard. For the teenager such a moralistic position is the logical extension of an adult society based on rationalism and strict codes of moral decency and acceptable, responsible behaviour. It is the adult world and its structures taken to its extreme, but obvious, conclusion.

Therefore, by telling ghost stories and making wide use of supernatural imagery, the teenage storyteller is not only committing an act of defiance to standards of fundamentalist Christian morality, but also to the adult world in general. What is more, by taking such clearly expressed pleasure in such stories, by telling them as funny as well as scary, the act of defiance is made the more effective. This is adding insult to injury.

This, of course, is what Bakhtin means when he describes fear as 'the extreme expression of narrow-minded and stupid seriousness, which is defeated by laughter' (Bakhtin, 1984, p.47). For Bakhtin, fear is an emotion of imprisonment, whilst laughter is a liberating force. The teenager is expected by the adult world to be frightened by ghost stories, just as adults are, conforming to their own patterns of behaviour, and so laughter is a liberating act of defiance. However, fear and laughter are not as incompatible as Bakhtin suggests.

Naturally, even teenagers primarily tell ghost stories to scare each other, even if this is part of a complex rehearsal for confronting fears or initiation into the post-pubescent world. There is, of course, a pleasure to be had in being frightened within a safe environment, but fear and laughter are not mutually exclusive, but instead part of a more complex relationship. It is quite possible to be frightened by the narrative, whilst finding specific details of that narrative, or descriptions within it, funny. Keith Cunningham sees the relationship between belief and non-belief in the performance of stories as a continuum, thus:

Believed------------------------------------Non-Believed
(Cunningham, 1990, p.4)

Cunningham notes that as we move along the continuum towards non-belief then there is an increased emphasis on the part of the storyteller on the performative aspects of the story. In other words, the story is told more for its performative effect and becomes more conscious of itself. A similar continuum could be placed alongside this to illustrate the relationship between fear and laughter.

Fear--Laughter

Likewise, as we move towards the laughter end of the continuum, the emphasis on performative detail becomes stronger. Towards the other pole (fear) the performance becomes less self-conscious. This, of course, is closely tied in with believability, since the more a story is told for entertainment, for laughs, the more the teller concentrates on his/her performance, and the less likely a story is to be accepted as true. Exactly where the storyteller places his/her performance on the continuum is an artistic decision governed by his/her understanding of context.

However, even in a story which is told purely to scare, perhaps a cautionary tale, humour need never be totally excluded. Of course, in longer narratives, laughter can serve as comic relief, releasing the tension and so allowing it to build up again more intensely later on in the story. It can also serve to emphasise the vulnerability and/or stupidity of characters within the narrative, so heightening the tension and fear through an implied dramatic irony.

Fear, then, is also an important element of teenage ghost storytelling, and, although it is at the opposite end of the continuum to laughter, the two are not at all mutually exclusive. Furthermore, it is worth noting that the fear is not the spiritual fear of the religious fundamentalist, but a more concrete fear. It is a fear of being physically or psychologically hurt, rather than fear of eternal damnation!

Conclusion

In conclusion, therefore, it can be said that the adolescent taste for violence, horror and the supernatural in their stories can be explained in a number of ways. There are interpretations according to an awakening sexuality, the psychological in addition to the physical transition and initiation into the adult world, including issues of mortality and a need to reassess one's purpose and position in the world in the light of this transition. All these are valid, but in terms of teenage storytelling there is an added layer of meaning, in that it is subversive and rebellious and this is perhaps its overriding significance and helps explain the adolescent cultural fascination with such matters.

In a society where one of our greatest fears is that of increasing violence, especially amongst the young, then the teenage oral narrative must find a way of giving a metaphorical v-sign to adult society. The fact that those on the moralistic right wing are so outraged by teenagers' supposed obsession with all things ghostly, gruesome and gory is a sure sign that the stories are doing their job effectively. If Bakhtin and Zipes are correct and the folktale is a liberating force and its purpose is to rebel and revolt against the perceived establishment, then we should hardly be surprised that the teenage narrative has succeeded in touching the raw nerve of adult sensibilities.

It is in this sense that teenagers' stories are so often 'unsafe'. They are risky and dangerous by virtue of their breaking of taboos and refusing to conform to accepted standards of taste, constantly running the gauntlet of decent adult society.

Notes

[1] For an example of this motif being adopted into the literary tradition, see

The Canterville Ghost by Oscar Wilde.

[2] In his book *The Trials and Tribulations of Little Red Riding Hood*, (2nd Edition. New York: Routledge, 1993), Jack Zipes has shown successfully that the story was originally a tale about a girl's rite of passage, the transition into womanhood, and of women taking control of their own destinies.

[3] 'The Castrated Boy', or CB story, as Carroll calls it, concerns the castration of a young boy in the toilets of a shopping arcade whilst temporarily separated from his mother.

[4] My emphasis.

[5] In our late twentieth century, technologically-advanced, Western society, where folklore is no longer circulated purely by oral means, but also by xerox, fax, the mass media, etc., then 'unofficial' may well be a useful term in helping us redefine our terms of reference.

5 The rôle of other media in the creation, maintenance and development of teenage oral narrative traditions

It is not really so very long ago that scholars were using the oral medium as a defining criterion of folklore. For the folklorists of the nineteenth and early twentieth centuries, this is indeed understandable since they perceived their task as being one of 'a rescue operation, a reconstruction of the past from relics in the memory of the old people' (Dégh, 1994, p.5). Folklore was seen as a product of a pre-literate society and the oral nature of the transmission of folktales in traditional communities was seen as definitive, and, indeed, in the face of growing industrialisation and developing technology, there was an undoubted attraction to the pastoral nostalgia that folklore represented. In his preface to *Folk Culture in a World of Technology* (Bausinger, 1990), the German folklorist Hermann Bausinger criticises this stance:

> In Germany folklore and folk life were not so much realities but anti-modernist constructions based on a repressive ideology and compensating for the alienation of modern life (Bausinger, 1990, p.xi).

Bausinger himself saw folklore as wallowing in what Dan Ben-Amos calls 'its romantic naiveté and idealisation of traditional life' ('Foreword' to Bausinger, 1990, p.vii).

However, this romantic view of folklore as the dying culture of a naive, simple and illiterate underclass and its narrow insistence on oral transmission, is not one confined to the Victorian and Edwardian scholars. We can also see its survival through to the 1960s and beyond. In *The Study of Folklore* (Dundes, ed., 1965), although the editor, Alan Dundes, himself admits that folklore can also be passed on in written form, eminent folklorists such as Francis Lee Utley (Utley, 1965) and William R. Bascom (Bascom, 1965) seemingly line up to declare their allegiance to the belief that 'all folklore is orally transmitted' (Bascom, 1965). In addition Ronald L. Baker notes that in

1966 MacEdward Leach was bemoaning technological advances as sounding a death knell for folklore and tradition (cf. Baker, 1976). In fact even as late as 1981, Jan Harold Brunvand was defining folklore as 'oral[1] tradition in variants' (Brunvand, 1981, p.3) and others have since followed suit.

However, there is now a broad recognition that folklore can indeed be transmitted in any number of ways. Of course, if oral transmission is the only, or prime, medium of communication in any society, then folklore will be transmitted in this way, but in a society that has at its disposal the computer, the fax machine, the telephone, etc., then we should not be surprised that these will be commissioned as vehicles for the dissemination of folklore in its many forms. Bausinger argues that folklore is, in fact, not ahistorical (Bausinger, 1990, p.7) and this is indeed true, since folklore, like any cultural construct, will be a product of its own time and will adapt both its content and modes of transmission to meet contemporary realities. Traditions, of course, are not fixed items, but are constantly changing and being reinterpreted by successive generations and different groups within the same generation. As Linda Dégh says: 'Folklore.....is the product of an ongoing historical process that consolidates the interaction of literary and oral....constructed and improvised creativity' (Dégh, 1994, p.1), and, indeed, even those of us who do not have access to fax machines or the Internet cannot escape the fact that in the Western world we now live in a largely literate society and that as such folklore will often be transmitted in written form.

The transmission of folklore through means other than oral is not a particularly recent development. Although the Victorian Folklorists were 'scholars who took it for granted that folklore was a self-contained, self-perpetuating art of an illiterate folk, free from literary influence' (Dégh, 1994, p.12), we know that literary traditions had an important influence on the folk culture of the time. Of course, the collectors of folk tales from Perrault through to Jacobs and Laing were involved in publishing their findings for popular circulation, they were writing for a largely middle class readership and not in order to more widely disseminate the stories amongst the people from whom they had been collected. However, this undoubtedly did happen to some degree. Developments in education had meant that literacy was on the increase amongst the lower classes, and research has shown that many items collected from 'traditional' singers were learned from published chapbook texts. Folktales were sometimes learned in the same way. Even many of the Grimms' storytellers at the beginning of the nineteenth century, both peasant and bourgeois, had learned their tales either directly or indirectly from written sources (cf. Dégh, 1994, p.18), and the popularisation of the literary fairy tale following the publication of *Kinder- und*

Hausmärchen in 1812 served to increase the accessibility of the literary fairy tale and this process. It would, therefore, be true to say that at least for the past two hundred years literary and oral traditions have existed side by side in an interdependent relationship enriching each other, and the notion of an undiluted, pure oral tradition is a piece of folklore itself. In fact, this process is no more obvious than in what are nowadays often termed 'the classic fairy tales'. If one were to eavesdrop on an adult telling a child the story of 'Little Red Riding Hood', the story would no doubt be a variant of one of the many literary versions of the tale and most probably that of the Grimms. In the case of 'Snow White', Walt Disney might also take an influential rôle. In any case, this 'Red Riding Hood' would be far removed from the oral version of the text collected in Brittany in 1885.

All of this, of course, is not to deny the importance of oral communication in the folklore process. As long as people continue to talk to each other and use speech as the most common tool of social interaction, then the oral communicative process will remain central to the folklorist's concerns. However, in a rapidly changing world, we must recognise that items of folklore will be passed on in any way that is possible and that technology is not necessarily the enemy of folk tradition. In fact, Bausinger argues that technology has always played an important rôle in folklore (Bausinger, 1990, p.12) and Linda Dégh quotes from Rudolf Schenda's paper 'Folklore und Massenkultur'[2]: 'Never did folklore fare better than under the flag of mass culture' (Dégh, 1994, p.2). And Ronald L Baker declares that 'a dominant mass culture does not necessarily mean the end of folklore' (Baker, 1976, p.367). We can even see from the large amount of narratives which are the focus of this study that even today's technology-obsessed adolescent is an effective communicator of traditional narrative folklore.

However, this study concerns itself with those teenage narratives which are in oral circulation and so it is not my intention to investigate in detail the transmission of folklore via other media as such. It would indeed be misguided to examine the dissemination of folklore by any particular medium in isolation, without reference to other forms of transmission. The various media operate in a complex inter-relationship, nourishing, informing and drawing from one another, and it is, therefore, rather my intention in this chapter to examine that relationship and look at ways in which the oral traditions of teenagers have been influenced by a variety of other media.

The literary tradition

It is probably the literary tradition that has the biggest influence on the oral repertoire. A good example of this is the story *The Monkey's Paw* by W W Jacobs.

In brief, it is a ghost story which tells of a man and wife who one day receive a visit from a long-lost friend. The visitor, who has been in the army in India, leaves in their custody a fetish, a monkey's paw which has the power to grant them three wishes. However, the paw also comes with a warning that the three wishes must never be made, since it will only cause pain and trouble. Nevertheless, the man is overcome by temptation and uses the claw to wish for two hundred pounds. Shortly afterwards they receive another visit, this time to inform them that their only son has been killed in an accident at work and the compensation payment amounts to exactly two hundred pounds. In their grief the woman persuades her husband to take the paw and wish for their son to be alive. Later that stormy night an increasingly violent knocking is heard on the door. The woman goes to open the door and as she is struggling with the bolts, her husband, in his horror, grabs the monkey's paw and wishes for his son to be dead. As his wife finally opens the door, there is nobody to be seen.

Whether the story is based on another tale that was already in oral circulation at the time of Jacobs's writing it, it is impossible to tell, but his knowledge of folk narrative must have been good, since the story is littered with folkloric motifs, images and structural devices.

It is also a very well-known and widely-read text and would be familiar to many British and Irish teenagers today. It is certainly a story that I personally can remember from my own teenage years and it is often used in the classroom these days as a standard text for English for twelve to thirteen year-olds. It is, therefore, not surprising that we should find the story in evidence as an oral tale. Whether or not the story was originally an oral tale is, in fact, irrelevant since we can be almost certain that it has entered the teenage repertoire from Jacobs's literary text and the fact that it closely mirrors oral narrative structure has simply smoothed the way for the story to be absorbed into an oral tradition. What is particularly interesting, however, is that by being subjected to the oral process, the story emerges in variant form from the original, not only in terms of the precise language, but also in terms of plot.

The notion of variance is, of course, a central concern for folklorists. Although it is a term born of the now outdated theories of each story being a variant of an original Urtext, the concept of folklore tending towards variance is still of prime importance today. Indeed Linda Dégh suggests that we should replace the term 'oral' with 'variable' in our definitions of folk narrative (Dégh, 1994, p.33). Let us, for example, examine the following version told by Kerry, aged twelve, from Mullion School on the Lizard Peninsula in Cornwall (Wilson 48).

'The Killer Motorbike'

In the country there lived a husband and wife, who were very happy. They had a son, who loved motorbikes.

So, coming up was their son's eighteenth birthday and his parents loved him so much that they bought him a magnificent motorbike. They didn't really want to buy it because they were so dangerous, but they knew how much he loved them.

So when the son came down on the morning of his eighteenth birthday, his parents showed him the magnificent motorbike. He was so pleased that he drove it straight away. He drove it everywhere, but then he was in a fatal accident. He crashed and he died.

His mum and dad were so upset. His dad tried to get on with life and lived things to the full, but his mum just wouldn't forget. She kept on moaning and crying. She was getting so ill with it and one day there was a knock at the door. (knocking sound). She opened it and there was a man dressed in a long dark cloak. He said, 'You want to buy a monkey-paw? It'll give you three wishes.'

She thought for a moment. Three wishes. Three wishes. Three wishes. She said yes. She said she hadn't any money. So the man at the door said, 'I will trade it with you for your lovely silk coat.' So she did.

The lady held the monkey's paw to her heart and thought, 'Three wishes. Three wishes.'

Her husband knew what she wanted to say, but he wouldn't let her have it, until one day she was almost on her death bed, he said, 'You may have your wish.'

So the lady opened the box, took out the monkey's paw and rubbed it three times...(some text missing here as tape ran out)...the son would come back from his grave. Her husband then said, 'Oh no, please, you shouldn't have said that.' But the lady was determined.

They was waiting for a couple of hours for something to happen and then they suddenly heard, down by the garden path, footsteps. But they weren't child's footsteps, they were the footsteps of an old person. They drew closer until they were right outside the room of the husband and wife. They heard a creak of the door (creaking) and slowly he walked in.

But before he could do so, the husband grabbed the box from the lady, rubbed it three times and said, 'Oh, I wish my son to go back to his grave.'

And the son went back to his grave and he said, 'You did this to me, father. You! I shall pay you back!'

Then the man said the third wish, 'I wish this monkey-paw was gone forever.' And it was.

The lady was upset to start with, but she soon started to learn she couldn't weep forever. The husband and wife soon lived happily ever after.

The first thing to be noticed is that the story now has a new title, 'The Killer Motorbike', which, with its twin emphasis on violence and machinery is more suited to modernity and the teenage context. There are also significant changes in the details of the plot of the text. Firstly, the monkey's paw is not introduced into the story until much later in the narrative. Instead the story begins with an episode not present in Jacobs's original, namely the son's birthday and the receipt of that adolescent icon, a 'magnificent motorbike'. However, here there is a cautionary message, because it is in a road accident that he is killed (not an uncommon motif in teenage narrative) rather than through an accident at work. It is only now that the monkey's paw enters the story when it is sold to the couple by a stranger (rather than an old acquaintance). As in Jacobs's story the monkey's paw is able to grant three wishes and it is the husband who is the reluctant partner, the wife herself making the wish by rubbing the paw three times and asking for her son to be alive again (the second wish in Jacobs's story).

As the son returns the husband makes the second wish (Jacobs's third wish) that his son were dead again, but before finally disappearing the ghost of his son issues a chilling warning, in contrast to the written text, where the son's ghost simply vanishes. It is at this point that the man makes his final wish to destroy the paw for ever.

This inconsistency between the two sets of wishes does have a certain significance. In Jacobs's story the monkey's paw has to be introduced at the beginning of the story, because the first wish for the money is necessary in order to precipitate the accident which causes the son's death. In the oral version this is not the case. The fatal road accident is such a common motif in teenage and other contemporary folk narrative that, folklorically speaking, the son's death is no more than a logical extension of his receiving the motorbike, in terms of the narrative. No other explanation is necessary. In a sense, the son's death is determined by the present of the motorbike in the same way that it is by the wish for money in the literary text. In both cases the parents are the unwitting instigators.

However, this now leaves the couple in Jacobs's story short of a wish - the wish to destroy the paw. Of course this is unnecessary since Jacobs explains to us that the paw is capable of granting three wishes to three men and the husband in the story is the third man. Once he has used his three wishes the paw no longer has any magic left in it. In the oral version, though, no such information is given, and so the third and final wish must be retained to bring the story to the same satisfactory conclusion with the destruction of the monkey's paw.

We can see, therefore, that in its transformation into an oral story a significant amount of plot variation has been introduced, whilst retaining the kernel of the original. As we might expect, the same is true of linguistic variation. Jacobs's rather formal, archaic and high-faluting style has been replaced with a modern idiom. However, Kerry's style is still quite formal and polished. The reason for this, I feel, lies in the way the story was collected. Contrary to usual practice, the narrative was forwarded on to me on a cassette by the Head of English at the school, a couple of weeks after I had visited. Therefore, Kerry's story was not spontaneous in the way it would have been had I collected it when I was at the school. Instead she had time to practise and prepare her story and this is clearly evident in the almost faultless performance. There is little, if any, hesitation, no self-corrections or reorientations and no mismanagement of information. This has all been removed through careful rehearsal.

What is most interesting about Kerry's story, however, is the way in which it has acquired many of the defining features of the oral story, or at least what she perceives to be the defining features. These may well have been self-consciously incorporated into the text during her 'rehearsal' period, but they might equally have been added subconsciously during the story's transformation from written to oral. It could even be a mixture of the two; it is impossible to tell. Nevertheless, it is not insignificant that Kerry's story acquires a specifically rural setting ('In the country there lived a husband and wife'), thus giving it the non-industrial setting that she associates with the folk tale. Repetition is also used to emphasise the significance of the three wishes. Furthermore, the folkloric quality of the number three is re-emphasised by the need to rub the paw three times in order to activate its magic, and if that were not enough, Kerry even supplies us with a neat and formulaic happy ending ('The husband and wife soon lived happily ever after').

Thus we can see how a story from a distinctive literary tradition has been absorbed into the teenage oral tradition to produce new variants and, in doing so, has acquired many of the trappings of the 'traditional folk tale'.

Furthermore, this is by no means an isolated case. The recent success of *Point Horror* and *Point Crime* publications[3] has shown that teenagers will read widely in these genres and many stories which enter their oral repertoires will inevitably have been gleaned from their reading. There are three stories in the accompanying archive which are clear examples of this and show that both books and magazines are common sources for stories.

Tammy begins her story (Wilson 79) with the admission, 'I read it in a magazine...', whilst Karen Young from Gillingham, Dorset qualifies her version of the well-known contemporary legend 'The Hook' (Wilson 12) by saying that she read the story in the *Readers' Digest*, a publication which regularly prints such stories, often submitted by readers as having actually happened. Likewise, Mark Duff from Lipson in Plymouth prefaces his narrative with, 'I've got this ghost book' (Wilson 65). In fact there are many cheaply produced anthologies of ghost stories on the market, often aimed at a predominantly male teenage readership, which provide a rich source of narrative material. It is impossible to say just what percentage of stories in the teenage oral repertoire have entered it from written sources, but it is not uncommon for a storyteller to confess to a literary source for a story when questioned, and neither is it rare for teenagers to bring books of this kind along to follow-up sessions I have run. These are then used to remind potential storytellers of material they may at some point share.

What is curious is that these ghost story anthologies seem to be mainly, though not exclusively, in the hands of boys. Of course, once a narrative has entered the oral tradition it will be circulated by both sexes, but the appropriation of the literary ghost story from anthologies appears to be a largely male activity.

Girls, on the other hand, have their own form of popular literature to work from. This appears in the form of the 'teen magazine', whose numbers on the newsagents' racks seem to grow almost daily and a whole new generation of titles has recently hit the market, including publications such as *Sugar*, *Bliss*, *Mizz*, *Big* and *Just Seventeen* to replace their forerunners such as *Jackie* and *Blue Jeans*. These publications are targeted at an exclusively female readership aged between approximately eleven and fifteen. They are essentially gossip magazines, and many of the pages are devoted to interviews, pin-ups and trivia concerning the current favourites of the pop music, television, film and fashion industries. A smaller proportion of pages are set aside for articles on self-image (fashion, make-up, etc.) and issue-based pieces from the serious (e.g. abortion, contraception, smoking, etc.) to the seemingly ridiculous (e.g. how to kiss properly, how to get the boyfriend of your dreams, etc.). However, there is always a certain number of column inches given over to letters, which appear not only on the problem page, but also as personal anecdotes. It is here that a variety of folklore (after the *Readers' Digest* fashion) will be disseminated under the guise of true personal experience narrative.

Some magazines will also carry 'photo-stories', comic-strip type narratives, but using photographs of actors with speech bubbles portraying vital parts of the story, usually of a romantic and occasionally supernatural nature. The photo-story, though, seems to be a phenomenon of the seventies and eighties and is nowhere near as evident in the new crop of magazines for the nineties. Nevertheless, these ghost stories can easily enter the oral repertoire and even sometimes use contemporary legends as their basis. I remember some years ago coming across a variant of 'The Vanishing Hitchhiker' in photo-story form. Again, once in the oral repertoire, these stories will be passed on by both boys and girls.

We can see, therefore, that narratives in printed form exert a strong influence on oral narrative traditions in the teenage context. However, the relationship between the two is not a simple one and the traffic is not all one-way. 'The Vanishing Hitchhiker' example shows that printed narrative draws heavily on its oral counterpart. In fact, what can happen from time to time is that stories which began life in oral form can be adopted into the literary tradition and, in doing so, reach a wide audience, and then are reborn into oral tradition with new variants. In this way, the printed narrative is simply another vehicle for the effective transmission of folklore that is already in oral circulation.

Also, it does not have to be complete narratives that traverse between the oral and literary. Sometimes only bits of stories, images and motifs may be adopted. It is nonetheless clear that in discussing oral narrative traditions amongst teenagers, we must also bring their reading habits into the equation.

The radio as narrative medium

Teenagers are avid radio listeners and make up a significant proportion of the listening figures. Considering recent technological advances, it may at first sight seem rather odd that teenagers would be so obsessed by something as low-tech as the radio, but we must remember that teenage listening habits vary widely from those of many adults. Where adults will tune in for a variety of reasons - music, news, information and even companionship (cf. Lovelace, n.d., p.22) - teenagers will listen to the radio for music alone. Bearing in mind that most teenagers do not have the financial power to buy large amounts of cassettes or compact discs, they will often, therefore, turn to the radio as the prime source for this very important aspect of their culture.

Martin Lovelace has already closely examined the transmission of folklore through radio phone-in shows (Lovelace, n.d., pp.19-30), but it has to be admitted that this is entirely an adult phenomenon; teenagers rarely participate in such shows, their experience of radio being a far less interactive one. Phone-ins on the mainstream pop-music stations tend to be limited to quizzes and competitions and there is little room for any storytelling exchanges. There is, however, one significant exception to this.

B.B.C. Radio One is Britain's most popular mainstream pop-music station and, despite recently declining figures due to competition from independent broadcasters, continues to command a large listenership, especially amongst the under-fourteen age group. As with most stations of a similar ilk, the general format of most programmes is one of end-to-end music. However, for some years during the 1980s and early 1990s the morning breakfast-time programme was presented by Simon Mayo who was later joined by two co-presenters. One of the highlights of the programme was a daily item called 'True Confessions', in which listeners were invited to write in with amusing stories of times when they had got away with practical jokes or not being entirely honest, etc. The slot took the form of a confessional and after the story had been read out the presenters would pronounce judgement on whether the contributor was 'forgiven' or 'not forgiven'. The success of 'True Confessions' resulted in a series of publications of the stories sent in, and recently has even been transformed into television format.

It is not surprising that at the height of its popularity the programme became the conveyor of a fair amount of modern folklore, and particularly humorous contemporary legends, which would be sent in by listeners and passed off as true personal stories. It is, of course, quite possible that the people who sent such stories in to Simon Mayo had heard them as having happened to a friend of a friend and, genuinely believing them to be true and too good a story to let pass, had decided to personalise them for the purpose of the show.

In January 1992 one such story was broadcast, which at the time was relatively unknown (I myself was unaware of the story's contemporary legend status), but has become very widespread over the last four years. The story tells of two young men on holiday in Cornwall. Returning from the pub one night they come across an old disused mineshaft and begin to speculate on its depth. They then notice a large concrete post lying on the ground nearby and decide to hurl the post down the mineshaft and wait until they can hear it hit the bottom. So, with great effort they lift the heavy piece of concrete to the edge of the mineshaft and drop it. At that moment they realise that tied around the concrete is a length of rope and as they turn around they see a startled goat charging towards them with the other end of the rope around its neck. Needless to say, both concrete and goat end up at the bottom of the mineshaft and the two men return, saying nothing of the incident.[4]

A few days later I found myself running a storytelling session at Ernesettle Library in Plymouth, during the course of which twelve year-old David Allcock told the same story. Unfortunately, I was unable to record the story at the time, but when questioned David freely admitted that he had heard it on 'True Confessions', at which a number of other people in the room said that they too had heard the story on the radio and had liked it. David's story was in the main identical to the broadcast version, but differed in one important element.

At the time the local news was full of reports that a number of houses in Gunnislake (a small village in East Cornwall on the Devon/Cornwall boundary) were under serious threat from subsidence from old mine workings. A number of householders had woken up to find that large mineshafts had appeared overnight in their gardens, and those householders were subsequently involved in legal proceedings against the local authority. In David's variant the story had been transferred to Gunnislake and the man in question was not a holidaymaker, but a local resident who had wanted to ascertain the depth of a mineshaft which had suddenly appeared at the foot of his garden. However, the post he used for this purpose was tied to his neighbour's goat. Furthermore, a number of David's friends agreed with his version of the story.

Clearly either the story and the news item had got muddled up in the communal subconscious, or David had deliberately changed the setting of his story to maximise efficacy and authenticity, but it is interesting that in such a short space of time the narrative, once having entered the oral tradition, began to take on a life of its own and appear in variant form.

It will also be interesting to see whether, now 'True Confessions' has been transferred onto television, stories will continue to be circulated in this way. Having seen a few minutes of the television version, my own feeling is that it is now being presented in a far more sensational style, as is often in keeping with popular television, whereas the radio version was much more low-key, and that it will not have the same influence on oral narrative traditions as it once did. On television the show is very public and involves direct interaction between Simon Mayo and the perpetrators of these acts in front of a live studio audience, so making it more difficult to pass off contemporary legends as personal narratives. The radio, on the other hand, was able to engender an illusion of privacy, intimacy and anonymity which is more conducive to this sort of storytelling. Undoubtedly the show, being based as it is on the personal experience story, will continue to be an important communicator of a variety of folklore, if not the contemporary legend.

The rôle of television

This is not to say that television is an ineffective medium for influencing the teenage oral narrative tradition, because this is not the case at all. Any parent will testify that the television serves a number of functions in pre-adult experience and is a very important presence and cultural influence. Furthermore, the changing pattern of contemporary family life from the extended to the nuclear unit, for example, has elevated the function of television as a medium of social and cultural interaction amongst children and teenagers. It is not unusual for young people to spend upwards of four hours per day watching television, and so we might expect a close relationship between their folklore traditions and this central medium of popular culture.

Over recent years on British television there has been a number of one-off programmes and series devoted to ghostlore, the supernatural and unexplained phenomena. Examples of this include *Strange, But True* (I.T.V.), *The Fortean Review of the Year* (B.B.C.2, January/February 1995) , *Out of this World* (B.B.C.1, 6 October 1994) and, most recently, *Fortean T.V.* (Channel 4, 1997), to name but a few. In fact, in December 1994 B.B.C.1's *Weird Night* devoted a whole evening of prime time television to programmes of this sort. Although many of these programmes have been considered minority viewing and broadcast after nine o'clock in the evening, the generally accepted watershed for adult viewing to begin, this has, of course, not prevented large numbers of teenagers watching them.

Out of this World is an interesting case in point. The programme itself was presented as a serious investigation into the paranormal, focusing on four separate case histories, one of which was 'The Ghost of Bluebell Hill'. This is a local legend from Kent and is briefly mentioned by Michael Goss in his paper on 'urban maniac' tales (Goss, 1990, pp.92-3), where he quite rightly comments on its similarity to 'Vanishing Hitchhiker' variants.

The programme included testimonies from people who had been driving along Bluebell Hill when a young woman with blonde hair ran out in front of the car and appeared to fall under the wheels. However, when the driver stopped to investigate, there was nobody to be found anywhere; she had disappeared without trace. The local police, it was reported, are quite used to distraught motorists reporting accidents of this nature.

This is also a story which was known to me through teenage storytellers, particularly from Kent. However, the first time I heard the story was from Louise, aged about twelve, from Gillingham in Dorset, and in spite of her confusion with the place name, her version is surprisingly close to those presented by the television programme, even down to the attitude of the police.

> A bloke is driving home late one stormy night. Suddenly he sees a young woman in the headlights. He tries to brake, but it is too late and he knocks her down. He gets out of the car in a panic and looks around, but can't see her anywhere. He drives to the Police Station to report the incident.
> 'Where did this happen?' asked the officer on duty.
> 'On Blueberry Hill,' replied the driver.
> 'Oh,' said the policeman, 'in that case that will be the Ghost of Blueberry Hill!' (Wilson 10)[5]

This story was told to me long before the programme was transmitted and I immediately assumed that the story was a variant (if a somewhat distant one) of 'The Vanishing Hitchhiker'. It was not until I was visiting the Isle of Sheppey in Kent in July 1994 that I discovered it was in fact a local legend that had somehow migrated to Dorset (see Wilson 11).

Of course, the similarities to 'The Vanishing Hitchhiker' cannot be denied and are, indeed, important; a male driver encounters a female pedestrian, often during bad weather, who vanishes into thin air and when the accident is reported to the police (or woman's parents), no surprise is shown. Gillian Bennett has already demonstrated how phantom hitchhiker stories tie in closely with traditional ghostlore (Bennett, 1984) and the same is true of 'The Ghost of Bluebell Hill', and it is in this way that the two stories are related: they correspond to similar patterns of traditional ghostlore.

Out of all the stories which were featured in the television broadcast it was 'The Ghost of Bluebell Hill' that kept resurfacing in sessions with teenagers after the programme had gone out, and this I believe to be the case precisely because the phantom hitchhiker motif echoes within it. Whether or not 'The Vanishing Hitchhiker' was known to individuals, the narrative reverberates with so much traditional lore that it begins to ring bells of recognition within the subconscious and becomes instantly memorable. Furthermore, it is interesting that since the broadcast I have heard the story in all parts of Britain and often following on from a telling of 'The Vanishing Hitchhiker', whether by myself or a teenager, indicating a clear recognition of the shared motifs of the two stories by adolescent storytellers. 'The Ghost of Bluebell

Hill' has now firmly entered the teenage repertoire on a national level - thanks to television.

Television, therefore, can also be seen to exert a powerful influence on the teenage repertoire of oral narratives. The short, manageable narratives often presented in programmes about the supernatural provide ideal material for the adolescent storyteller and soon become assimilated into the existing traditions. None of this is surprising considering the importance of the television as a popular cultural medium, but we must also remember that television, more than any other medium, has the ability to speak to a massive range of people in all corners of the country, and indeed the world in these days of satellite and cable television, and so is a remarkably efficient means of disseminating folklore. As in the case of 'The Ghost of Bluebell Hill', the television has the capability of turning a location-specific local legend, little known outside its native region, into a story that can be found in repertoires all over the country. This is not to say that television is a central player in the homogenisation of folklore, eradicating local and regional variations. In fact, quite the opposite is true; television, by effectively transmitting folklore over long distances, is a prime mover in the creation of new variants within previously confined traditions, because this is what will inevitably happen to 'The Ghost of Bluebell Hill'. A wide range of variants will gradually emerge throughout the country on account of one half-hour television broadcast.

The rôle of cinema

The cinema has now for a number of generations been an important cultural influence on young people. However, frequent visits to the cinema were (and still are) often beyond their financial limits. Nevertheless, the advent of the video cassette player as a standard household appliance has changed all that. Not only do teenagers now have access to more films, but also to a wider range of films, including those which are publicly restricted to adult viewing. This increased availability of films would, we might expect, be reflected in teenage folk culture.

However, the traffic seems to be largely in the opposite direction. It is well established that films (and television) regularly draw upon folk narratives and motifs for their plots. Paul Smith and Sandy Hobbs have compiled a bibliography of films which make use of contemporary legends (Hobbs and Smith, 1990), which gives a fair idea of the wide influence of these types of narrative on the cinema. It does not seem usual for cinema to provide material for, or disseminate stories in any big way into, the teenage repertoire. This may well be because films (unlike television which tends to work in shorter snatches) generally concentrate on telling narratives of up to two hours or more in length, which are generally unsuitable for acclimatisation into oral tradition. There are, of course, films which do attempt to tell a number of separate stories within them and there are many single incidents within film plots that may be appropriate to teenage oral tradition, but by and large cinema does not provide raw material to the extent of other media.

This is not to say that cinema bears no influence on their oral narratives but rather the influence manifests itself in four different ways. Firstly, teenagers, like anybody else, will readily articulate ideas spawned from recent cultural experience and so it is not unusual for adolescents to spend time discussing films and recounting their plots. However, such narratives are usually short-lived, ephemeral aspects of conversation and do not develop into part of a continuing tradition, so being outside the scope of this present study.

Secondly, the use of traditional narratives and motifs within films may revitalise similar narratives which may have lain relatively dormant for some time. For example, the popularity of the 'Freddy Kruger' series of films[6] may in part account for the enduring popularity of the numerous teenage narratives which touch on the 'maniac-threat' and mutilation (eg. 'The Mad Axeman', 'The Licked Hand', 'The Babysitter', 'Johnny, I Want My Liver Back', etc.). Or perhaps the reverse is also true, in that these films are so popular because they echo existing folkloric obsessions of the age group. The relationship is, of course, an extremely complex one.

Thirdly, films are often used as reference points by teenagers for stories, particularly by story-listeners. For example, in Steven Spielberg's *Gremlins* (Columbia-EMI-Warner, 1984) there is a short, but memorable scene where a character 'destroys one of the multiplying Gremlins by throwing it into the microwave oven, where it explodes' (Hobbs and Smith, 1990, p.145). This is, of course, a variant of the well-known contemporary legend often known as 'The Poodle in the Microwave' (cf. Wilson 83-85 and Healy and Glanvill, 1992. p.4). Furthermore it is a film that a great number of teenagers will have seen in the years immediately preceding their adolescence. It is, therefore, to be expected that when a variant of this contemporary legend is told, it is greeted with cries of recognition from the audience making reference to the film. This is also evident with the Freddy Kruger character. The telling of a 'maniac story' will sometimes elicit comments such as 'It's just like Freddy' from the audience, or even the storyteller may make the reference as a descriptive aid to his/her audience, as in a variant of 'The Babysitter' story from Kay, aged thirteen, from Lipson, Plymouth, when she describes the assailant as having a 'Freddy Kruger face' (Wilson 42).

Films, then, are often used as important reference points in the telling of oral narratives by teenagers, to clarify, illustrate and identify.[7]

Finally, cinema can be seen to bear an influence on oral tradition in that there are occasional instances of characters from films finding their way directly into the narrative, as opposed to simply being used as a reference. Instead of being a device for the storyteller or audience, it becomes a central and internal part of the narrative text. A good example of this phenomenon is the following variant of 'The Mad Axeman' as told by a male storyteller at Pyworthy Youth Club, Devon on Hallowe'en Night, 1992.

Right, there was these newly-weds and they'd just been married and they said, 'Mmm, let's go up to Dartmoor,' and they were driving along and the lady gets really bored, so she goes, 'Let's play some music,' so the bloke (imitates turning on radio and music).

And they're driving along (more music imitation).

And they're still driving and they come to this place and.., but there's some fog and there's this river and he goes (sound of car and bursting tyres) and he looks down the car and he's got one puncture there and one back there. And he goes (look of disappointment)

And the lady's next door (more music sounds) and the bloke goes, 'Have you noticed something?' and the lady goes (more music sounds). And he goes, 'Look I've got punctures!' And the lady goes, 'The jack's in the boot,' and the bloke goes, 'Aren't you going to help me?' And she goes (more music sounds), and the bloke goes, 'Great!'

And then suddenly there appears this (grunting noise) and what's happened is there's Mad Max, right, and he came along and he just grabbed Nigel and put him against the car and out comes the axe and Tracey looks out the window and she goes (screams), like that, opens the door, comes out and she sees the blue flashing lights (siren noise) and it comes along (screeching brakes) and the policeman goes, 'Keep moving, keep moving.' (more screaming sounds)

She's like that all the way up the hill and you can see Mad Max (more grunting) and then suddenly this man, he comes out of the boot of the car, and he's like a gorilla with this tommy-gun (grunting sounds) and Mad Max looks and he grabs him and slings him over his shoulder and carries him by the arm and he's dragging him down the hill and then the bloke, the gorilla (grunting) and then there's (gun noises) and then you see Mad Max dragging him and there's this trail of blood going up the hill and everything.

And then the policeman comes along, walking up, and then suddenly the blood stops and it's never seen again. (Wilson 20)

This jokey performance is very clearly over the top and exaggerated to the point that the storyteller gets so carried away in the search for laughs that he eventually loses sight of the narrative, which detracts from the competence of his performance and so the story ends rather weakly and unsatisfactorily. However, what is most interesting is that the character of the Mad Axeman, which is how the storyteller almost certainly first heard it, has undergone a slight linguistic metamorphosis to become Mad Max, a character popularised by actor Mel Gibson in the series of films of the same name. In fact the character in the films, although prone to violence, is not the psychopathic maniac of 'The Mad Axeman', but rather the hero of the piece. Nevertheless, the storyteller has deemed it appropriate to draw directly on a figure from popular film culture for his narrative. In many ways this is an astute and consistent choice, since his performance style, making full use of sound effects and acting out certain parts of the story in preference to verbalising the narrative, is arguably reminiscent of cinema. He is telling the story as if it is an action film; the narrative is very punchy and moves swiftly, there is much use of visualisation in the telling and at one point he even tells us that 'you see Mad Max dragging him...', as if he were describing the action on the screen in front of us. It is almost as if his rôle has at this point become commentator rather than storyteller.

It would seem, therefore, that although the cinema does not generally provide stories that can pass easily into teenage oral narrative tradition, it continues to be a significant influence in a variety of ways.

Conclusion

It is quite clear that modern folklore is transmitted in a number of different ways and not simply by means of face-to-face oral communication, although this may remain the most important method of circulation. Even in this present study which concentrates on the oral narratives of teenagers, a group which, moreover, does not usually have direct access to many of the most advanced communication technologies, it is imperative that we take into account a whole variety of popular media and assess their influence on that oral tradition if we are to aspire to anything resembling a true and accurate picture of the current state of things. Although oral narrative tradition clearly exists and thrives amongst teenagers in contemporary Western society, it does not do so in isolation and arguably no folk narrative tradition ever has, at least since the advent of written forms of language. The methods used to disseminate folklore amongst a particular group will clearly reflect all those methods available to that group for the articulation of a number of different cultural messages. As narratives are transmitted in an ever-increasing variety of ways as technologies develop, we must look at all these as potential and actual vehicles for folklore circulation, development and creation. By looking at the ways in which literature, radio, television and cinema influence current teenage narrative traditions, we are able to go some way to understanding the complex relationship between folklore and popular, mass-communicated culture.

Notes

[1] My emphasis.

[2] In *Tradition and Modernisation*, Nordic Institute of Folklore, Turku, 1992.

[3] An attempt to produce non-issue based popular fiction for a teenage readership. They were originally published in the United States and subsequently remarketed and published in the U.K by Scholastic Publications, a reputable educational publisher. They have generated a certain amount of debate amongst parents, teachers, librarians and publishers, and have enjoyed considerable popularity amongst teenagers since they first appeared at the beginning of the nineties.

[4] This story appears in Healey and Glanvill, 1992, p.11 and was also used as the basis for an incident in the film *Hear My Song*.

[5] Although this story is only a summary of Louise's narrative, as I was unable to record the actual performance, it was jotted down almost immediately afterwards and so is reasonably accurate to what was actually said.

[6] Freddy Kruger is a horrific character who terrorises innocent members of the public with his long, razor-sharp finger nails in such films as *Nightmare on Elm Street*.

[7] The question of recognition, of course, can be used either to debunk a story that is told as true, (for example, the effect of an audience member making reference to *Gremlins* when a storyteller is telling a supposedly true version of 'The Poodle in the Microwave' is to challenge the

assertion of its truth), or it can be used to claim connection to the storyteller and the story and, thereby, raise one's status.

Part Three
THE STORIES

6 The glutton's errand: a structural analysis of 'Johnny, I Want My Liver Back!'

Some years ago now, when I first began working in secondary schools as a storyteller, a colleague told me that he had noticed that one particular story seemed to be enjoying a heightened wave of popularity at that time amongst teenagers. The story in question concerned a young boy who was sent on an errand by his mother to buy some liver from the butcher. However, the lad instead spent the money on sweets and, realising the gravity of his situation, dug up the corpse of his granny, removed the liver, and took it home to his mother. That evening the ghost of his granny returned to exact revenge on the boy and the story ended with a 'jump'.

At the time the story was unknown to me, but as I began to make enquiries amongst the teenagers I had begun to work with, I discovered that the story was indeed very widespread in a number of variants. Although the story has seemed to wane in popularity to some degree in more recent years, it remains a cornerstone of the teenage repertoire. Further investigation also suggests that, although the tale is also quite common amongst younger age groups (for example the seven- to ten-year-olds), it is virtually unheard of amongst the adult population. In my experience it is rare to encounter a teacher who is familiar with the story, even when the whole of his/her class is conversant with it. In fact, when I told the American scholar Jack Zipes about the story, he had never heard it before, but was so excited by it that he insisted that I tell it to his young daughter when we next met. Of course, she knew the story already as, she claimed, did most of her contemporaries.

On this score, it might seem likely that the story is, therefore, relatively recent in origin and that it is unknown by adults since it was not in existence twenty years ago. However, one person told me that she remembered the story from her childhood in Canada in the 1960s and another that she had heard it during the 1940s in Michigan. It would appear, therefore, that the

109

story is, at the very least, fifty years old. The following version, as told by Tony Martin from Abingdon was the first telling of the story I collected.

His mum wanted this boy to get her some liver, but the boy went to get him some sweets. So he dug up a dead body, then he got the liver out and he took it home and he bought some sweets and then they ate the liver, and that night his mum and dad went out without him knowing. And well, he was upstairs in bed, doing homework, and he heard this:
Johnny, I want my liver back.
Johnny, I'm outside your bedroom.
Johnny, I'm in your bedroom.
Johnny, I want my liver back.
Johnny, I'm on your bed.
Johnny, YOU'RE DEAD!
(Wilson 32)

This version was told to me by Tony at the end of a lesson at his school and, therefore, although it contains all the key features of the story, remains artificially short. It would also be worth quoting in full the following, fuller version as told by Jamie of Okehampton at his youth club, when the pressure of time was not so great.

There was this lad and his mum and dad asked him to go down to the shop to buy some liver and the mum gave him the money and he set off down the road. He kept on down the road and he passed a sweet shop and he goes in and buys some sweets instead of a liver.
So he walks on past the church, so he goes, 'I've got an idea', or something. He goes into the churchyard and digs up his gran. Then he gets hold of a little pen-knife, cuts his nan's liver out and runs home. He gives the liver to his mum, she cooks it for tea and...'Mmm nice dinner', and all that.
So a couple of hours later his mum and dad went out to a meal, see, and Johnny was up doing his homework and downstairs her could heard:
Johnny, I want my liver back.
Johnny, I'm on the first step.
Johnny, I'm on the landing.
Johnny, I want my liver back.
Johnny, I'm in your bedroom.
Johnny, I want my liver back.
Johnny, I'm on the pillow case.
Johnny, I want my liver back.

Johnny, I'm on your head.
Johnny,.....BOO!
(Wilson 33)

As we can see, Jamie's story is essentially the same as Tony's except that Jamie has included more detail (e.g. identifying the corpse as that of his granny), the occasional joke ('Mmm nice dinner') and even has the time to slowly build up the tension to achieve maximum effect with the concluding shout.

Textual versus contextual analysis

The process of oral transmission of folk narratives has been likened to a large game of chinese whispers. As a story gets passed on from person to person each storyteller adds a little something. Each time the story is told it is slightly different, since an oral text is, by definition, a fluid text. This is, in part, used to explain the existence of different variants of the same story in different parts of the world, and it is the theories of textual analysis that have formed the bedrock of folklore studies until relatively recently. The problem with this analysis is, of course, that it presumes that somewhere, at some time, there exists, or existed an original form of the story from which all subsequent variants developed. The theories as to the origins of folktales are manifold, but in the nineteenth and early twentieth centuries they all rested on notions of genealogy, that the folktale originated in the dim and distant past, where the purest (and, by implication, the most superior) forms were to be found. Indeed folklorists from the 'Finnish' School spent much time and effort attempting to create definitive Urtexts and to plot their journeys through history[1]. The verbal artistry associated with performance was largely ignored and, although we have a fine collection of folktale anthologies as a result, much of their work has proved to be ill-founded.

Performance-centred theories have, over the past twenty or thirty years, come partly as a reaction to this earlier thinking, as scholars have begun to realize the important shaping influence of performative and paraperformative details and this has now come to dominate current developments. However, Daniel R. Barnes is eager to warn us against dismissing textual analysis purely in favour of contextual considerations and favours a more mixed approach (Barnes, 1984, p.67), and this is an argument to which I too would subscribe.

Whilst agreeing that a performance-centred analysis is of paramount importance to our understanding of oral traditions, different approaches will inevitably give us a fuller picture. For example, if we wish to establish

111

relationships between different stories, then a performance-centred analysis of 'Johnny, I Want My Liver Back' would illuminate for us the contextual relationships between this narrative and other narratives told during a single storytelling event; why a particular story follows on from another and what is its particular contribution to the greater event. These intertextual relationships would not be shown by a purely textual approach. However, on the other hand, whilst accepting the futility of the quest for an Urtext, there is still some validity in examining texts for shared motifs to establish tale types.

By investigating character types, narrative incidents, settings, etc., it is quite possible to establish links between a variety of texts. By this method it could be argued that the more shared motifs, the more likely two narratives are to be variants of one another. Although the two quoted examples of 'Johnny' are clearly different performances produced under different conditions, they are still obviously performances of the same story. It is by looking at the central motif that the tale type of a particular text is decided. Of course, there may always be some argument as to what the central motif is, but it is in this way that 'Rumpelstiltskin' (Grimm, 1993, pp.247-9) and 'Tom-Tit-Tot' (Carter, 1990, pp.113-17) can both be classified as being variants of 'Tale Type 500: The name of the helper' (Aarne-Thompson, 1961).

In this way we can establish a clear link between 'Johnny' and 'The Golden Arm' (Wilson 1-3) through the number of shared motifs. Both stories concern a lone male (usually) who, through greed, robs the grave of a relative, removing a part of the body, in order to alleviate a dire situation (punishment/bankruptcy). The ghost then returns to avenge the indignity suffered by the corpse and the narrative ends with a sudden shout. The central motif in both stories seems to be the return of the ghost, which firmly establishes the two stories as belonging to 'Tale Type 366: The man from the gallows' (Aarne Thompson, 1961). Stith Thompson describes the story thus:

> This story of 'The Man from the Gallows' (Type 366) is well known in Western Europe. Its greatest popularity seems to be in Denmark, though it is told in England and as far south as Spain. There are frequent German variants, but it fades out as soon as one moves east of the German border. Variants have been carried by travellers to the Malay peninsula and to the Hausa in Africa. A poor man, desperately in need of meat for his family, finds a thief hanging from the gallows. He cuts the meat from the legs of the thief, takes it home and has it served at a feast. The dead man comes and demands the return of his flesh. In most versions the man who stole the flesh is carried off. Some variation is

made in the story from place to place. Sometimes it is the heart, or even a piece of clothing of the hanged man is stolen (Thompson, 1977, p.42).

Although this passage betrays Thompson's adherence to the 'Finnish' School by his interest in how the story has travelled, it also shows a distinct relationship between 'Johnny' and 'The Golden Arm', a relationship which may seem obvious, but would, nevertheless, not necessarily be articulated during the course of a purely contextual analysis. In addition we are now able to establish that 'Johnny' is not the completely 'new' story we might have thought it to have been, but has its roots in a much older tradition. When Joseph Jacobs published his version of 'The Golden Arm' in *English Fairy Tales*, he noted that the Grimms had collected a story 'which tells of an innkeeper's wife who had used the liver of a man hanging on the gallows, whose ghost comes to her and tells her what has become of his hair, and his eyes, and the dialogue concludes: SHE: Where is thy liver? IT: Thou hast devoured it!' (Jacobs, 1967, pp.252-3). Clearly Johnny's ancestors were alive and well in Germany at the beginning of the last century!

Textual into structural analysis

Of course the success of an analysis by type and motif depends largely on the selection of the central motif. In other words, we have to decide what the story is about, in order to draw parallels between it and other stories of similar intention. If we decide that 'Johnny' is essentially about the return of a ghost to avenge an indignity, then we have no problem in linking it with 'The Golden Arm'. However, we could just as easily argue that this is merely the framework around which a wider issue is explored. That is to say, 'Johnny' is essentially a story about gluttony; it is through the boy's excessive gluttony that he comes unstuck and, thus, there is a strong cautionary element to the story.

There is, indeed a tale type devoted to gluttony, namely 'Tale Type 333: The Glutton' (Aarne-Thompson, 1961) and, more interestingly, it is to this group of stories that 'Little Red Riding Hood' belongs. It may seem rather odd that 'Red Riding Hood' should be classified as being a story about gluttony; Jack Zipes convincingly argues that originally the story was about a young girl's passage into adulthood and her ability to thwart an attempted rape through her own cunning (Zipes, 1993, pp.24-5). However, by extending a type-motif-based textual analysis to a comparison of narrative structure in 'Johnny' and 'Red Riding Hood' we are able to show yet another side to the teenage tale, namely a strong inter-relationship between these two stories.

When trying to draw parallels between oral narratives, 'Red Riding Hood' is a very problematical text to be working with, since, probably more than any other folktale, it has been rewritten and altered by generations of writers and the version known to most of us is now far removed from the original oral tale. I will, therefore, refer to two relatively unknown 'Red Riding Hood' texts for the basis of my analysis. The first is a reconstructed version by French folklorist Paul Delarue from Nièvre about 1885, entitled 'The Story of Grandmother', and is widely accepted as being relatively faithful to the original oral version of the story (see Appendix 3 and Zipes 1993, pp.21-3). The second is an Italian variant called 'Uncle Wolf'[2] (Calvino, 1980, pp.152-4).

On the surface, it would seem that the stories have relatively little in common, in terms of their central motif; the first is symbolically highly sexual and concerns violence and a young girl's rite of passage, whereas 'Uncle Wolf', 'with its rudimentary elements of gluttony and excrement' (Calvino, 1980, p.725), is essentially a cautionary tale against greed, gluttony and ingratitude. However, the stories enjoy a large enough number of shared motifs (the young girl, her mother, the wolf, the errand with food, the attack etc.) for us to see quite clearly that the two stories emanate from the same tradition. Furthermore, if we are to compare the structures of the stories, it is even more obvious that the narratives are linked. Both stories begin with the setting of a domestic situation. Then follows the girl being sent on an errand, which has a conversational interlude with the wolf. The errand then continues and at the house the main conflict between the girl and the wolf ensues. The story ends with a stylised accumulation of tension which is resolved in favour of one or the other. The narrative patterns of the two tales can be seen below:

'Red Riding Hood'	**'Uncle Wolf'**
Setting of domestic situation	Setting of domestic situation
Girl and Mother - Mother as provider of food.	Girl and Mother - Mother as provider of food.
Girl sent on errand.	Girl sent on errand (1).
Girl meets and converses with Wolf in wood. Conditions are made.	Girl meets and converses with Wolf in house. Conditions are made.
Girl continues errand.	Girl sent on errand (2).
Main conflict between girl	Main conflict between girl

and Wolf.
Resolution of conflict -
Girl returns home and
escapes.

and Wolf
Resolution of conflict -
Girl returns home and
is eaten.

Structurally, therefore, both narratives are almost identical.

If we now bring 'Johnny' into the equation we can also see that this story also fits the pattern. The motif of the grandmother, which is common in 'Johnny', is the only one it shares with 'The Story of Grandmother', but there is a number of motifs that 'Johnny' shares with both 'Red Riding Hood' variants, namely, the mother, the child, the errand, the unsavoury food, the 'progression of fear' (Calvino, 1980. p.725), etc.. However, it is when we compare 'Johnny' and 'Uncle Wolf' that the similarities become more obvious. In both cases the central theme is one of gluttony; it is the child's greed that is the cause of their downfall. Furthermore, the child is no longer the innocent victim in the story, but rather the culprit. Instead it is the wolf/corpse that is the blameless injured party. In addition, we can apply the same structural analysis to the two texts and find the same level of similarity.

'Johnny'

Setting of domestic
situation
Boy and Mother - Mother
as provider of food.
Boy sent on errand.

Errand interrupted
(sweet shop).
Boy exhumes corpse and
removes liver.
Parents eat liver.

Main conflict - ghost pursues
boy to bedroom.
Resolution of conflict -
Ghost kills boy in bed.

'Uncle Wolf'

Setting of domestic
situation.
Girl and Mother - Mother
as provider of food.
Girl sent on errand (1).
Girl meets and converses
with Wolf in house.
Conditions are made.

Errand interrupted
(eats pancakes).
Girl collects dung, lime
and muddy water.
Wolf eats dung, lime and
drinks water.

Main conflict - wolf pursues
girl to bedroom.
Resolution of conflict -
Wolf eats girl in bed.

We can also establish a clear link between the stories through the dramatic intention. That is to say that 'Johnny' is almost always told as a jump story and the formulaic ending which slowly increases the tension is ideally suited to this, as has been shown with 'The Golden Arm'. However, if we look at the structure of the ending in 'Johnny', we can see that 'Uncle Wolf' uses the exact same strategy. The assailant's gradual progression towards its victim is punctuated by the repetition of a key phrase:

'Johnny'	**'Uncle Wolf'**
I'm on the first step.	I'm on the roof.
Johnny, I want my liver back!	I'm going to eat you!
I'm on the landing.	I'm on the chimney.
Johnny, I want my liver back!	I'm going to eat you!
I'm in your bedroom.	I'm on the hearth.
Johnny, I want my liver back!	I'm going to eat you!
I'm on the pillowcase.	I'm in the room.
Johnny, I want my liver back!	I'm going to eat you!
Johnny, I'm on your head.	I'm at the foot of the bed.

It is then only a short step to the formulaic repetition used in the climactic build-up in 'The Story of Grandmother'. However, Calvino's version of 'Uncle Wolf' is not a 'jump' story, ending instead with the moralistic proclamation, 'Uncle Wolf always eats greedy little girls.' Nevertheless, as Zipes has shown, the transformation of a folktale into a story with a greater emphasis on moral instruction for children is not inconsistent with the influences that the literary tradition has exerted on oral literature (Zipes, 1993, pp.17-88). Not only is it perfectly conceivable, but also quite probable, that 'Uncle Wolf' was indeed often told as a 'jump' story and that the replacement of the 'jump' with the moral coda merely signifies the general influence of the literary tradition and the personal preference of the storyteller from whom the tale was collected. Certainly the structural evidence seems to point towards this. Further evidence for this hypothesis comes from Zipes who argues that 'Red Riding Hood' was probably also told as a 'jump' story.

> Evidence indicates that the teller would grab hold of the child or children nearby when the final line in the well-known dramatic dialogue with the wolf was to be pronounced - 'the better to eat you with!' We must remember that storytelling was a dynamic process, with give and take between narrator and listeners (Zipes, 1993, p.23).

It would seem, therefore, that through its structure, 'Johnny' can also be related to the tradition of 'Red Riding Hood.'

Conclusion

Quite clearly the teenage story of 'Johnny, I Want My Liver Back' is a complex cocktail of a variety of narrative traditions. An analysis of the story in performance would illustrate how the story fits into a storytelling tradition. In other words, we can link it to other teenage ghost narratives through the circumstances under which it is often told. At the same time we can apply a type and motif analysis and show how the story is essentially a variant of the older folktale 'The Golden Arm' or the modern folktale 'The Missing Finger'. However, with a structural analysis we can also relate the story to 'Little Red Riding Hood' and show how 'Johnny' has been influenced by and partly evolved from conceivably the best-known fairy tale in Western Europe.

Of course, it is only through a variety of analytical processes that we can begin to understand the complexities of oral narratives and their processes of development. Clearly, folk narratives are not simple items which evolve from single pure sources, but rather a mish-mash of different influences both textual and contextual, and as folklore studies move, quite rightly, ever more towards performance-centred theory, we must also be careful not to totally dismiss the efforts of previous generations of scholars. Their mistake was not perhaps their interest in textual questions, but merely the blinkered obsession with which they pursued it.

Notes

[1] For a general introduction to a range of early folklore methodologies, see Finnegan, 1992, pp.29-50.

[2] Permission to reprint the full text of 'Uncle Wolf' in an appendix was not obtained and so readers should refer directly to Calvino, 1980, pp.152-4 for this story.

In essence the story tells of a young girl who misses out on eating pancakes at school and whose mother promises to make some instead, if she will pay a visit to Uncle Wolf to ask for the loan of his skillet. Uncle Wolf, who has had no visitors for a long time, is suspicious of the girl and only agrees to lend the skillet if the girl in turn promises to return it with a pile of pancakes, a loaf of bread and a bottle of wine.

The girl's mother obliges and gives her daughter the food and drink to give to Uncle Wolf. However, the little girl instead eats all the food and drinks the wine herself, replacing it with lime, donkey dung and dirty water. As soon as Uncle Wolf tried the food and drink, he spits it out in disgust and threatens to take revenge on the girl for having tricked him.

The girl runs home where her mother sends her to bed and locks the doors and windows to keep Uncle Wolf out. Unfortunately, she forgets to block up the chimney and Uncle Wolf gains access to the girl's bedroom this way, each time declaring his increasing proximity as he comes down the chimney, onto the hearth, in the room, at the foot of the bed, etc. The story ends with the girl being eaten by Uncle Wolf, because, as the coda to the story says, that is exactly what happens to gluttons!

9 'The Singing Bone': a traditional tale in a modern context

We have seen in the previous chapter how a 'new' story, 'Johnny, I Want My Liver Back', has evolved according to the structures and conventions of familiar traditional narrative and yet has modified itself to fit into a teenage narrative tradition, where it has thrived (and continues to thrive) for the past fifty years or more. In this chapter I wish to examine related issues but from a different direction, in that I would like to look at how a well-documented traditional story has survived in the contemporary adolescent context and the changes that the story has undergone, whilst remaining true to the type. My reference will be to the texts I have collected.

The particular story in question is 'The Singing Bone', which has appeared in its many variants in a large number of collections of folk tales over the past two hundred years, although it has, most surprisingly, not attracted a great deal of scholarly attention from folklorists. I would, therefore, first of all like to examine the story in its historic-traditional context.

'The Singing Bone' in its historic-traditional context

It is probably true to say that the story's life as a literary fairy tale began with the publication of the Grimms' *Kinder- und Hausmärchen* in 1812, where the story appears as Number 28, 'Der Singende Knochen'. This story was collected by the Grimms 'von Dortchen Wild in Kassel am 19 Januar 1812 am Ofen im Gartenhaus, von Nentershausen'[1] (Bolte and Polivka, 1913, p.260) and appears in various rewritten versions in subsequent editions of the collection (see Grimm, 1992, pp.108-9).

The 1812 version primarily tells of two brothers who set out on separate quests to gain the hand of the King's daughter in marriage. However, in a fit

119

of jealousy the unsuccessful brother kills the other, throws the body off a bridge into a river and returns to the King's castle to claim the princess for himself. The corpse is washed downstream where it is discovered by a musician on his way to the King's castle to play music for the princess's wedding. From the body of the dead brother the musician makes a musical instrument, but when the said instrument is played at the wedding celebrations, it sings a song of its own accord, that song telling the story of the murder that has taken place. The wedding is thus halted and the murderous brother subsequently punished.

It is this version by the Grimms that Lutz Mackenson uses as his starting point in his paper 'Der Singende Knochen' (Mackenson, 1923). Although much of Mackenson's discourse is dominated by the misguided notion of the story's link to a German mythological past inhabited by Gods and Heroes and the now outdated and pointless quest for an Urtext from which all subsequent variants stem, his analysis of the type and its central motifs is thorough. Mackenson gives a skeletal form of the story, which we could do worse than adopt as a working definition of the essential narrative.

> Es berichtet von einem Morde, der durch das Lied eines in irgend einer Weise aus den beresten des Getöteten hergestellten Musikinstrumentes enthüllt wird.[2] (Mackenson, 1923, p.3)

However, Mackenson also acknowledges that the story is very widespread:

> Das Märchen vom singenden Knochen (Grimm Nr 28) gehört einem Märchentyp an, der über ganz Europa verbreitet, auch Fassungen aus Afrika, Indien und Brasilien aufweist.[3](Mackenson, 1923, p.3)

Indeed the story is so widespread that it earns a place in the Aarne-Thompson *Types of the Folk-Tale* as No.780. Mackenson himself summarises an impressive number of textual variants to conclude his study and Joseph Jacobs also published a version of the story in *English Fairy Tales* (Jacobs, 1967, pp.43-7) under the title of 'Binnorie'.

Jacobs's story, however, differs from the Grimms' version in that it tells of two sisters, rather than brothers, who are princesses themselves. The youngest, and most beautiful, wins the heart of one of the elder sister's suitors, and in her jealousy the elder sister contrives to push the younger into the river, where she drowns.[4] The body is finally discovered by the miller and his daughter in their mill-dam, and as they bring the body onto the bank a 'famous harper' passes by and sees the scene. He returns a few days later to make a harp from the bones and hair of the corpse. Once again the harper takes the instrument to the King's court, where it sings of the treachery that has taken place.

It has, however, been pointed out that Jacobs's version was taken from one of the many ballad versions of the tale, which were widely published as broadsides and collected by Francis Child (Child Sargent and Kittredge eds., 1904, pp.18-20). Here the story appears as Child No.10 under the title 'The Twa Sisters' and he includes a large number of varying texts from both England and Scotland. In fact, it seems that in Britain the story was most common in ballad form. Mackenson acknowledges that the ballad form was very widespread in both Britain and Scandinavia (Mackenson, 1923, p.14) and also that within the ballad there is to be found less narrative variation than in the prose narrative, presumably due to the stricter confines of the verse form (Mackenson, 1923, p.15). However, Child also tells us that the story, at least in the nineteenth century, was still widely known in the form of a folk tale:

> Though the range of the ballad proper is somewhat limited, popular tales equivalent as to the characteristic circumstances are very widely diffused. (Child Sargent and Kittredge eds., 1904, p.18)

The problem, of course, with both the Grimms and Jacobs is that their versions of the tales tell us precious little about the oral nature of the story. We have little or no information about the collectors' informants, no knowledge as to how widespread and commonly-told the stories were, and in how many other major variants, and no record of the original oral texts, since the published versions are radically edited and censored literary renditions appropriate to the potential readership of the time and contemporary fashion and expectations. Indeed, Jacobs's text is so absurdly romantic and archaic that it is almost laughable in a modern context and it is very hard to believe that anybody actually spoke in that manner.

However, it is important not to dismiss the texts out of hand. They are the only records we have and they do at least tell us that the story did exist as an oral folk tale in some form. They also allow us, by comparing the two narratives, to identify some of the central and integral motifs in the story, which will help form the basis of the future analysis of modern texts.

Bearing this in mind, we can say that the following motifs and elements in the story are shared by most variants of the type, and so go a step beyond Mackenson's previously quoted resumé, in helping us define the type.

a) the story centres around two people - brothers in the case of the Grimms and sisters according to Jacobs and Child, although Mackenson points out that many other types of relationship can be found in variant texts, such as brother/sister, stepmother/stepdaughter, husband/wife, etc. (Mackenson, 1923, p.5). Either way the two central characters have some kind of relationship with each other, usually a familial one.

b) One of the pair is murdered by the other. The motive for this is very often envy or jealousy, either for a lover, or for some material possession. Mackenson observes that the motive very often hinges around the desire for an object (Mackenson, 1923, pp.6-7). The murder (or, sometimes, accident) often occurs 'in Zorn infolge eines Streites' ('in anger following a quarrel') (Mackenson, 1923, p.7).

c) The body is fashioned into a musical instrument, which when played will sing a song telling of the murder that has taken place.

d) By these means the murder is uncovered and the murderer 'fingered' in the presence of figures of authority. Mackenson also notes, 'Oder der Mörder selbst ist der ahnungslose Entdecker seiner Untat' ('Or even the murderer himself unsuspectingly uncovers his misdeed') (Mackenson 1923, pp.8-9).

Therefore, having now examined the older, 'traditional' texts, and in particular those that appear in Grimm, Jacobs and Child, we can now turn our attention to an examination of how 'The Singing Bone' has fared in the modern teenage repertoire and the changes that it has undergone.

The Falmouth text

Early in December 1992 I was invited to run a storytelling session in Falmouth Youth Club in West Cornwall. The session began with my telling a number of ghost stories which quickly prompted the young people themselves to volunteer their own narratives. There had initially been a slightly uneasy feeling at the club that evening due to the fact that there had been a violent incident there the previous week. However, as story upon story began to be told, all misgivings gave way to a greater enthusiasm and an increasing number of people joined the group.

Unfortunately, the circumstances at the time did not lend themselves to my recording any of the stories being told that evening, but I had been especially excited by one particular story told to me by fourteen year-old Emma Grimshaw, and I very much regretted not having been able to record her performance. I was, therefore, very grateful for the opportunity of returning to the youth club to run some further sessions the following February. This time I made a point of collecting the story that had so interested me.

There was this girl and she's got a boyfriend called Davey and one night he came over 'cos it was her birthday or something and he gave her some pearls and she said, 'Oh, thanks a lot.'

Next morning he came around and he goes, 'Oh I need the pearls back, I need the money.' And she goes, 'No, no, it was a present from you.'

And he got the pearls, he ripped them off her neck and he killed her and made a piano out of her bones.

And anyway, he gave the piano to the girl's parents and they put it up in the attic.

And one day, they brought it down, after a year, and the mother pressed one of the keys on it and it goes:

'Mother, Mother, you're playing on my bones,
Someone killed me and stole my precious stones.'

And then the mother called the father and he pressed one of the keys and it goes:

'Father, father, you're playing on my bones,
Someone killed me and stole my precious stones.'

And then Davey came round, who was the girl's boyfriend, and he goes to it, and it says:

'Davey, Davey, you're playing on my bones,
Someone killed me.. YOU KILLED ME!'

(Wilson 37)

In his critique of folk and fairy tales, *Breaking the Magic Spell*, Jack Zipes argues:

In each historical epoch they (folk tales) were generally transformed by the narrator and the audience in an active manner through improvisation and interchange to produce a version which would relate to the social conditions of the time (Zipes, 1992, p.28).

We might, therefore, fully expect 'The Singing Bone' to have undergone a similar process of change (by being subject to those same factors that facilitate change) as it has been assimilated into a late twentieth century adolescent tradition, and there are certainly wider differences between the nineteenth-century texts and Emma's story than between any of the nineteenth-century texts themselves. In his list of the kinds of oral change that can occur in folktales, Stith Thompson asserts that 'obsolete traits may be replaced by modern' (Thompson, 1977, p.436). Nevertheless, beneath the modern references, Emma's story conforms closely to our type definition and is quite clearly recognisable as a modern variant of 'The Singing Bone.'

Firstly we have the story revolving around the relationship of two people, this time not siblings, but boyfriend and girlfriend. With this we have the introduction of a romantic element, which also exists in the older narratives, and yet I would suggest that the boyfriend/girlfriend situation tells us more about the storyteller than it does about the similarity of texts. The boyfriend/girlfriend relationship sets the story firmly in the world of the modern teenager. Gone are the courtly aspects of the older tales, and instead they are replaced by a modern setting with modern characters. Emma is bringing the story up to date and making it relevant to herself and her audience. Nevertheless, the two central characters have a relationship with each other and this is important to the progression of the narrative.

Secondly, one of them (the girlfriend) is killed by the other (the boyfriend), and the suggestion is that she has been murdered rather than killed as a result of an accident. Either way the tragedy occurs after a quarrel over a material possession. The girl is killed over that twentieth century female icon of wealth, privilege and sophistication, a pearl necklace. The pearl necklace, therefore, is endowed with this added cultural meaning and so can be seen as a further example of the modernisation process.

A further reading of this incident could of course interpret the episode as a symbolic rape. The pearl necklace, as an image of sophistication, is also, therefore, an image of maturity, a symbol of the girl's passage into womanhood. However, no sooner has Davey acknowledged the girl's new status as a woman, than he demands a reciprocal gesture on her part. In other words, if he is to recognise her womanhood, then she must also be prepared to surrender it back to him. When she refuses, he forcibly takes it from her in a most violent way.

Thirdly, as in the nineteenth-century texts, the body is fashioned into a musical instrument. This is perhaps the central event around which all else hinges and it is significant that in Emma's story, the instrument in question is not a harp, which is a symbol of the antiquarian past, but a piano, which has a quite different symbolism. In addition to being a relatively modern instrument, the piano is a symbol of domesticity. It is not long ago that many homes would boast a piano as a sign of cultivation and respectability (and even bourgeois aspirations), irrespective of whether anybody could play it, and to some degree this still persists today. It has become a domestic icon for the respectable working and lower middle class home, and by giving the piano as a present to the girl's parents, Davey is covering his tracks most effectively by appearing as the paragon of respectability and decency himself.

The piano, therefore, is not simply consistent with the modernisation process, but it is also part of Emma's strategy to claim the story as her own, filling it with familiar popular icons and symbols which have additional meanings for both performer and audience.

The final part of the story, the singing of the song, is very formulaic and echoes traditional folk narrative strategies. The song itself consists of a simple couplet[5] which is repeated three times during the course of the story, with the simple alteration of the names at the beginning of the couplet. This repetition is important because it is through this that the effectiveness of the final 'jump' is achieved. The audience is lulled into an expectation that the song will finish with the simple naming of the murderer, and so when the 'jump' comes it is never anticipated.

We have already seen that a concluding shout to make the audience jump is a very popular device in teenage oral storytelling. However, we have also seen, for example in Jacobs's 'The Golden Arm' (Jacobs, 1967, pp.138-9), that this is not a modern device as such, but very traditional. Therefore, the existence of the 'jump' per se does not indicate the modernity of Emma's text, and yet it is interesting that the story has acquired this ending, which does not seem to be employed in any of the older variants. Although the device itself is very traditional, its inclusion can nevertheless be seen as a part of the modernisation process, since Emma is once again endowing the story with the language of her own oral culture; the use of the 'jump' is part of the tale's acclimatisation into the teenage repertoire.

We have seen, therefore, that our contemporary variant of 'The Singing Bone' has undergone a thorough process of updating. All of the images that suggest a pre-industrial past have been replaced by symbols and icons from twentieth-century Western popular culture. In fact no defining element of the story has escaped modernisation. However, in spite of this, the story has remained faithful to its traditional concerns, motifs and structures and has continued to be recognisable as belonging to the same family of variants as the nineteenth-century texts of the Grimms and Jacobs.

Of course, one of the obvious ways in which Emma's narrative differs from the earlier prose texts is in the length; Emma's story is considerably shorter than either the Grimms' or Jacobs's. However, caution must be exercised here, because with the nineteenth-century variants we are dealing with literary and not oral texts. As far as we know, Jacobs was rewriting the story from ballad form and the Grimms could quite easily have expanded an oral version of the story into a fuller text suitable for publication.

Moreover, we must, in Emma's case, take full stock of the context of the storytelling event where the tale was told, since it has already been established that the ground rules for a particular storytelling event, which are socially negotiated between participants, can affect the performance of a story. For example, where the situation arises that a large number of people are waiting to tell a story, then a rule exists that no one storyteller should dominate the proceedings and that everyone should get a chance to take their turn. This was certainly the case at Falmouth, where a small, but eager group of storytellers, each with a number of stories to tell, awaited their chance to perform. It was, therefore, appropriate that, given the limited time available, all storytelling performances should be as economical as possible. Although this was never actually articulated, the rule was in operation throughout this session.

Furthermore, and perhaps most importantly, it must be remembered that this was the second time she had told me the story and I specifically requested it for the purposes of recording. Therefore, Emma was aware that I was familiar with the narrative and specifically that I knew to expect a shout at the conclusion. She was, thus, able to take for granted some of the detail, exposition and explanation, which had been so important at the first telling. She also did not need to slowly build the tension during the telling to make the 'jump' effective, as the element of surprise had already gone. Although I had asked her specifically to tell the story as she had the first time, there was a certain amount of paraphrasing, if not quite a summary, in the performance.

Bearing in mind the traditional pedigree of this story, I might have expected to find the story very widespread and common. This is certainly the case with many other stories in circulation amongst teenagers which contain strong traditional elements, such as 'The Golden Arm', 'Johnny, I Want My Liver Back!', 'The Mad Axeman', 'The Vanishing Hitchhiker', etc. However, although I eventually found that the story was widespread, in that I was able to collect versions in distant corners of the country, the story is not commonly told. In fact, as I travelled the country and asked other teenagers about the story, I continually drew a blank. The only place that I got a positive reaction was in Falmouth itself, where the story seemed to be reasonably well-known. It certainly seemed odd that such a well-documented traditional tale should survive in modern form only in a particular area of West Cornwall. However, I did eventually collect texts of 'The Singing Bone' which are worth examining as they throw further light on how the story has been transformed.

The other variants

The first of these variants was one which was not collected by myself, and so is not included in the accompanying appendix of texts, but is important as a comparison to the Falmouth text.

At the end of February 1994 I made a visit to Northern Ireland and made a point of meeting with Linda M. Ballard at the Ulster Folk and Transport Museum, who, I had heard, had collected some stories from teenagers in the Province in the early 1980s. She was very modest about what she described as a very limited collection made spontaneously one afternoon at a community centre. There was very little material, she added, although I would be very welcome to look through the transcripts.

Unfortunately, I did not have the time to do this on this particular visit, but a couple of months later I received a package containing the transcripts from Clodagh Brennan Harvey, then at the Institute of Irish Studies at Queen's University, Belfast, who was aware of the research I was conducting.

From a quick glance at the material, I saw that in some ways Linda had been right. There seemed to be only about fifteen minutes of conversation. Nevertheless, I began to recognise some old favourites amongst the stories being told. Then towards the end of the manuscript, quite unexpectedly, I came across the following variant of 'The Singing Bone'.

2nd Voice: My daddy told me it years and years ago. You see there was this here woman and her husband died, she had two children, well she had one and she adopted one you see, the wee boy. And em and you see she had this here lovely rose and John was the wee boy.
3rd Voice: What time is it?
2nd Voice: It's five o' clock.[6] And John wanted the rose, you see. So she wouldn't give it and he killed her and he threw you know her body over the wall. Well next door there was a woman and they didn't know it was a witch and it was the wee boy's birthday.
1st Child: I know that one. She knocked her into the grave or something.
2nd Voice: It was the wee boy's birthday and the mammy said to the woman next door 'Would you make me something for John for it's his birthday.' So she made an old piano and he brought it in and all, and he thought this here was great and all, til have a piano you know, and he started to play it and the tune came -
(sings) 'Oh mammy, oh mammy he's playing on my bones,
John killed me, John killed me, and stole my lovely rose.'
And the bones they weren't,.....

and his mammy came in you see, and he said 'Mammy come here till you hear this here, it's frightening me.' So it went again, and his mammy just killed John for killing the wee girl.

1st Child: John killed the wee girl and with the bones he made it into a piano. With the bones the witch made it into a piano with the bones, and it started to play a song - 'Oh mammy....' That there song, that there thing's years old.

L.B.: Hm?

Child: That there poem's are out years and years.

In many respects the story is very different from both the older version and the Falmouth text, and yet the story is quite clearly 'The Singing Bone' and bears all the defining elements previously identified.

We have the two central characters around whom the story revolves, only this time they are identified as 'two children'. The implication is that they are pre-pubescent, much younger than the characters in Emma's story, as they are introduced in relationship to their parents and not as individual people. The relationship between the two children is that of brother and sister, which is more consistent with the Victorian variants and so the sexual element in the Falmouth text is removed and the story reverts to its themes of jealousy and sibling rivalry. The fact that the young boy is adopted is presumably to distance him from the rest of the family as he is the murderer. Strictly speaking, he is no more guilty of sororicide than his mother is of filicide. In terms of the plot this makes their actions more credible, if not morally acceptable.

The girl is murdered by the boy and once again it is an act motivated by jealousy. However, it is not envy of a twentieth-century icon such as a pearl necklace, but of a rose, a symbol of romantic beauty rather than material sophistication, and associated with traditional narrative imagery. The body is then disposed of over the garden wall, where it is made into a piano by the next-door neighbour. This is an interesting incorporation of an additional character. Presumably the boy, being only a child, would not have the necessary skills to make a piano, whereas an adult would. However, the neighbour also needs a motive to undertake such a bizarre task, and so an obviously traditional solution is found - she is, of course, a witch. No blame or guilt is ever attached to her and she remains a simple functionary in terms of the narrative. Her identity as a witch merely explains her actions.

Once again it is a modern piano that the bones are made into and the boy receives this as a birthday present from his mother. At this point the story follows the same line as the other variants. When the piano is played it sings the song of the murder that took place and the murderer is identified. In fact, in this variant, although I have no record of the tune to which the song was sung, the text follows the same structure as the Falmouth text and there are no significant linguistic variations, as can be seen below.

N.I. Text: Oh mammy, oh mammy, he's playing on my bones
Falmouth Text: Mo-ther, Mo-ther, you're playing on my bones

N.I. Text: John killed me, John killed me and stole my lovely rose.
Falmouth Text: Some----one   ki-lled me and stole my precious stones.

The main difference is that in the text from Northern Ireland the song is only sung twice, which is unusual, but there are only two people who could play the piano, since we are told at the beginning of the story that the father has already died. In addition the story does not end with a jump, but with the boy being killed by his mother. This, however, is not seen as murder, but merely as the doling out of just punishment by a figure of authority. This again is consistent with Mackenson's conclusions about the earlier narratives, as he identifies the punishment of the murderer as an integral part of the story (Mackenson, 1923, p.27), which, although implied, has disappeared from the Falmouth text in favour of the 'jump' ending.

It seems, therefore, that the version collected by Linda Ballard in Northern Ireland varies significantly from the other texts, yet, whilst having clearly undergone some process of modernisation, which makes it more redolent of Emma Grimshaw's version of the story, it has retained a large degree of traditional motif and imagery.

It would be tempting to assert that the variations in the two modern stories are due to cultural differences, that they are typical of regional variation. However, to say that one story is the Cornish variant of 'The Singing Bone' whilst the other is the Northern Irish version would be a great mistake. The practice of classifying folk tale variation and motif by region (except, of course, in the case of local legends which make use of distinctive and specific local features, or in stories that rely on location-specific references) is misleading, especially in a world where technology increasingly allows quick and easy communication across the whole globe. All we can say is that Emma Grimshaw's story is a Cornish narrative by virtue of the fact that it was told in Cornwall, and by the same token the story collected by Linda Ballard is Northern Irish. We must also remember that each variant is unique, as each set of paraperformative details is unique, and that we cannot talk about identical variants, but only variants that share a greater or lesser degree of similarity. The folly of regional classification in the context of modern folklore study can be seen by the next 'Singing Bone' variant, which I was told in Cornwall, this time by Lee, aged twelve, from Redruth School.

Lee is a member of a class made up of children who have been identified as having severe behavioural problems. In a normal classroom situation they would tend to be disruptive and have only very limited concentration ability. However, they clearly share a vibrant oral culture and seem to have little problem telling and listening to stories over prolonged periods. Lee told the story with no prompting from myself and he afterwards said that the story had been told to him by his 'uncle', who turned out to be a close friend of his father's. It is, therefore, interesting that in Lee's case the story has entered his repertoire from a non-teenage source. Unfortunately I was unable to record the story at the time and, although the following summary is of limited use, it is, nevertheless, a fairly accurate summary of Lee's telling. Furthermore, we can see from it quite clearly that, as a variant, it has more in common with the narrative from Northern Ireland than it does with that from Falmouth.[7]

> There was this man and woman and two children, a boy and a girl. The boy was called David. One day they were walking in the woods and the father picked a rose for the girl. The boy wanted the rose and he killed her and stole it and then made a piano out of her bones.
> When the dad played it, it sang:
> (rhythmically spoken)
> 'Father, Father, someone killed me and stole my great rose.'
> When the mum played it, it sang:
> 'Mother, Mother, someone killed me and stole my great rose.'
> When David played it, it sang:
> 'David, David, someone killed me and stole my great rose. YOU DID!'
> (Wilson 38)

This text is indeed more reminiscent of the Northern Irish story in that the central images of the story are the same. The boy and the girl are brother and sister and seen in relationship to the parents; the character group is identified as a family unit and again the children are implied to be of pre-teenage years. Furthermore, the murder is committed out of pure envy, as opposed to the financial need in Emma's story, and the object of the envy is once more a rose. After the murder has taken place the narrative follows the predictable pattern of the manufacture of the piano, the song and the identification of the murderer.

However, on some of the minor details Lee's story corresponds closely with Emma's. Firstly there is the fact that the boys have the same name (David-Davey)[8]. Secondly, it is the murderer himself who manufactures the piano from the bones as part of the process of disposing of the body. Thirdly, the song is sung three times, since the father has not already died, and finally, the story ends, not with the punishment of the murderer as such, but rather with a 'jump'.

Lee's story, therefore, lies somewhere between the two previous versions. Its central images and motifs are closer to the story from Northern Ireland and so we can say that it is essentially more similar to that variant, yet its minor details correspond more closely to the other example from Cornwall.

Let us now turn our attention to the final version of 'The Singing Bone' which I have collected, and which shows a greater degree of divergence from both the Victorian and the modern examples. It was collected from a twelve-year-old girl from Sheerness on the Isle of Sheppey, and again was told at a time when I was unable to record the event. In fact, the storyteller herself, who heard the story from 'a friend of her sister's', was a little vague about it and so told it as a summary of what she could remember. Therefore, all I have is in the form of a summary of a summary, and as such is next to useless for a contextual examination of the story. However, even with this most basic of forms, we are able to compare what information we do have with the other variants. The story runs something like this:

> There was a husband and wife and he suspected her of having an affair.
> So he removed a string from the piano and strangled her. He then made a
> string out of some of her skin and used it to replace the missing string in
> the piano. However, when the piano was played, it sang the story of the
> murder. The story ended with a jump.
> (Wilson 39)

Unfortunately, there is much information missing, such as the precise wording of the song, which the storyteller could not remember; she was only sure that it ended with a shout to make the audience jump. However, we do still have enough to be able to identify it as a variant of 'The Singing Bone', even though, strictly speaking, there are no bones mentioned in the story.

As before the narrative centres around two people who have a relationship to each other, in this case it is a husband and his wife. As in all the modern versions I have seen, the two people are of different genders and it is the male who kills the female, which, of course, adds an extra layer of meaning to the story which does not exist in the Victorian retellings, namely that of the issue of power relationships between the sexes. In this version, although the motive behind the killing is one of jealousy, it is not jealousy for material possession, but jealousy of a sexual nature. The story is consistent with the other modern variants in that the instrument in question is a piano, but here it is introduced much earlier in the text as it (or at least part of it) is identified as the murder weapon and so has a dual function. Once the murder has taken place, it is not the bones which are used to build the piano from scratch, but simply a piece of her skin that is used to replace the string that has been removed. It would seem that the primary concern of the murderer here is not to safely dispose of the body, but rather to restore the piano to full working order. The result, nonetheless, is the same, as the piano sings the story of the events whenever it is played.

Whilst this may seem to differ radically from the other versions where the bones are central to the instrument's manufacture, this part of the story is still consistent with tradition, as it seems to be related to some of the English ballad forms of the story that appear in Child's collection, as in the following example, where, in addition to the breast-bone being used as the frame for the instrument, various parts of the body are also put to effective use.

> What did he doe with her fingers so small?
> He made peggs to his violl withall.
> What did he doe with her nose-ridge?
> Unto his violl he made him a bridge.
> What did he doe with her veynes so blew?
> He made him strings to his violl thereto.
> (Child No.10. Text A. Broadside 1656 - 'The Miller and The King's Daughter')

Also in the following Scottish text the bones are never mentioned, but it is simply hairs from the deceased's head that are used to restring the musician's harp.

> He's taen three locks o her yellow hair,
> An wi them strung his harp sae fair.
> (Child No.10. Text B.)

Child himself notes that it is not necessary for the bones to be used in the manufacture of the instrument:

> According to all complete and uncorrupted forms of the ballad, either some part of the body....is taken to furnish a musical instrument......or the instrument is wholly made from the body (Child Sargent and Kittredge eds., 1904, p.18).

The story ends in the same way as the two variants from Cornwall, with a 'jump'. So we might say that even this story, which is the least similar to the other available texts, is still consistent with the wider narrative tradition.

Conclusion

From our investigation it would seem clear that 'The Singing Bone' still exists in modern teenage oral narrative tradition. It is not a particularly common story, but it is widespread, having been collected as far apart as Cornwall, Kent and Northern Ireland. Where it does exist, we find, as might be expected, that the stories have undergone a significant amount of revision and modification due to modernisation. However, all the texts retain a large number of traditional elements and motifs and follow the same narrative structure, so enabling them to be identified as belonging to the same type. The amount of modernisation that has taken place varies from text to text, but the clearest sign that the story is in healthy circulation is that each of the texts shows a good degree of variation from one another. Just as Mackenson found in his study of older texts, 'The Singing Bone' today exists in many variants and, of all places, continues to thrive in the repertoire of the late twentieth century adolescent.

Notes

[1] 'from Dortchen Wild (Henriette Dorothea Wild [1793-1867]) in Kassel on 19 January 1812 by the stove in the outhouse at Nentershausen.'All translations from German are by the author, unless credited otherwise.

[2] 'It tells of a murder which is uncovered through the song of a musical instrument that is in some way made from the remains of the dead person.'

[3] 'The fairy tale of "The Singing Bone" (Grimm No.28) belongs to a tale type which is distributed throughout the whole of Europe, variants also being known from Africa, India and Brazil.'

[4] Parts of the story are also reminiscent of the famous American ballad 'My Darling Clementine'.

[5] See variants of 'The Juniper Tree' in Grimm and others for use of the

bones/stones rhyming formula (Grimm, 1992, pp.171-9).

[6] Note the skill with which the storyteller is able to answer the unrelated question without losing the thread, pace or rhythm of the performance

[7] Redruth, incidentally, is only about twelve miles up the road from Falmouth.

[8] It is interesting that in all three modern variants the murderer is the only character who is given a name.

8 Personal narratives in the teenage repertoire

It has already been established that the need to tell stories is a part of our basic humanity, that the 'readiness or predisposition to organise experience into a narrative form' (Bruner, 1990, p.45) is 'an essential component of our humanness' (H. Rosen, 1985, p.24). Storytelling, or the ability to create, recreate and enjoy many different types of story is not the preserve of the very old or the very young, but is equally important to the ambitious politician, the student, the housewife, the factory worker, and, of course, the modern teenager. Richard Bauman calls oral storytelling 'one of the most fundamental and potent foundations of our existence as social beings' (Bauman, 1986, p.114). We are all storytellers and carry with us a fair number of stories in our portable, cerebral repertoire, simply waiting for the right context to arrive to enable them to be told. However, not all of us tell traditional wonder tales. Likewise, we don't all know local legends in any great detail. We can't all remember jokes, let alone tell them effectively. Furthermore, even if we do have a large repertoire of these stories, we can't always rely on having the opportunity to tell them.

However, there is one type of story that we all tell, that makes up a large part of all our repertoires, and that, of course, is what is often called the personal experience story. In her introductory essay to the genre of the personal narrative in *The Handbook of American Folklore* (Stahl, 1983), Sandra K D Stahl says, 'it would be a rare adult who has not at one time told such a story or who did not have at least one or two such favourite stories in a ready repertoire' (Stahl, 1983, p.268). It would also be a rare child or teenager who did not have a fund of such stories for an appropriate context.

There are, of course, many different kinds of personal experience stories. There are stories which are momentary and topical. They may be of immediate relevance, but are unlikely to be told more than once or twice and will have a life of no more than a few days. Into this category can be put those stories of unexceptional, everyday events, such as experiences of the working day or the previous evening's television. These may be called Type A stories.

There are also stories which will acquire a semi-permanent currency, in that they may be retold on a number of occasions by the storyteller, becoming part of his/her portable repertoire. The life of these stories may be as long as a particular period of the storyteller's life or may even become part of the permanent bank of narratives that will be told on occasions throughout the rest of his/her life. However, they will not outlast the storytellers themselves. Such stories may be identified as being of Type B.

Thirdly, there are what we might call Type C narratives. These are those stories which may begin as first person personal narratives, but will get adopted into the repertoires of other storytellers, where they may be told about the original storyteller, but will instead be narrated in the third person. These stories may well survive longer than their originators and have the potential to take on a life of their own, as will be seen later in this analysis.[1] Whether a story will develop its full potential as a durable, independent Type C story or wither into the obscurity of a Type A story, will to some extent depend on the success of its first and subsequent tellings. As Stahl says, 'if it (the story) effectively entertains, teaches, or awes the audience, then the teller is likely to repeat it whenever the context ..... is appropriate' (Stahl, 1983, p.269). At the same time, however, the storyteller will make a decision as to whether they want to retain the story as part of their repertoire, irrespective of its success, but based on his/her recognition of its durability or even their own preference. For example, a particular story may be extremely well received at its first telling, but the storyteller may choose not to repeat it on subsequent occasions, having recognised that it would no longer retain its vitality or relevance.

For the purposes of this study I shall be concentrating on Types B and C of the personal experience narrative as previously defined, for two reasons. Firstly on a practical level, Type A stories are, by their very transient nature, extremely difficult to collect and so play no part in the accompanying archive. Secondly, it is with those stories of Types B and C that we begin to see an absorption into a narrative tradition, and they are therefore of particular relevance to this study.

Although the personal experience story has long been the mainstay of oral and social historians, narratologists and linguists, it has until relatively recently been woefully neglected by folklorists. Only in cases where the personal narrative has had a secondary purpose, such as conveying information about a folk belief, superstition, custom, etc., did folklorists show any interest, and even then only the content of the narrative was considered worthy of serious study. Fortunately the balance has been redressed of late, mainly thanks to the work of a number of scholars such as Linda Dégh, Roger Abrahams, Richard Bauman, etc., but most notably Sandra K D Stahl, who sees folklore's erstwhile uncommitted relationship with the personal narrative as being due to the apparently idiosyncratic nature of such stories. The fact that they display 'what appears to be non-traditional content' (Stahl, 1977a, p.11) and resist otherwise accepted systems and indices of folktale classification makes the personal experience story notoriously difficult to pin down and pigeon-hole.

On the surface the personal experience story is exactly what it purports to be, namely, a single, real-life experience or sequence of experiences, organised into narrative form and retold by the person to whom the experience happened.[2] Of course, this is an over-simplification, as will be seen later, but it is this very idiosyncratic nature of the personal narrative which has caused a problem for folklorists who are interested in the transmission of tradition lore.

However, Sandra K D Stahl has shown that the personal and the traditional are not necessarily diametrically opposed (see especially Stahl, 1977a). Stahl argues that whilst the content of the personal narrative may be non-traditional, the personal experience story makes wide use of traditional narrative structures. Furthermore, the traditional aspects of the story will become more obvious as a story gets recreated by the original storyteller and adopted and transformed by new storytellers, until the story comes to play a full part in an oral tradition. According to Stahl it is this balance between the idiosyncratic and the traditional that is of prime importance; when the scales finally tip in favour of the traditional, then the personal narrative becomes folklore.

Nevertheless, this analysis in itself is unsatisfactory, because it suggests that a story only becomes traditional as it is repeated, and yet I would argue that in many ways a personal experience story displays many traditional elements at its first telling. It is the subsequent retellings, though, which will establish it as part of a tradition. Stahl indeed recognises this;

> We could say that some elements are traditional the first time the story is told. Other elements become increasingly traditional as the story is repeated by the teller, and still others may become traditional in the more conventional folkloric sense if the story is adopted as a whole item by another teller and circulated 'in oral tradition' (Stahl, 1977a, p.12).

Of course, no story, not even a personal experience story about a unique set of occurrences, can be said to be truly original. When an individual organises an experience into narrative form, what resources do they have at their disposal, if not a set of traditional structures and formulae, a whole system of subconsciously acquired paralinguistic devices, which help give meaning to the narrative and increase its communicative effect? Let us, for example, look at the following story from Dean Taylor, aged fourteen, from Audley Park Secondary School in Torquay, Devon.

> O.K. My name is Dean Taylor, Sir, and I've come from up Northlands. The story I told was about being up North and all streets were dirty and all that 'cos of all the pits, all the coal dust. It would get all the washing dirty and all that. We couldn't go swimming on the beaches 'cos of all the coal making it dirty and all that.
> The strike up there....we had no money. My dad works down the pit and when the strike was on we had no money and we had to eat tomato ketchup soup. 'Cos nobody had no money.
> So that's all I've got to say.
> (Wilson 95)

Here is a story which has a very understated narrative. In fact it is basically a reminiscence, a description of a past situation and the narrative within it is barely discernible. Nevertheless, this story about Dean's earlier life in a Northern mining village makes use of traditional narrative structures.

In his opening metacommunicative statement Dean very economically announces the start of his story, ('O.K.'), introduces himself, ('My name is Dean Taylor, Sir, and I've come up from Northlands') and also sets the scene for his narrative, ('The story I told was about being up North...'). He then proceeds to give us the main bulk of his story, making use of repetition to emphasise its 'point'. The main narrative is divided into two sections. The first is concerned with setting the context in which the narrative takes place, concentrating on the grimness of the situation, hence the repetition of 'dirty'. The second concentrates on the main narrative, which is about life during the Miners' Strike of 1984-85. Here, the overriding point is that of poverty, the cause of the central image of the 'tomato ketchup soup'. Therefore, Dean repeats 'had no money' three times in as many sentences, so that we do not miss his point.

All through the short narrative Dean is very selective about the information he offers to his audience. He could have told us any number of things about his life, but he makes a conscious decision, in the context of his new life in Torquay, to concentrate on details which he understands as being

138

culture-specific, or indeed self-specific. That is to say, he sees the dirt and such a level of poverty as being alien to his current situation, and so having added poignancy. The purpose of this will be examined later in this chapter.

Finally, to finish off his story, Dean employs a further piece of neat metacommunication ('So that's all I've got to say'). Not only can nobody be left in any doubt that the story is now concluded, but also the almost curt nature of the ending serves to emphasise the previous sentence (''Cos nobody had no money'), which, as previously explained, is the whole point of the story.

Therefore, we can see that, even with a personal narrative such as Dean's, which actually takes pride in and underlines the idiosyncrasies of its content, the storyteller relies upon a series of traditional narrative structures and formulae such as metacommunicative openings and endings, repetition and careful information management, as a vehicle to effectively convey his story.

If personal experience stories are largely traditional in structure, then the same is also true of the performance of such narratives. Bauman says 'performance as a mode of spoken verbal communication consists in the assumption of responsibility to an audience for a display of communicative competence' (Bauman, 1977, p.11). In other words the storyteller takes on board the fact that his/her story will be judged and evaluated by the audience on the basis of the expertise displayed by the storyteller. This, of course, not only relates to the actual delivery of the story, the linguistic skill shown, but also to his/her ability to interpret the paraperformative details of context. Again, as Bauman says;

> The emergent quality of the performance resides in the interplay between communicative resources, individual competence, and the goals of the participants, within the context of particular situations (Bauman, 1977, p.38).

Therefore, if we are to examine the traditional aspects of performance of personal narratives, we should see how such stories fit into the model of the performance continuum:

```
INFORMAL------------------------------------------------FORMAL
UNCONSCIOUS----------------------------------------CONSCIOUS
LOW-INTENSITY------------------------------HIGH-INTENSITY
<-----------teenage------------><-----------professional------------>
Bus-stop                                              Arts Centre
Cloakroom                                               Theatre
<------------------TRADITIONAL PERFORMANCE--------------->
<-----------PERSONAL EXPERIENCE NARRATIVES--------->
Type A----------- - - - - - - - - - - - - - - - - - - - - ->
Type B- - - - - ----------------------- - - - - - - -   - - - ->
Type C-  -  -  -  -  -  -  -  -  -  -  -  -  -  -------------------------->
```

We can see from the above model that all types of the personal narrative are told at the informal, conversational end of the continuum. As we progress along the continuum and the performances become more formal and stylised, Type A stories begin to drop out of the equation and Type B stories predominate, and as we reach the high-intensity end of the continuum then Type C stories have begun to take precedence, although Type B stories are still in evidence.[3] At this end of the scale we would be talking of contexts such as after-dinner speeches and professional raconteurs (such as Peter Ustinov, for instance) on stage and television, and would normally be well outside the teenage experience. As with other forms of storytelling, the teenager will tell personal narratives within the lower half of the performance continuum.

The performance of personal experience stories, then, fits neatly into our model for all traditional narrative performance. A storyteller telling a personal story of any kind will take into account the same paraperformative details of time, space, event, nature and size of audience, location, the preceding stories, etc., in not only selecting the appropriate story to be told, but also, having made that selection, will place his/her performance at a suitable point on the continuum, so precisely patterning and influencing the specific performance of the story.

We can also attempt to identify the existence of a storytelling tradition in which the telling of personal narratives plays an important part. Stahl claims that we should be looking at such storytelling traditions rather than story traditions in our examination of the personal narrative, and quotes genres such as the tall tale as relying on 'collective knowledge of the personal narrative tradition' (Stahl, 1977a, p.18). Drawing on Bauman's research among La Have Islanders (Bauman, 1972), she suggests that 'the selection of an experience....and the fashioning of it into a narrative are traditional aspects of storytelling' (Stahl, 1977a, p.19). It is important to recognise that, in our modern, Western society, storytelling survives in an essentially social (rather than sacred) tradition, and that the importance of the personal experience story within social discourse bears testimony to its importance within this storytelling tradition.

Thus, although a personal narrative may seem on the surface to display content that is new, unique, idiosyncratic and non-traditional, its 'performance will involve a number of other traditional aspects such as traditional structure, use, attitudes or idioms' (Stahl, 1977a, p.14) and will often be part of an established and accepted storytelling tradition.

The content of personal experience stories

As already stated, it is generally inherent in the very nature of the personal narrative that its content concerns a unique set of events and a single individual or specific individuals. As such it is often presumed that the content of personal experience stories is non-traditional. Whilst this may often be the case, we must be careful not to exclude aspects of tradition from our analysis of narrative content.

In their paper on family lore (Kotkin and Zeitlin, 1983), Amy J Kotkin and Steven J Zeitlin list the following themes as those that cover the type of content, as opposed to the content itself, occurring in family narrative traditions.

1) Wild antics
2) Poverty and hardship
3) Lost fortunes and opportunities
4) Notorious deeds
5) Heroic action
6) Courtship and marriage
7) Family migrations
8) Natural disasters and near deaths
9) Supernatural occurrences
10) Eccentric behaviour
(Kotkin and Zeitlin, 1983, p.93)

To a large extent the same list can be applied to personal experience stories, although in the teenage context certain categories, such as 'supernatural occurrences', will inevitably have a greater weighting than 'courtship and marriage', which may be practically, if not entirely non-existent.[4] It can also be said that stories may cover more than one

141

category; for instance, Dean Taylor's story already quoted is essentially a story about 'poverty and hardship', but because of the context in which it was told, it is also by implication about 'family migrations'.

Before proceeding any further, it is necessary to define more closely what exactly we mean by personal experience stories. It is often assumed that personal narratives can only ever be told in the first person. However, this is not necessarily the case. We have already seen how a personal narrative can develop through countless retellings into a piece of widely communicated folk narrative. If Person A tells Person B a personal narrative and then Person B goes and tells the same story to Person C, only this time in the third person, but still concerning Person A, then how is the story different? Certainly the personality of the storyteller is different and will, with repeated tellings, put his/her own stamp on the story, and the context of the second telling may also have effected changes in the narrative, but essentially the story is the same. It recounts the same set of sequential events about the same person, and if told shortly after the first telling and in a similar context, when the memory may still be fresh, it is even possible that the two tellings may share similar linguistic features.

It could also be argued (and often is) that a story can never be purely personal, because any story must have a 'point', must communicate with other people for it to be deemed worthy of being told in the first place. The personal narrative must address communal beliefs as well as individual ones, centring upon a shared agenda. On the other hand, Jerome Bruner argues that an element of the personal is evident in all stories, because a 'story is somebody's story' (Bruner, 1990, p.54). In other words, any story is a curious mix of the personal and the communal, albeit in varying ratios. Of course, for our own purposes, we must recognise that as a story gets retold and, more importantly, moves from storyteller to storyteller, a story which may have begun life as a personal experience story (Type A or B) will reach a point where it becomes totally independent of its original source (Type C) and achieves 'legendary' status. Therefore, we may define the personal experience story as a story which may be told in either the first or third person, but which retains a personal element and clear links between the experience and the originator, irrespective of whether the story is actually true or not. In practice this usually means that the protagonist of the story is no more than a couple of steps removed from the storyteller.

By this token, not only can Dean Taylor's story be easily recognised as a personal narrative, but also stories such as the following fragment from Anne-Marie Emond of Ernesettle, Plymouth:

My Auntie Jan put the poodle in the microwave and cooked it.
(Wilson 83)

Here, this short fragment suggests a longer, more substantial narrative, but is a story told about someone who is personally known to the storyteller. Furthermore, the story is that of a well-documented contemporary legend, usually known as 'The Poodle in the Microwave' (cf. Brunvand, 1981, pp.62-5). This is particularly interesting because it shows that not only can personal narratives develop into independent stories, but that the process can also to some extent work in reverse, in that widespread traditional narratives can be personalised and acquire the trappings of the personal narrative. This is especially true of contemporary legends where the presence of a friend of a friend (FOAF) or, as in Anne-Marie's case, a friend/relative, or even occasionally the first person, is often added to give authenticity to the story. Likewise, a good story, which may be in widespread circulation, may be personalised and told as a first person narrative as part of the process of a storyteller absorbing a story into his/her own repertoire. This is most obvious in the non-teenage context of the after-dinner speech, the tall tale or the banter of the stand-up comedian. Linda Dégh and Andrew Vázsonyi have even brought attention to the point that there comes a moment when it is difficult to say whether a particular text is a personal narrative which has become a legend, or whether the reverse is true (cf. Dégh and Vázsonyi, 1974).

Linked closely to the contemporary legend, particularly in the teenage repertoire, is, of course, the ghost story, and consistent with Kotkin and Zeitlin's list, many of these are told as personal narratives. Such stories are usually termed as 'memorates'[5] and have particular significance for us in studying aspects of tradition in personal experience stories. Stahl explains that the memorate 'has long been accepted to identify personal accounts of experiences with the supernatural' (Stahl, 1983, p.269). Such stories illustrate aspects of tradition in two important ways. Firstly, the stories concern traditional folk belief (ghostlore) and, therefore, give validation to such belief, and secondly, as a follow-on from this, memorates are inevitably filled with motifs and imagery from traditional ghostlore. As Stahl says, 'memorates represent personal testimonials either supporting or denying the validity of established elements of culture' (Stahl, 1983, p.270).

Stahl, however, does not ultimately seem to accept the memorate into the fold of the personal narrative. She argues that the traditional content of the memorate disqualifies it from being a personal experience story, which she defines as being 'a prose narrative relating a personal experience; it is usually told in the first person and its content is non traditional' (Stahl, 1977b, p.20).

This argument, however, is, I feel, flawed since, as has been shown, traditional content and the personal narrative are not incompatible. Furthermore, by excluding memorates from our definition we would singularly fail to recognise the full importance of the personal narrative in the teenage repertoire.

The majority of the Type B and Type C personal narratives of teenagers are memorates and, of those that are secular in nature, most are told in the third person. It seems that there may be a simple reason for this. Firstly, considering the importance of the supernatural within the teenage narrative tradition, it is not surprising that this is also reflected in their personal experience stories. As Stahl herself says, 'through personal experience stories we articulate and then test the values that identify our selves' (Stahl, 1983, p.275). This is echoed by the experience of Betty Rosen of working with teenagers in a London secondary school. In *And None of It Was Nonsense* (B. Rosen, 1988), she allows us a taste of some of the personal narratives she recorded from her students, and there follows a whole series of memorates, many incidentally in the third person (B. Rosen, 1988, pp.13-14). This activity, she claims, is universal because 'each child is subject to the narrative of his own living' (B. Rosen, 1988, p.13).

Secondly, if personal narratives are drawn from real-life experience, then it might reasonably be supposed that the older the person, the more stories they have in their personal repertoire. Furthermore, bearing in mind that every story must have substance, a 'point', in order to have a reason for being told, it often requires a distance between the event and the first telling for the true significance of that event to be understood. For example, yesterday's experience may seem of little consequence today, but in five years' time, viewed in the context of subsequent experience, its full importance may be realised. Therefore, considering the relative youth of the teenager, it is not surprising that many personal experience stories are third person narratives inherited from older members of the family or even teachers. Where teenage stories are told in the first person they tend to be either memorates or stories linked to specific significant, and often shared, experiences, and as such often occur in cycles (see Wilson 96-99).

It is clear, therefore, that when discussing personal experience stories, it is important not to limit ourselves to a narrow definition of first person stories of non-traditional content. Rather we must look towards elements of the personal in teenage storytelling, which are very prominent. Whilst accepting that the content of such stories may often be unique and original, and that it is essentially through structure that we can universally define them as traditional, we must also understand that the content of the personal

144

experience story can also display, either partly or wholly, elements common to what might be conventionally defined as traditional narrative.

The purpose and function of teenage personal narratives

Having discussed at length our definitions and aspects of tradition within the personal experience narrative, let us now turn our attention to the function of such narratives with specific reference to the teenage context. At this point it may be useful to compile a list of functions after the fashion of Kotkin and Zeitlin's run-down of content types. It would seem that the telling of personal narratives and the use of the personal in narratives amongst teenagers serve one or more of the following functions:

a) To raise the status of the storyteller
b) To reinforce the identity of the group/family in the story
c) To reassert the identity of an individual within the group or isolate another individual
d) To build social cohesion/intimacy between teller and audience
e) To add authority/authenticity to an otherwise incredible tale
f) To validate belief or a previous assertion
g) To convey a cautionary or moral message
h) To help the continual flow of conversation
i) To convey information about an unfamiliar culture

Let us begin by looking at the two stories already quoted. Dean's story about his experiences during the Miners' Strike can only be fully understood in terms of its function if we are first to place it in context. When this particular telling took place I had been working for a couple of days in the school as a resident storyteller and had set Dean's class the task of telling a personal narrative. Dean had been praised by his teacher for the story and, when I visited the class, he was keen that I should listen to him. At this time Dean had only recently moved down to Devon and he was very much considered an outsider. This was further enforced by the fact that he spoke with a strong Geordie accent and clearly found it quite difficult to make friends. He was a very personable boy, but was never socially at ease. Furthermore, Dean's class was a remedial set for 'low-achievers'; it was probably a rare occurrence for Dean to be praised by his teacher for a piece of work. Quite rightly, his telling oozed with pride. Therefore, the main function of his performance was to raise his own status (Function A), whilst also conveying information about life in the mining village (Function I). As a person who was used to being treated as low-status, and having already had

145

his status raised through his teacher's praise, he was eager to have it further increased by receiving the praise of the 'visitor' (an even greater accolade). He is eager to please (notice his politeness in the first line), and his whole telling is geared towards singling himself out from the rest of the class. His experience is special and unique.

There is also an additional function in Dean's story and that is to reassert the identity of himself and his family through the content of the story (Function B). As an outsider Dean is keen to establish his identity within the group and this he does by sharing information about his own cultural background, which again singles him out as being special and so worthy of social acceptance by the rest of the class. My suspicion is that when the story was first told, this was the primary function. Only after he had been praised for his telling, did Function A come into the frame, and in his performance to me Function B takes on a secondary rôle (after all, I'm even less part of the social group than he is) and function A becomes of prime importance. By this example we can see, therefore, that not only is a personal narrative told with specific functions in mind, but also that the relative importance of these functions can change according to the context in which it is told.

Anne-Marie Emond's short story, however, fulfils quite different functions. The clue for this is primarily in the brevity of her narration. Anne-Marie's story is in a way merely a suggestion of a longer story, a statement stripped down to its bare essentials. This is because it is not intended to be a complete story; there is no wish to take up any valuable time with the telling, as its prime function is that of a conversation filler, to help the social intercourse of the storytelling session along whilst somebody else prepares a more substantial contribution (Function H).

However, the story did not come out of the blue. The context of the telling was that of a storytelling session in the local library, consisting of young teenagers telling mainly ghost stories and contemporary legends. Immediately preceding Anne-Marie's interjection I had told another variant of the same story, but had not personalised it in any way or sought to authenticate it, merely introducing it as a story that people often tell as having really happened, in the hope that it might prompt some variants from the young people. Therefore, Anne-Marie's story serves the function of giving validation to my previous statement about the story (Function F). The sub-text of her narrative is, 'Yes, it is true, because I know somebody who actually did that very thing.' Furthermore, by personalising the story - it is not just somebody she has heard of, but someone whom she intimately knows, a close relative - she is also adding authority to a story which might otherwise not be believed (Function E). In my own comments about the story I had hinted at my scepticism about the truth of such stories, but we can assign to

Anne-Marie an additional sub-text of 'and I can't be mistaken because I got it from a very reliable source.' Again, therefore, we can see how even a very brief story such as this can carry out a number of functions at varying degrees of intensity.

Let us now turn our attention to the group of related stories (Wilson 96-99) which were told to me by a group of students from Brannel School, near St Austell in Cornwall and which serve quite different functions once more.

There is a number of interesting points to these stories, not least that they are all told as first person narratives. All four stories are, in fact, precisely what we might expect from personal experience stories, namely that they are real-life experiences fashioned into narrative structures and so recreated by the people to whom the events happened. Also these stories are told as a cycle; they were told one after another in sequence, all relate to the same time and location (whatever the singular events of each narrative, they are all independent stories set during the previous year's school camp), centre around the same set of characters, and whilst each individual narrative serves its own functions, the group of stories as a whole also has overall purposes. In a sense we are dealing with four episodes, which, although they are stories in their own right with different storytellers, are also part of one larger story.

The stories were all told to me during what was my second visit to the class. This is important because it meant that I was already known to the students and they were relatively at ease in my presence. It is also important to point out that every member of the class had taken part in the school camp which forms the larger suggested narrative linking the four stories. Moreover, every person mentioned in the stories was also present, forming part of a smaller social grouping within the larger grouping of the class. We might, thus, expect the stories to betray a complex web of interpersonal group relationships.

In fact, this points us towards the primary purpose of the cycle as a whole, which is to build social cohesion within the group (Function D). The stories are all part of a shared experience and so become a common cultural reference point for all the class. Additionally the experience is specific to that class, an experience that binds them together as a unit. They are identifying themselves as a social unit by the very virtue of their participation in the experience.

However, in doing this, the storytellers are very careful not to exclude me as an outsider. Their delivery is not aggressive and exclusive, but friendly and inclusive. The sub-text is not so much to emphasise my separateness from the group, but to share with me a key element of their group identity. The storytellers are working to build a level of intimacy between teller and audience (or rather audiences; myself and the rest of the class). This, of course, is another aspect of Function D.

In her essay 'A Literary Folkloristic Methodology for the Study of Meaning in Personal Narrative' (Stahl, 1985), Sandra K D Stahl suggests that by the very sharing of personal knowledge, personal experience stories 'facilitate the creation of intimacy' (Stahl, 1985, p.47). In this way the storyteller can make connections with an audience that is not part of the same social group. At the same time, however, Stahl also recognises the importance of a shared folklore within a specific social group. She makes a clear distinction between communal folklore, which is not culture-specific, although it is often thought to be so by its transmitters, and private folklore which is culture-specific and is only universal structurally speaking (Stahl, 1985, p.48). She also notes; 'Those who share a body of private folklore often cherish the exclusive nature of that lore for the sake of the intimacy it engenders' (Stahl, 1985, p.48).

In the context of the session at Brannel school, these stories could not have been told during my first encounter with the class, because it was only after they got to know and trust me a little better that they felt able to invoke a certain intimacy and invite me, at least on one level, to be a part of their social group.

Let us now focus on the purposes of the four individual texts. Although quite different stories, all four narratives share three common purposes, albeit to different extents, and those purposes are to assert the identities of the people in the stories as a cohesive social group (Function B), to build social cohesion amongst both this smaller and the larger social group (Function D), and to raise and lower the statuses of various individuals within the group (Function C). Interestingly enough, it is always the group identity that is important rather than that of the individual storytellers.

The first story (Wilson 96) is the longest and tells of two encounters with rats, one dead and one alive, whilst on the school camp.

It's the first day of school camp and we were all picked to go in our tents and it was me, Anthony and three other boys; Shane, Craig and Jamie.

I was sitting on my bed eating our packed lunches and I put my drink beside my bed. My bed was beside Shane's, we had about a foot gap between us. I put my drink down, I saw this rat - it was under my bed and it had blood coming out of its eye and it had a cut down at the side and I said, 'There's a rat under your bed', and Shane goes, 'Yeh, I believe you.'

I go, 'Go on, have a look', so he looks round.

148

He goes, 'Ugh, rat', and Jamie goes, 'Let's have a look', and he runs out, saying we've got a dead rat in our tent. Everyone was coming round looking in our tent. When I came out with the rat, Shane was going, 'I killed it!' When I brought it out, they all run away because they were afraid of it. I brought it out in some loo roll and chucked it over the hedge.

The last night we were there, we had all been to Padstow and Jamie had bought a big lolly and he left it in his bag because he was going to take it home for a present for someone.

I was in bed and I couldn't sleep and everybody else was asleep and I was just looking at the end of the tent and there was this little bit of light come in the tent and I was watching it. There was a half circle in black with a little tail sticking out and it came straight for me, so I picked up a welly and threw it at it.

I go, 'Jamie, Jamie, wake up, there's a rat here.' I was looking under my bed to see if it was there, and we had plastic groundsheets to keep our clothes dry and it was going under one of them.

In the end I think it ran away or something because we didn't know where it was. We went back to sleep and in the morning Jamie got up and all his clothes were wet and the lolly was wet as well.
(Unidentified Male, aged c.13, Brannel School, St. Austell, 30.4.93.)

Of all the stories it is also the one that has the weakest narrative, in that it actually deals with two separate stories that are connected merely by their subject matter. This is because, as the opening story in the cycle, its prime function is not to tell a good entertaining story with a strong 'point', but rather to set the scene, to establish the identity of the larger social group (the class) by introducing the backdrop of the school camp, and also that of the smaller social group by identifying the characters who will take part in the stories. Of course, the content of the narrative is not totally inconsequential - it would be classified in the Kotkin-Zeitlin list as 'wild antics' - since it establishes the mood of the stories to come. In fact, this first story is essentially by way of an introduction, establishing the social groupings and defining the individuals within them, and so paves the way for the succeeding narratives.

The three stories that follow are all much shorter, more concise, and more clearly structured as stories, relating single-event episodes of the school camp. However, they are still concerned with interpersonal group relationships. The next story (Wilson 97) is a very clear example.

I bought this giant bag of gobstoppers and I was giving them all around. Everybody was having one. Then it was time for us to go to sleep.

I woke everybody up at about one o' clock in the morning and handed out more gobstoppers in our tent and Jamie says, 'What?'

I said, 'Have a gobstopper.' So he puts it in his mouth and goes to sleep, then I give one to everybody.

When they're all asleep and about three o' clock or so I give out more and there's Craig still asleep, snoring with his mouth open, so I drop one in.

By the third time everyone was getting pissed off. Jamie said, 'Get lost', Shane was swearing his head off, Craig was still sleeping. Then I go back to sleep.

Just before it was morning, I was just about to give out the next lot and Shane gets out and says, 'If you give me another gobstopper, I'm going to kick your head in.'

(Unidentified Male, aged c.13, Brannel School, St. Austell, 30.4.93.)

As a successor to the first expositionary narrative, the storyteller here needs waste no time in setting the scene and is able to launch straight into the details of the narrative. He begins by raising his own status, but not as a storyteller, but rather as a character within the story, identifying himself as the magnanimous hero; 'I bought this giant bag of gobstoppers and I was giving them all around.' The story then goes on to tell of how he regularly woke everybody up, throughout the night, to give out more gobstoppers until one of the group finally loses patience. It is the character of Craig who comes off worst from the story; his status is lowered by making him the comic character. Firstly, he is identified as a snorer. Furthermore, when he fails to wake, a gobstopper is simply dropped into his open mouth (presumably we are meant to believe that he consumes the gobstopper without being aware of it) and so becomes the victim of a practical joke. Later on in the narrative we are also informed that Craig is still asleep and so is further isolated, having slept through the whole episode and not consciously participated in the events.

However, the story is not simply about having a joke at the expense of Craig. The character of Shane is subsequently raised. Whilst Craig is asleep, Shane, we are told, 'was swearing his head off.' This active/passive contrast between the two boys serves to highlight Shane's involvement in the activities and so raise his status. It is also Shane who is given the punchline to the story; 'If you give me another gobstopper, I'm going to kick your head in!' This not only endows Shane with the gift of wit and physical prowess (it is presumably thus inferred that he is capable of such an act), but also of

150

illustrating the point of the story, namely that even the acknowledgement of such unbridled generosity has its limits.

It is now the turn of Craig to hit back with another story (Wilson 98), which attempts to redress the balance in a similar way, by raising his own status and lowering that of other characters.

> We were in a tent and we were all talking about stuff and we were doing wrestling and I picked up a welly and threw it at Anthony (Copper) and it fell on Shane's bed cover and it had all clothes laid out on it and they all went everywhere and Copper fell off and he picks up the welly boot and throws it back to me. I duck and it hits Jamie smack on the gob.
> (Craig, aged c.13, Brannel School, St. Austell, 30.4.93.)

Craig's short narrative tells of an incident when a wellington boot was being thrown around the tent. He is able to reassert his own identity as high status within the group in two ways. Firstly, he identifies himself as being the instigator of the episode; 'I picked up the welly and threw it', so negating his image of passivity as constructed in the previous story. Secondly, he emphasises his own agility. When the boot is thrown at him, he ducks and seems to be the only character who emerges from the episode totally unscathed. It is Shane and Jamie who are each singled out for ridicule in this story. Shane suffers the indignity of having his belongings scattered everywhere and Jamie literally loses face at the very end when the wellington strikes him 'smack on the gob'. Even Copper, whose real name is Anthony, does not escape unscathed as he falls over in the middle of the mayhem. This story, therefore, concentrates solely on the identities of the characters in the story.

The mentioning of Copper as a nickname for Anthony acts as a prompt for the final story of the cycle (Wilson 99).

> I call this one 'The Legend of Copper'. This was why we named him Copper.
> Simple reason was, when we was on school camp, we all had our beds a foot apart and we had our sheets, but Anthony was laid on his bed. His leg was a bit funny, so we kept racking it up and collapsing the bed and he started to cry a little bit because we kept scatting up his bed. Someone broke the spring by jumping on it. He sat on the bed and he went straight to the ground. We had scat up his bed completely.
> So then he goes out and says, 'I'm going to go and play with an electric fence.' He conducts electricity, so we call him Copper.
> (Unidentified Male, aged c.13, Brannel School, St. Austell, 30.4.93.)

Of all the stories it is the one that is most structured, in that it is framed by formal opening and closing formulae; 'I call this one "The Legend of Copper"' and 'so we call him Copper'. In its telling it also concentrates on the imparting of the relevant information, never deviating from its purpose. Of course, the function of the story is to isolate Copper as an individual within the group and hold him up for ridicule (Function C). We are told that 'he started to cry a little bit' as he was being picked on and that his nickname originated from a comment he made whilst being intimidated.

However, whilst these stories isolate certain individuals and praise others, we must also remember that the stories were all told in good humour. The function of them is also to reassert the individuals' identity as part of the group. This is particularly true of this last story which on the one hand makes fun of Copper, but on the other hand turns him into a 'legendary' figure. The group is able to make fun of Copper precisely because he is part of the group.

Sandra K D Stahl suggests that there are two types of personal experience storytellers, the 'self-oriented' and the 'other-oriented' (Stahl, 1983, p.270). The self-oriented storyteller emphasises the importance of their own actions in the story and the importance of their presence at the happening. An example of this would be the tall-tale. The other-oriented storyteller plays down the personal involvement, which is incidental, merely giving authority to the narrative. It is the events that are important in the story, for example, in the memorate, where it is the element of the supernatural that makes the story worthy of being told.

Of course, it would be more helpful to talk about self-oriented and other-oriented performances rather than storytellers, since individual storytellers readily alternate between types, but Stahl's analysis is useful to bear in mind.

If we look at our Brannel cycle of stories, they are clearly self-oriented performances, but the self is not only the performer as an individual, but also the small social group of boys as a whole. It is their presence together at the events which gives the stories substance.

Now let us turn our attention to an other-oriented performance, this time a memorate told in the third person by Daniel, aged thirteen from St Stephen's Youth Club near St Austell, Cornwall (Wilson 72). His story clearly serves as a moral warning or cautionary message.

One day when my step-mum was about ten or eleven, she went on this ouija board and spirits said that she would die on 30 December, on her birthday. Instead of her dying, her gran did.

To some degree, of course, all stories exhibit a moral stance in the same way that all stories contain an element of the personal. As Jerome Bruner says; 'To tell a story is inescapably to take a moral stance, even if it is a moral stance against moral stances' (Bruner, 1990, p.51). However, in telling his story, Daniel is quite unambiguous about the moral stance he is taking, making a virtue of it (Function G). For many people the ouija board represents the unacceptable side of the supernatural. It is dabbling with the occult, an active involvement with the supernatural as opposed to a passive one, where ghostly experiences just happen to people. Daniel's story aptly illustrates the dire consequences of such involvement - experimentation with the occult only leads to tragedy. At the same time the story is fulfilling the function of validating a belief or previous assertion (Function F). Undoubtedly all memorates do this because they give credibility to a belief in the supernatural, but Daniel's story also, in the context of being told after a number of other 'true' ghost stories, is giving validation to the previous storytellers' narratives.

The personal experience stories of teenagers exhibit a wide range of functions to varying degrees of intensity, whether they are first or third person, secular or supernatural, idiosyncratic or traditional. It is also appropriate that this analysis of function should finish with Daniel's story because it is a personal narrative that has found its way into his repertoire via a family source, which is vital to our understanding of the teenage tradition.

Family lore in the personal repertoire

Narrative traditions within the family constitute an aspect of folklore that has already received some attention from scholars. The family is seen as a relatively secure social unit within which folklore is regularly transmitted, and this is made more acutely relevant in a modern society where traditional social communities are generally in decline and being eroded. If family lore is folklore transmitted within the social unit of the family, we might then validly question whether family lore has a place in our study of teenage traditions. However, a cursory glance at a sample of teenage narratives will show us that stories which clearly began life within a family tradition find their way into a more public repertoire.

Family stories are nearly always personal experience stories in our wide definition of the genre, in that they are nearly always narrative constructs of significant experiences of a member of that family, living or dead. Inside the family such stories and storytelling events where these narratives are performed, fulfil many important, and often ritualistic, functions. Yet when family stories get exported to a wider public audience they acquire personal experience status on a further level.

Not only, for example, is Daniel's story a personal experience story of his stepmother, it is also a personal experience story of his family. The family becomes a single unit in itself to which the storyteller publicly declares his/her allegiance. In this way the storyteller, by telling a family story to an outside audience, is claiming the experience for him/herself because it is an experience that happened to the family of which s/he is an integral part.

Above all, family stories are about identity, particularly when told within the family. We need only look at the occasions when such storytelling events take place to establish this. The most common occasions for families to exchange stories are at times of reunion, especially holidays and feast days, where they serve the prime function of reasserting the identity of the family and re-establishing the gathered individuals as a single social unit by recreating shared experiences and a common heritage through the narratives. This is done through stories which centre on individual personalities from within the family and on periods of transition within family history, which reinforce the continuity and indestructibility of the unit (see especially Kotkin and Zeitlin, 1983, p.92). Indeed there are many elements that link family storytelling to sacred traditions as well as social ones, such as certain stories being assigned to certain storytellers, the repetition of stories that have been heard many times before, and other facets of ritual. Family storytelling actually bridges the gap between sacred and social narrative traditions.

Of course, not all family stories are sacred stories. Whilst there are stories in any family's repertoire that would never be told outside of the family, there are also some stories which are easily transferred from the family into the public repertoire.

Sandra K D Stahl argues that there are two types of folklore, communal folklore and private folklore (Stahl, 1985). The former is public and widespread, whilst the latter is private and group-specific. Communal folklore may well be thought to be private, but is generally in wide circulation, whereas private folklore is 'exclusively shared (and cannot be corroborated outside the group) and it is privately or even personally generated through group interaction or personal experience' (Stahl, 1985, p.48). To develop this argument we could say that family narrative lore can also be divided into the two same categories. Communal family lore is those stories which are easily exportable to a more public forum, where the meaning of the story has relevance outside of the family as well as inside it, although that meaning may well change depending on where it is told. For example, a family story of an ancestor's deeds during the war may essentially be a story about heroism, which, of course, can have relevance both inside and outside the family.

However, if told inside the family it will probably have the effect of allowing the audience to share in that heroism, whereas if it was told publicly, the effect would be to allow the audience to merely aspire to it.

Private family lore, on the other hand, is those stories which stay firmly within the family context. This may be for a number of reasons. Perhaps they are stories which show an individual member (and, therefore, by implication the whole family) in a bad light, which may act as a cautionary message within the family circle, or they may be stories which express private emotions and, therefore, put the family in a vulnerable position. Stahl argues that the personal experience storyteller is indeed more vulnerable because personal narratives deal with confession and self-revelation (Stahl, 1983, p.274). They may also be stories whose meaning simply gets lost in the public forum, being heavily steeped in private lore. Furthermore, any family will need to retain a certain amount of family lore as private because the existence of such stories helps serve the function of binding the family together as a social unit. That is to say that secrets unite families by making them unique and special. As Stahl says; 'Those who share a body of private folklore often cherish the exclusive nature of that lore for the sake of the sense of intimacy it engenders' (Stahl, 1985, p.48).

However, the division between private and communal family narrative lore is not as straightforward as the above argument may appear to suggest. Exactly how a piece of family narrative is defined will very much depend on the storyteller. A private story to one may be a public story to another. Very much also depends on the context; a private story one minute may suddenly be transformed into a public story the next, if the context is appropriate.

Let us take the example of a memorate. On the one hand, a certain member of the family may consider a story of supernatural experience one that makes the central character appear foolish, and would, therefore, view it as private. On the other hand, another family member may see the story as one of a unique experience, thus raising the protagonist's status. Also, the story may be felt to be appropriate amongst a number of similar stories, but considered as slightly ridiculous in a more formal context.

We can see, therefore, family narratives are defined as such in that they originate within the family and serve very specific functions within it. However, they are not strictly confined to familial contexts and may equally be told in the public forum.

Family stories within the adolescent repertoire serve two principal functions; firstly to raise the status of either an individual within the story, the family unit, the storyteller him/herself or a combination of the three, and secondly, to provide validation for an otherwise incredible narrative.

If a particular story, for example, concentrates upon an individual's heroic action (self-oriented narrative), then it will, of course, serve to raise the status of that individual. Furthermore, if this immediately follows a similar story, it could also be seen as competitive, part of what we might call the 'my-dad-is-better-than-your-dad' syndrome. Naturally, a story of this kind also serves to raise the status of the family, because it implies that the family (of which the storyteller is part) is full of heroic and exceptional characters. However, stories which do not centre on any particular individual (other-oriented narrative) also raise the esteem of the family in that they suggest that this is a family which does interesting things, or to which interesting things happen.

The status of the storyteller is often raised in two ways. Firstly by association, which is to say by identifying him/herself with the family, they acquire their positive attributes. Secondly, as in any storytelling performance, the storyteller is assessed by the audience according not only to the standard of the performance, but also to the quality of the narrative itself. If a storyteller is able to tell a good story in addition to telling a story well, then some of the credit will inevitably fall upon him/her.

This, I feel, may hold the key to why so many family stories find their way into the teenage repertoire. At a time when so many young people rebel against and reject the 'traditional' institutions of the establishment such as the family, we might reasonably expect the opposite to be true. On the surface it does seem rather odd that, amongst their peers, teenagers not only gain credibility by the effectiveness of their rebellion against the family, but also by portraying it in a positive light. If we accept that the storytelling process raises the status of the performer, however, then in the family repertoire there exists a whole fund of material, which has been tried, tested and developed, and which the teenager can plunder for his/her own use. Additionally, bearing in mind that teenagers will have limited experience of their own from which to draw for personal narratives, it is only to be expected that they would use stories from the lives of those adults closest to them.

Nevertheless, we must not lose sight of the fact that most family narratives to be found in the teenage repertoire are memorates. For the teenage storyteller there is clearly much to be gained from either relating memorates or by simply personalising stories of supernatural experience. This is because a 'true' ghost story always carries more weight than one which cannot be validated. Furthermore, the validation of a supernatural experience by an adult is of greater significance than that of a child. The adult represents the world of supreme rationality, which, although being something to rebel against on one level, offers a perfect authentication for irrational events. Whilst it is easy for the audience to challenge and contradict the evidence of a

156

child, an adult's testimony is something totally different, something not easily disbelieved. After all, the rational adult, unlike the child, will not easily be convinced by the inexplicable, and so the truth of their stories must be beyond doubt.

In this sense the adult from within the family serves the same function as the FOAF (Friend of a Friend) in the contemporary legend genre. Brunvand says that 'urban legends gain credibility from specific details of time and place or from references to source authorities' (Brunvand, 1981, p.3), and such a story 'is true; it really occurred,... and always to someone else who is quite close to the narrator...' (Brunvand 1981, p.4).

The nature of truth in the personal narrative

It is often presumed that when we are talking about personal experience stories, we are also dealing with true stories. Whether the story is told in the first or the third person, it is always presumed that the events actually did happen, that is to say that the personal narrative is a reconstruction of real-life events into a narrative framework. Even in the tall-tale, where the whole point is that the story is stretched beyond believability, it relies for its ultimate effectiveness on it being told as if it were true. There would appear to be a contract between performer and audience that when a personal narrative is being performed, there is a general acceptance that the story is true.

However, the matter is not as clear-cut as it may at first appear. We have already seen that memorates serve to validate otherwise irrational and incredible events. Likewise, stories are sometimes personalised in order to give them authenticity, as in our earlier example from Anne-Marie Emond. Therefore, the personal narrative may be used as a cloak to dupe the audience into believing an untruth.

This leads us onto the issue of lying. There is no reason at all why we should always accept that our storytellers are not consciously telling us blatant falsehoods. Richard Bauman argues that lying is, in fact, an essential component of the personal experience story (Bauman, 1986, p.21). Since such stories 'are a vehicle for the encoding and presentation of information about oneself in order to construct a personal and social image' (Bauman, 1986, p.21), so raising the storyteller's self-esteem and esteem in the eyes of others, we should expect that the storyteller is likely to exaggerate positive aspects in order to raise his/her status, the central character (in the case of third person personal narratives), or the family. In fact, Bauman suggests, the audience readily expects a certain amount of lying in a true story for this very reason, and so presumably takes this into account when assessing the believability of a story. Lying, he says, can be divided into two categories, 'outright lying' and 'stretching the truth', the latter, in the case of the personal narrative, being more acceptable than the first. For example, when Anne-Marie Emond told her story (outright lie), it was greeted with derision by the audience and she had to aggressively reassert the story's truth in order to prevent losing all credibility with the listeners. Obviously, the outright dismissal of a personal experience story as a lie is the worst reaction a storyteller can expect from an audience. It is part of the performer/audience contract that even if a story is not strictly true, then it is an insult to step beyond the accepted range of the audience's gullibility.

In contrast, when Dean Taylor told his story, it was readily accepted as the truth, even though the audience suspected that certain aspects of it may have been slightly exaggerated for the purpose of achieving maximum effect. It is precisely because of this expectation and tolerance by the audience of a certain degree of manipulation, that storytellers will often underline the truth of some of the less credible aspects of a narrative, such as, 'This is a true story' (Wilson 69), 'And I reckon it was true' (Wilson 70) and 'Now this is a hundred per cent true and I'm not lying you' (Wilson 71).

There is a further way in which fiction finds a home in the personal narrative, even when the storyteller firmly believes in the absolute truth of the story. Any personal experience story is a recreation of events from memory, and not only can memory be inaccurate, fallible and selective, but it can also be creative. It is, for instance, not uncommon for two people who were at the same happening to quarrel over the precise nature of events, because everybody has his/her own version of the truth, which is coloured by personal perception and memory, since truth is subjective. Furthermore, even when there is no argument, our memory readily creates new pieces of information to fill the gaps in what we actually remember. For example, in the cycle of stories from Brannel School, all the storytellers make extensive use of direct speech, and yet there is no way that any of them can actually recall the precise words that were spoken. Whilst they are all sure that certain things happened and certain things were said, they are only able to reconstruct speech and events into a meaningful approximation of the truth. In analysing one of his own autobiographical stories, Harold Rosen comments; 'So the words I use telling the story are fabricated but very faithful to the events' (H. Rosen, 1993, p.147). Thus none of us can rely on our memories to recreate stories of absolute truth.

This inevitably raises the question as to whether any story is true. In this sense we must indeed accept that all stories contain varying degrees of fiction. Truth, argues Bauman, is, like everything else, dependent on context; 'Consideration of truth and belief will vary and be subject to negotiation within communities and storytelling situations' (Bauman, 1986, p.11). We must also recognise that story itself imposes untruth on narrated events, since narrative is an organisational construct. Unlike stories, life does not have clear-cut beginnings and endings, clearly defined and distinguishable episodes, but goes on, as we go on, from one experience to the next. Narrative restructures life into manageable, meaningful chunks for us. Where a story begins and where it ends is an artistic decision made by the storyteller (see H. Rosen, 1993, pp.142-3 and p.148).

Not only does the narrative construct impose its own fiction on real-life events, but so does the storytelling. We have already seen how the more a storyteller consciously performs a story, the more s/he employs the resources and techniques associated with performance, then the less the story is told as true (see Cunningham, 1990, p.4). If a storyteller plays down the performative qualities, presenting a seemingly spontaneous, rough and unselfconscious rendition, then this 'lends an air of sincerity and immediacy to the storytelling, qualities that might be undermined by an extremely polished performance' (Stahl, 1983, p.272). Therefore, the very act of performance imposes an additional level of untruth upon the narrative, which is increased with the formality of that performance. Performance is merely a recreation of experience to give it meaning (and thus an integral part of it), but not the experience itself.

The question of truth is one that has troubled folklorists and critics alike for a very long time.[6] Too much time and effort seems for many years to have been devoted to establishing clear distinctions between truth and fiction in narratives. Linda Dégh and Andrew Vázsonyi, however, make the effective point that the legend 'takes a stand and calls for the expression of opinion on the question of truth and belief' (Dégh and Vázsonyi, 1976, p.119). This hints at the real importance of truth in personal experience stories. It returns us once more to the notion of a contract between performer and audience as to the nature and assessment of truth within any particular narrative. It is not so much important to determine whether stories are true or not, but more that performer and/or audience consider them to be so. This is particularly relevant to a study of teenage narratives, since so many deal with events that may appear irrational and unlikely. They continually stretch the bounds of credibility, and so the issue of truth lies completely within the dynamics of the performer-audience-context relationships.

Conclusion

It is clear from this analysis that personal experience stories play a very important rôle in the teenage narrative repertoire. However, in order to fully understand this we must broaden our definition of personal narratives to include third person, as well as first person, stories and independent legends which have been through a process of personalisation. In fact, we might include in our definition any story which retains a strong element of the personal or the personality of the originator. In addition we must also take close account of the rôle of the family, in that the family repertoire often acts as a rich source of third person personal narratives to be appropriated and retold at teenage storytelling events.

Finally, it is particularly pertinent to understand that truth as a central element of the personal narrative is rarely an easily defined issue in the teenage context, relying heavily on a number of unique and specific factors. Above all personal experience stories allow us to give meaning to experience and take our own stances, an issue of great relevance to adolescents on the cusp of adulthood and responsibility. In the words of Harold Rosen, 'personal stories in all their forms could be said to be a kind of self-made curriculum' (H. Rosen, 1993, p.145).

Notes

[1] Stahl sees these three different kinds of personal experience story rather as separate stages of development of the personal narrative at which the story may acquire a number of traditional elements. See especially Stahl, 1977a.

[2] Richard Bauman, however, suggests that it is not the case that events happen and then we recount their story, but rather that we tell the story in order to create events by giving experience meaning. See Bauman, 1986, p.5.

[3] Of course, Type A stories are also sometimes used in formal performances by way of introduction to more established narratives.

[4] Except, of course, in the private discussions of sexual conquest and rumour.

[5] A term originally invented by W von Sydow, the Swedish scholar in

1934.

[6] Bauman gives numerous examples from Socrates onwards in Bauman, 1986, p.11.

9 Riddles and the riddling process

The origins and notions of riddles and the riddling process have occupied folklore and linguistics scholars for the whole of the twentieth century, and whilst much valuable work has undeniably been done, the concept of the riddle has usually been examined as a separate phenomenon of vernacular language, rather than as part of a strong and developing oral narrative tradition. Indeed it may be argued that the study of riddles has no place within an investigation into narrative traditions, that riddles are not stories at all. Riddles, like stories, may be orally transmitted, linguistically shaped pieces of communicative folklore, but they do not possess the narrative complexities of the story, such as sequencing, plot, character development, etc.. Whilst it may be true that the two forms are separate in that our conventional notion of a story expects a series of events and occurrences to be organised into a narrative framework, we must, nevertheless, recognise that riddling and storytelling traditions (and, thus, riddles and stories) are interlinked in a number of ways and that an understanding of a riddling tradition can only serve to enhance and inform our understanding of wider narrative practices and conventions.

Probably the most obvious combination of riddling and storytelling traditions is in the use of riddles within stories. The riddle is a common enough motif in traditional narrative, often occurring in threes and usually as a test of the principal character's strength of intellect, either as a contest[1] or as a challenge (e.g. to prove worthiness, especially where that worthiness is otherwise in doubt[2]). In fact, the answering of riddles in traditional narrative can be seen very often as a rite of passage into intellectual maturity. This specific rôle of the riddle has long been recognised, but it also points to something more significant, namely that riddling and storytelling traditions often exist side by side. It would not be uncommon for a story with internal riddles to spark off a series of riddle exchanges between performer(s) and audience within the context of a storytelling session. The story may well work metacommunicatively to herald a riddle sequence. In the context of the whole storytelling session, moreover, the brevity of the riddle form offers a welcome balance with longer, more complex narratives. As the renaissance of storytelling gathers momentum in Britain, many professional storytellers will carry a number of riddles in their repertoire to provide precisely this balance of material within a performance. Within our own traditions, wherever storytelling takes place then there also exists the potential for riddling and vice versa, because the two forms are socially inseparable. Thomas A. Burns likewise argues that the 'occasional prerequisites for riddling are often........shared with other genres of traditional expression, notably tale and song' (Burns, 1976, p.142).

Additionally, stories and riddles are textually linked as well as contextually, in the sense that, although a riddle may not strictly speaking be a narrative, it often implies one. There is always a potential for narrative lurking behind the riddle. For example, when Andrew Norris asks the riddle,

> Two legs sat upon three legs,
> With four legs standing by.
> Four then drawn by five
> Read me a riddle you can't
> However hard you try.
> (Wilson 101)

he is hinting at a story about somebody sitting on a milking stool, milking a cow. In another version of the same riddle, the narrative is made much more obvious;

> One day there was this two-legs sat upon a three-legs and (with) the two-legs was a one-leg. In came a four-legs and took the one-leg and the one-leg was taken away. The two-legs went after the four-legs and the two-legs and the four-legs and the one-leg were never seen again. What were they?
> (Wilson 102)

Here the main body of the text is framed by opening and closing metacommunicative formulae ('One day' and 'What were they?') as in longer folktales, and in examples such as these the narratives are never far behind the riddles that imply them.

Other riddles have even clearer narratives and very much centre themselves around the story, as, for example, in this riddle from David Price.

> There's this man and he's travelling towards this field and when he hit the field, he knew he was going to die, and he had a pack on his back. What do you think that is?
> *A parachutist whose parachute has failed to open.*
> (Wilson 130)

This is typical of many of the logic riddles which find a prominent position in the teenage repertoire and will be examined in more detail later in this analysis.

Riddles and riddling, then, are linked to stories and storytelling in both text and performance and it is the purpose of this particular chapter to examine teenage riddling within the context of a narrative tradition.

There have over the years been many attempts to define the riddle in its many forms. Mark Bryant resorts to the Oxford English Dictionary definition as a 'question or statement intentionally worded in a dark or puzzling manner, and propounded in order that it may be guessed or answered' (Bryant, 1994, p.5). Whilst this may be an adequate starting point for Bryant in compiling his collection, it is so general that it is of little use to us, particularly since it takes no account of the cultural and social rôle of the act of riddling. On the other hand, Bryant also quotes Ludwig Wittgenstein, as claiming that riddles did not exist, because there was no such thing as an unanswerable riddle (Bryant, 1994, p.4). Wittgenstein is, of course, posing a philosophical question rather than a folkloric one, but a definition of a riddle as being by its very nature unanswerable is even wider of the mark, as will be argued later.

Iona and Peter Opie tackled the problem of definition by identifying a number of different types of riddle (Opie and Opie, 1959, pp.73-86). The true riddle they defined as:

> a composition in which some creature or object is described in an intentionally obscure manner; the solution fitting all the characteristics of the description in the question, and usually resolving a paradox (Opie and Opie, 1959, p.74).

and around this central definition exist rhyming riddles, punning riddles (which rely on double meaning for their effectiveness), conundrums, - e.g. What is the difference between a warder and a jeweller? One watches cells and the other sells watches (Opie and Opie, 1959, p.79) - wellerisms, - strictly speaking more closely related to jokes than riddles, e.g. What did the big tap say to the little tap? You little squirt! (Opie and Opie, 1959, p.82) - and catch riddles, which are really anti-riddles, pretending to be riddles, but the solution, in fact, being very straightforward (see, for example, Wilson 129).

Mark Bryant also uses his OED definition to similarly identify a number of different types of riddle, although his list is longer due to the fact that he is also dealing with literary and pictorial traditions of riddling.

However, Thomas A. Green and W. J. Pepicello identify Robert Petsch as the founding father of modern riddle analysis (Green and Pepicello, 1984), when in his paper, 'Neue Beiträge zur Kentniss des Volksrätsels' *(Polestra,* IV), he identified five essential elements of the riddle;

1) an introductory frame
2) a denominative element
3) a descriptive element
4) a block element
5) a concluding frame

It is, claim Green and Pepicello, this notion of the block element that has formed the basis of the subsequent analyses of Bascom, Georges, Dundes, Abrahams et al.

Green and Pepicello indeed take the concept of the block element one step further by arguing that the focal point of the block element is ambiguity, and proceed to examine its rôle in riddling strategies. They identify five different types of ambiguity present in riddles, which are:

1) Metathesis - the reversal of sounds as in the Opies' examples of conundrums.
2) Spoonerisms - related to metathesis, but arguably more central to tongue-twisters.
3) Lexical ambiguity - relying on different meanings of the same word.
4) Morphological ambiguity - using different words which sound the same.
5) Syntactical ambiguity - either the answer or the question having two different meanings with an identical linguistic structure.
(Green and Pepicello, 1984, pp.193-6)

Their analysis is very useful in identifying types of riddle in relation to different strategies employed, yet it still does not help us in an examination of the social function of riddles and riddling. Elli Köngäs Maranda, however, guides us along the correct path in her essay, 'Theory and Practice of Riddle Analysis' (Köngäs Maranda, 1972), an examination of a collection of

Melanesian riddles, when she suggests quite simply that a riddle 'consists of two main parts: the riddle image, that is the riddle posed, and the answer, which is simply the riddle answered by another party' (Köngäs Maranda, 1972, p.54).

Although very useful in helping us classify different types of riddle, the problem with much previous riddle analysis is that it is very much question-oriented. In his essay on African riddling traditions (Haring, 1974), Lee Haring points out that the main failing of Robert Georges's and Alan Dundes's otherwise useful structural analysis of the riddle (Dundes and Georges, 1963) is that 'it refers only to the question part of the riddles' (Haring, 1974, p.204). It presumes that the question is the most important part of the riddle and the answer is merely attendant upon it. Moreover, the answer is often completely ignored in analysis, even Green and Pepicello focusing their study on the rôle of the questioner, the performer, rather than the audience. However, Köngäs Maranda quite rightly reminds us that there are two parts to every riddle. This is why the Wittgensteinian concept of the riddle, according to Bryant, is wide of the mark. The theory is so question-oriented that he even denies the existence of an answer in relation to genuine riddles. However, riddle answers are as important to the equation as the question, and, furthermore, I believe that in the context of teenage riddling, we have much to gain from giving full weight to this much-neglected element of the riddle. Therefore, in relation to the teenage riddling process, I am proposing an analysis that centres itself on the answer or, rather, the answering.

In relation to the archive accompanying this study, it would be wrong to presume that those riddles which have the greatest common currency amongst teenagers are those which appear most often in this archive. This is not the case at all and, in fact, very often the opposite is true. A clearer indication would be how many people immediately knew the answer to a particular riddle without having to think about it. It is in the very nature of the riddle that the solution must not be known in advance; the same riddle will never be told twice in the same session, unless different answers are sought each time. In this sense it is the answer, or the ability to answer the riddle, which determines the question, because every riddle must have a question, even if it is merely a conceptual question (Köngäs Maranda, 1972, p.54).

However, the rôle of the answer in the riddling process can only be fully understood if we recognise that the main difference between a riddle performance and other kinds of narrative performance lies in the subtle shift in the performer-audience relationship. As Köngäs Maranda says, 'the presentation consists of the interplay of two parties' (Köngäs Maranda, 1972, p.54). Whilst this is true of all narrative performance in that the audience always plays a rôle in shaping the narrative, in riddling the audience's rôle is far more consciously participative. Admittedly, there are many performances of other kinds of narratives that employ varying degrees of conscious participation on the part of the audience, and yet it is a defining feature of the riddle that participation is essential to a successful performance. Although both parts of the riddle are interdependent, it is the answer that is the most important part of it. Without an answer the riddle has no point, because the purpose of the riddle is to elicit an answer. Although the answer may be determined by the question, it is the latter that is shaped by the answering process. Moreover, it is not enough for the audience to participate by simply guessing the answer; for the performance to be complete, the audience must provide the correct solution. This central, high-profile rôle for the audience is perhaps unique to the riddling process and is a defining element of the genre.

This calls into question a further tenet of previous riddle analysis. It has long been assumed that successful riddling hangs upon the notion of a contest between performer and audience, a competitive scenario that pits the wits of one against the other. The Opies define the skilful riddler as one 'who switches quickly from one type of riddle to another, never letting his opponent know the kind of question he is being asked' (Opie and Opie, 1959, p.84), thus suggesting that the success of a riddle can be assessed by the degree to which the riddler has been able to outwit or wrong-foot the audience. The very term 'opponent' suggests a battle of wits. Also, Thomas A Burns talks of 'riddling contests' (Burns, 1976, p.142) and Mark Bryant claims:

> Riddles have many uses, but the most widespread throughout their history has been deciding contests of wit. Such contests have varied from light-hearted entertainments to dramatic battles with a man's future or life itself at stake (Bryant, 1994, p.9).

Whilst we must be careful to make a distinction between the rôle of riddles within traditional narrative and within social reality, it is also inevitable that any question-oriented riddle analysis must conclude that the genre operates as a competition.

However, Köngäs Maranda notes that 'these parties may be in competition, although this situation seems to be extremely rare' (Köngäs Maranda, 1972, p.54) and I would like to suggest that, at least in the teenage context, the riddle is not a competitive genre, but a co-operative one. Lee Haring also notices this tendency in some African riddling, saying that 'many African societies make it a rule of the game that the answer to a riddle must be learned, not guessed' (Haring, 1974, p.200), suggesting that it is quite acceptable, indeed necessary, in this context for the answer to be known. He also draws on John Messenger's study of Anang riddles (Messenger, 1960). Messenger proposes that 'the enjoyment of a riddle derives from the sharing of it by members of a group rather than from the challenge to the imagination it presents' (Messenger, 1960, p.226), thus promoting a 'group solidarity' (Haring, 1974, p.201) through the shared knowledge of the riddle.

This is not to exclude all notions of competition from teenage riddling. As previously stated the riddle relies on the audience not already knowing the solution for its effectiveness, and there is clearly some degree of satisfaction to be had by the riddler from baffling the audience. However the ultimately successful riddle is not one that is not, or cannot be, answered, but rather one to which the solution is correctly supplied by the audience. Unlike the 'question and answer' joke, the riddle is not undermined by the supply of the answer, but rather enhanced by it, because a riddle without an answer has no point. It is, in effect, a non-riddle. It is, therefore, the responsibility of the riddler not only to ask a riddle to which the answer is not previously known, but also to ask one to which the audience will, albeit after a period of time, be able to deduce the answer correctly. An unnecessarily difficult riddle will inevitably produce flippant answers from an audience as it becomes increasingly frustrated at its inability to make a progress towards the correct solution. Nothing undermines a riddle more than an audience that refuses to take the riddle seriously. It is, therefore, incumbent on the riddler to pose a riddle that is ideally suited to that particular audience, being neither too easy, nor too difficult. In this sense the question is determined by the need for an answer.

The riddle is, it could be argued, an incomplete story; the riddler begins the story , but the audience must supply the ending. In fact, the riddler cannot provide the ending, for that would be to step outside his/her rôle and so reduce the efficacy of the riddle. The performer, therefore, relies totally on the audience's ability to conclude the story (or, at second best, at least to understand and be engaged by the conclusion), and without that it fails. To this end it is not unusual to see a riddler help guide the audience towards a successful conclusion if they are experiencing difficulty, by providing a series of clues. Even if the clues become increasingly obvious, as long as the riddler does not provide the solution, a degree of success can be salvaged. Indeed even Abrahams and Dundes in their question-oriented analysis (Abrahams and Dundes, 1972) argue that the very way in which the riddle question is framed provides a major clue to the answer sought, since

> Each riddle announces itself as being of a certain type by its conventional phrasing. This conventional frame creates a pattern of expectation on the

part of the hearers, allowing them to hazard a guess at the answer, since the range of possible answers is limited by the riddle's conventional mode of proposition (Abrahams and Dundes, 1972, p.140).

We can see, therefore, that far from being a contest, the riddling process is a co-operative exercise. The successful solving of a riddle is a celebration of shared knowledge between performer and audience, rather than the triumph of one over the other. The riddle is a joint project with a common purpose between performer and audience, and when that is realised, when the question and answer are fused, then that joint achievement can be celebrated. Rather than issuing a challenge, the riddler, by posing a question, invites the audience to provide an answer and so be party to the sharing of knowledge. This notion of the co-operative riddle is particularly important to an understanding of teenage riddling, and this becomes clear when we look at the function of the riddle.

The function of the riddle

It comes as no great surprise to find that a wide range of riddle types are to be found in the teenage repertoire. In terms of Green and Pepicello's breakdown into strategies of ambiguity[3], we find examples of lexical ambiguity such as the following from an unidentified twelve-year-old girl from Audley Park Secondary School in Torquay.

> Patches and patches
> Without any stitches
> Answer my riddle
> And I'll give you my britches.
> *Cabbage patches.*
> (Wilson 114)

This relies on the two different meanings of the word 'patch'. We also find incidences of morphological ambiguity, one of the best-known examples being this one from a twelve-year-old boy from Ivybridge Community College:

> A man in the desert. Around him is a solid concrete box and around that, a hedge. All he has is a plank of wood. How does he escape?
> *He rubs his hands until they are sore. He uses the saw to saw the wood in half. Two halves make a whole, so he climbs through the hole. Then*

he shouts until he is hoarse, then jumps on the horse and rides away
over the hedge.[4]
(Wilson 131)

Here the riddle relies on the homophonous qualities of sore/saw, whole/hole and hoarse/horse.

Additionally, in the next example from a twelve-year-old boy from Falmouth Community College in Cornwall, we can identify a combination of morphological ('One was twenty and the other was twenty-two/too') and syntactical ambiguity ('then they married each other').

> Two twins were born in March but had their birthdays in May. One was twenty and the other was twenty-two and then they married each other.
> *The twins were born in the town of March in the month of May. One*
> *was twenty and the other was twenty too, and they both married each*
> *other because they were both vicars officiating at each other's wedding.*
> (Wilson 119)

Likewise if we are to use the Opies' classification system we will find plenty of true riddles such as

> It comes and comes, but never comes.
> *Tomorrow.*
> (Wilson 105)

from a fourteen-year-old girl from Estover School in Plymouth, which depends upon the apparently self-contradictory notion that once tomorrow arrives it becomes today. There are also examples of descriptive rhyming riddles, such as that already quoted from Andrew Norris (Wilson 101). We can even identify catch riddles like this one from Joanne Simons, which was delivered at the end of a riddling session to maximise its effectiveness.

> What do you brush your teeth with, sit in and sleep on?
> *A toothbrush, a chair and a bed.*
> (Wilson 129)

In addition there are examples of what Mark Bryant calls trick riddles (Bryant, 1994, p.7), a type which includes riddles which have the answer within the question (e.g. Wilson 115) and those which set a mathematical problem such as the following:

If you have two haystacks at the front and thirteen haystacks at the back and you put them together, how many do you get?
One big haystack.
(Wilson 120)

However, all these riddle types rely on varying degrees of linguistic experimentation, a piece of carefully constructed metalanguage which allows performer and audience to play around with words, sounds, structures and meanings. They are 'a device for discussing essential features of the language in question' (Köngäs Maranda, 1972, p.57) and so provide us with a clue to their function in the teenage context.

By referring to her substantial archive of Malaitan riddles, Elli Köngäs Maranda successfully argues that riddles are also a 'device for discussing change' (Köngäs Maranda, 1972, p.59). In contrast to myths which have a sacred and ritual function and thus 'seem to reenforce the established order' (Köngäs Maranda, 1972, p.53), she sees the riddle as primarily a social form which seeks to 'question "the establishment"' (Köngäs Maranda, 1972, p.59).

As previously outlined, riddles are about playing with language; they only work because they bend the rules of language, play tricks on us by presenting alternative and contradictory realities through language. Since language is a tool for helping us shape our concepts of the world, by experimenting with language, we are challenging those very accepted concepts. Riddles are, in effect, a traditional way of subverting established realities.

Riddles in the teenage repertoire serve two distinct functions. Firstly, this experimentation with language can be seen as a vital part of the learning and maturing process. It is through the medium of language that we operate as social beings and, therefore, as teenagers make their entry into the adult world with all its new social traditions and demands, then it is important that the individual is linguistically equipped to cope with these challenges in order to survive. To experiment with riddles is, thus, a way of learning the complexities and possibilities of language in order to equip oneself for adult social realities. That is to say that the development of appropriate language skills is an essential part of the complex initiation process into adulthood, and this is, at least in part, fulfilled through the riddling process. However, if the acquisition of sufficient linguistic skills enables individuals to survive socially in the adult world, then it also offers the possibility of developing strategies to take control of and ultimately shape one's own future.

If riddles offer glimpses of new realities, as Köngäs Maranda would argue, then they are as much about changing the status quo as helping us deal with it. Whilst equipping us for survival within an established order, riddles are also subversive in nature; they literally turn the world upside-down. We have already seen, in the analysis of the use of violent and supernatural imagery in teenage narratives, that the notion of rebellion against an adult authority is often a driving force behind much adolescent verbal art. Riddles offer this very same potential for subversion and this is nowhere more obvious than in the riddle type that we may call the logic riddle.

The logic riddle

The logic riddle is a form of the riddle which is often neglected by folklorists and yet is extremely significant within the context of the teenage repertoire. In fact, it is probably the most popular type of riddle amongst adolescents. Abrahams and Dundes are the exception rather than the rule in not ignoring it, but identifying the type as 'the detective story' (Abrahams and Dundes, 1972, p.139). To define it is not straightforward, but we could say that, generally speaking, logic riddles offer a simple, single-stranded, short narrative, describing an action or situation, from which a single, vital piece of information has been deliberately excluded or obscured. The missing information offers an explanation for the actions or situation and it is incumbent upon the audience to deduce what that information is. It is not unusual for the posing of the riddle to be followed by a question and answer session, in which the audience can ask any question to the riddler in order to solve the riddle, to which the riddler may only answer in the affirmative or the negative. The following example, from a twelve-year-old boy from Ivybridge, Devon, is a variant of possibly the best known riddle of this type. It is a riddle which I often use myself in a session as a fuse to spark off more logic riddles, which explains why it is not more abundant in the archive - as previously explained, it is the very nature of the riddle that it is almost impossible to collect more than one variant of the same riddle within a single session.

> A man lives at the top of a block of flats and gets the lift down to work in the morning. When he returns home, he only goes to the top when it is raining. Why?
> (Wilson 133)

As we can see, the narrative is much more evident than in the simple 'question and answer' type riddle, and yet there is a piece of information missing which renders the narrative incomplete. Why is the man only able to return by lift to the top floor of the block of flats when it is raining? The answer is that the man in question is very small (missing information) and so, although he is able to reach the ground floor button in the lift in the morning, he is not tall enough to reach the button for the top floor upon his return. Except, of course, when it is raining, on which occasions he carries with him an umbrella which enables him to press the top button! This may seem like a rather far-fetched and unsatisfactory answer to an obscure riddle. Indeed this is true in a way, since other riddle types depend on presenting confusing, but complete, information, which the answer seeks to clarify. However, this is not the case with logic riddles. Whilst the answers serve to clarify the question by completing the narrative, the narratives themselves may be equally unlikely. The object of the riddle is not so much to look at everyday realities in a new light by providing rational solutions to apparent contradictions, but rather to challenge everyday rationality through logical application.

In teenage verbal art the adult world of authority is represented by rationality, that which can be explained. This, of course, is part of the adolescent fascination with all things supernatural. The logic riddle, in a sense, reacts against this rationality by taking it to the extreme. The narrative can only be completed by logical explanation, which is different from rational explanation, since in logic riddles, although the narrative is completed by the solution, the situation is often no less weird and unlikely for it. Logic enables the narrative to transcend acceptable reality, because it is a way of making the impossible possible. On the other hand, the rational would demand a solution that is explicable, something that fits into the realities of everyday life.

Let us take another example from Eggbuckland Community College in Plymouth.

> A man goes into his house, climbs the stairs and turns off the light. In the morning he shoots himself. Why?
> (Wilson 134))

The answer is that he is a lighthouse keeper and that, having automatically switched off the light before going to bed, he has caused the deaths of innocent sailors. In remorse he commits suicide. Here we have a seemingly everyday situation which is interrupted by an act of violence. Yet there is any number of possible explanations. However, it is not the point to provide the most obvious explanation, to attempt to rationally explain the act, as is the adult tendency; the point is to guess the solution which the riddler has, which may be obscure, but makes logical use of all the elements of the riddle. In this example from Totnes;

> A man is walking along the road when he comes across a puddle of water with a carrot and two lumps of coal in it. The sun is shining. What has happened?

174

A snowman has melted.
(Wilson 135)

The rational and most obvious (and most boring) answer would be that someone has been along the road previously and dropped the carrot and the coal from their shopping in a puddle from an earlier downpour. However, any audience familiar with the form will realise that the riddler is deliberately pointing towards the most obvious solution, when a more obscure, but logical and more satisfying answer is sought. The logic riddle replaces adult rationality with logic, and so can be seen as a reaction against the rational world of the adult. This goes at least some way to explaining the popularity of logic riddles amongst teenagers; that they defy the adult interpretation of what is acceptable, 'sensible' reality and offer a more bizarre, but logical alternative.

Aspects of tradition and the question of the 'fixed text'

No analysis of riddling would be complete without an examination of the rôle of tradition in that process. It has long been established that riddles are amongst the most traditional elements of our modern verbal repertoires, being 'one of the best-attested ancient folklore genres' (Abrahams and Dundes, 1972, p.129). Certainly within the oral tradition there is relatively little in the way of invention and creation of new riddles, and many riddles, unlike more substantial narratives, remain faithful to earlier variants.

In their analysis of children's riddling the Opies noted that

> Many of the riddles.....are 150 years old;.....a good handful of the riddles have been exercising young wits for a full 300 years; and just a few date back almost to the middle ages (Opie and Opie, 1959, p.73).

They were able to provide earlier versions of many of the riddles they collected, including this variant of Andrew Norris's milking riddle from *A Book of Merrie Riddles*, published in 1631 (No.59).

> Clinke clanke under a banke
> Ten above foure and neere the stanke.

Likewise Mark Bryant recognises the traditional pedigree of riddling when he says that 'the history of riddling is a rich and varied one and stretches back far into the antiquity of our culture' (Bryant, 1994, p.xi). Indeed we can trace some riddles even further back than the Middle Ages as suggested by the Opies. When a twelve-year-old boy from Totnes asks

> What has four legs, then two legs, then three legs?
> *A person.*
> (Wilson 104)

he is only posing a variant on the riddle asked to Oedipus by the Sphinx in Greek Mythology:

> What being, with only one voice, has sometimes two feet, sometimes three, sometimes four, and is weakest when it has the most?
> (Graves 1991: 132)

It is because riddle texts can be traced back through many centuries with little variation that it is often presumed that riddles circulate as fixed texts, and variations from a fixed text are due to the fallibility of memory. This notion of the existence of a fixed Urtext, from which all variants spring, has now been superceded in relation to the longer oral narrative, but has taken somewhat longer to expire when applied to riddles. I suspect that this is in part due to the relative brevity of the riddle, so making it possible to remember it verbatim, as opposed to say a legend which it would be perverse to learn word for word, and in part due to the fact that the riddle has had a long literary history, having been published in a number of mediaeval and early modern texts. However, Elli Köngäs Maranda, amongst others, disputes this theory, arguing that riddles are recreated in the same manner as all verbal art, in that they are not produced verbatim, but rather that people learn grammatical structures and linguistic frameworks in which to recreate the riddle;

> a person who knows a language does not mechanically repeat ready-made sentences but builds sentences according to certain rules....he learns words related to their meanings, and rules of formation and transformation (Köngäs Maranda, 1972, p.56).

The existence of identical texts, Köngäs Maranda claims, is purely due to coincidence because people recreate texts according to the same set of rules. The brevity of the riddle text makes this far more likely than in longer, more complex, narrative text.

I would fully agree with this analysis, but with one qualification. Whilst it is true that all oral art, including riddles, is reconstructed according to a set of

176

given linguistic and generic rules and that identical texts exist because of limitations to the different possibilities of recreating short statements of shared meaning, we must also accept that the internal rhythms of the language of a riddle are an aid to the recreation of identical texts. This is particularly true of rhyming riddles where a textual deviation may upset the rhyming and rhythmical scheme of the riddle.

Nevertheless, we must not confuse identical texts and fixed texts. Fixed texts do not exist in oral narrative, but the rules that govern the creation of texts may sometimes result in linguistically identical texts, although it must also be remembered that since each performance context is unique, then so is each performance, even if the text is identical to one used in a previous performance. The more rules (e.g. rhyme and rhythm), the more likely we are to experience identical texts. That is not to say that even with rhyming riddles variation is not possible; it is just that the rules may limit the amount of variation.

Consider the following riddle collected by Peter and Iona Opie from a twelve-year-old girl from Shropshire:

> Little Nancy Netticoat
> Wears a white petticoat,
> The longer she lives
> The shorter she grows,
> Little Nancy Netticoat.
> *A lighted candle.*
> (Opie and Opie, 1959, p.77)

and compare it to the following variant collected by myself from Gillingham, Dorset.

> Ninny, Nanny Netticoat
> In a white petticoat,
> The longer I stand
> The shorter I get.
> *A candle.*
> (Wilson 106)

Although we can see very clearly that the two are variants of the same riddle, there is, in fact, a great deal of variance between them. Not only is there the question of the extra coda line in the Opies' version, but if we superimpose the two texts we can see that there is just slightly more linguistic variance, on the basis of a simple word count, than there is identicality.

Word variation comparison

Opie	Little	Nancy	Netticoat
Wilson	Ninny	Nanny	Netticoat
Identical/Variation	x	x	+

Opie	Wears	a	white	petticoat
Wilson	In	a	white	petticoat
Identical/Variation	x	+	+	+

Opie	The	longer	she	lives
Wilson	The	longer	I	stand
Identical/Variation	+	+	x	x

Opie	The	shorter	she	grows
Wilson	The	shorter	I	get
Identical/Variation	+	+	x	x

Opie	Little	Nancy	Netticoat	
Wilson	-	-	-	
Identical/Variation	x	x	x	

Identical = 8   Variation = 10

We would also be able to establish at least the same level of variation amongst different versions of other rhyming riddles (e.g. Wilson 137-138).

In other riddles we can also detect other types of textual variation. Let us, for example, look at these two variants of the same riddle, collected on successive days in Dublin schools.

> One train leaves Dublin for Galway at 100 m.p.h. Another leaves Galway for Dublin at 50 m.p.h. When they meet, which one is nearer Dublin?
> *They are both in the same place when the meet.*
> (Wilson 122)

and

> An electric train leaves Dublin for Cork and a steam train leaves Cork for Dublin. When they meet, which one is nearer Dublin?

178

They are both in the same place when they meet.
(Wilson 123)

Essentially the two riddles (trick riddles type) are the same, in the sense that they both offer the same set of circumstances (a slow train and a fast train travelling towards each other in opposite directions) and attempt the same trick on the audience. The variables are, of course, the descriptive elements of the riddle, namely, the names of the destination cities and the manner in which we are told of the different speeds of the trains. Of course, if the riddle were told in England (as I'm sure it must be), we would expect the destination cities again to be different and likewise the riddle could just as easily be told about other modes of transport, say a car and a bicycle, without the substance of the riddle being affected in any way.

This would, therefore, seem to indicate that Köngäs Maranda is correct in arguing that riddle texts do not circulate as fixed texts, because it is against the nature of oral art for this to happen. Instead, each time a riddle is told, it is recreated as new according to a set of rules and conventions. Whilst texts may often be identical due to over-repetition and the brevity of riddles, we can still detect evidence of significant variation, even where we might least expect it.

Conclusions

Riddles and riddling have hitherto been mainly restricted to the realms of childlore, at least in contemporary Western culture, and yet they are also to be found alive and well within the oral narrative tradition of teenagers. Here we can find a wide range of riddle types and variants of many individual texts can be found in sources from a number of centuries ago. It is quite possibly within the genre of the riddle that traditionality is most evident.

The popularity of riddles amongst teenagers can be explained as two-fold. Riddling is an important part of the learning process, an effective way of developing the language skills necessary for operating socially in an adult world. That is to say that riddling can be viewed as a rite of passage to the intellectual and linguistic maturity required for the post-liminal society. However, riddling is also about change, presenting new realities and new versions of existing ones. In this sense it appeals to the rebellious nature of the adolescent and this explains the particular popularity of trick riddles and especially logic riddles which challenge the rationality of adult authority. Most important, however, to our analysis, is the notion that teenage riddling is a joint effort, a co-operative rather than a competitive process, which celebrates a common intellectual strength.

Notes

[1] For example, in Greek Mythology Oedipus defeats the Sphinx in a riddle contest and so unwittingly wins the hand of his mother.

[2] See, for example, 'The Wise Little Girl' (Carter ed., 1990, pp.28-31) for a variant of a well-known tale type whereby a poor girl becomes worthy of marrying the king on account of her ability to answer riddles.

[3] For purposes of collecting, I have not included examples of metathesis or spoonerisms in the archive, as these, at least in function, seem to relate more closely to jokes than riddles, and so fall outside the limits of this study.

[4] Wilson 132 offers an interesting variant on this in that it is not told as a riddle, but as a straightforward narrative, the question and answer being combined into what is, in effect, a jocular tale, designed to produce a humorous reaction from the audience.

Conclusions

This study is an investigation into an aspect of teenage folklore. It is not a study of teenage folklore in its entirety. For example, it is not concerned with song, music, rhymes, dance, visual communication, jokes, superstition, blasons populaires, etc., but purely with the oral narratives which pass between teenagers, sometimes in conversation, sometimes in more formal situations at sleep-over parties or around camp-fires, but always as a form of social currency.

Furthermore it is not even a study of teenage oral narrative in its entirety. It is merely a beginning, but, I hope, none the less important for that, for it is a study that has been both helped and hindered by the lack of previous scholarly research in the field. Certainly a fair amount of work has been done on teenage popular culture and various subcultures, but very little (with one or two notable exceptions) has been done from the point of view of performance and folklore studies. What has been done, and most of that has focused on the United States rather than Europe, has tended to be generically motivated. For example, contemporary legend scholars have touched on teenage storytellers as they have recognised that adolescents play an important part in the transmission of such stories, and students of ghostlore have also investigated elements of teenage storytelling, since that has a prominent place in the repertoire. However, this has always been motivated by a desire to investigate contemporary legends or ghost stories. Of course there is nothing wrong with that, but very little has been done about teenage storytelling as an identifiable tradition. Nor has much work been undertaken concerning teenagers as storytellers and the rôle of tradition within their oral narrative discourses.

There is also, since the Opies first began publishing the findings of their research into childlore, a sizeable amount of work that has been done in this field. However, this has tended to focus on younger, pre-pubescent children.

Folklorists have often not been quick to recognise that teenagers are neither children nor adults, and so likely to have their own cultural agenda and concerns. Although it may cause teenagers themselves no great concern, they have in the past been substantially neglected by the folklore community.

On the one hand this has meant that what has been written remains in largely manageable proportions, but on the other hand I have very much had to find my own way and set my own agenda without the guidance of the efforts of previous scholars.

This study, therefore, is intended as an introduction to the field of teenage storytelling in Britain and Ireland at the end of the twentieth century. It is certainly not a definitive study of the subject, but is based on a relatively small collection of about five hundred texts collected by myself from teenagers from all over Britain and Ireland. As such it simply shows that teenagers are telling stories, and provides a snapshot of the kind of repertoires from which they draw.

I could, of course, have carried on writing well into the next millennium, collecting, analysing, comparing and so on. Therefore, in order to keep the task in manageable proportions I have attempted to cover a wide range of issues within this analysis without laying claim to having covered every angle. To some degree, other issues and texts are discussed in the annotations to the accompanying collection of texts. I hope it will serve to stimulate further debate and interest among scholars.

However, having accepted these limitations to this study, I think there is a number of conclusions that can be made from the material collected and the ensuing analysis, and my aim is now to draw together those conclusions.

Teenagers as storytellers

It has long been presumed that teenagers are not active storytellers beyond the merely conversational. Researchers into childlore noticed that the traditional rhymes and games so cherished by those children at primary school seem to quickly evaporate at the adolescent stage. Furthermore it is generally believed that teenagers do not have the linguistic skills, maturity and competence to tell the more sophisticated traditional exchanges popular amongst adults, e.g. tall tales, etc. In fact, it is assumed that the onset of puberty is accompanied by a rejection of and cynicism towards all things traditional.

There is, of course, an element of truth in all of this, but it still paints an inaccurate picture. It is true that much childlore plays little part in teenage folklore, that much of it is rejected as the child approaches adolescence, which is naturally all part of the growing-up process, and yet the sophistication required to participate in many adult exchanges is also not yet present. Nevertheless, it should not be surprising that teenagers are able to find their own appropriate level of sophistication and thus create their own folklore. There is no clean, distinct transition from childhood to adulthood, but a liminal state which folklorists have so often chosen to ignore.

There is also some truth in the belief that teenagers will reject all things traditional. In my own experience of working in schools, I know that the first mention of storytelling will often produce a negative reaction, one that has 'this is not for us' written all over it. However, we have to be clear that this is not a rejection of tradition per se, but rather a rejection of adult notions of tradition. Teenagers, of course, want to be in control of their own traditions and when folklore, as a discipline, ignores the existence of teenage lore, then it is hardly surprising that teenagers themselves dismiss folklore as irrelevant to their lives.

We must also remember that by and large people are unaware of their own folklore traditions, and this is equally true of teenagers. Folklore and tradition belong to childhood or adulthood, teenagers believe, because that is what adults tell them. However, teenagers are as rich in tradition as any group in society, although these traditions may be different. It is, of course, absurd to imagine any group, whether defined by age, race, class, profession, etc., as not having their own folklore, so why should teenagers be any different?

The answer is, of course, that they are not and I hope this study shows that teenagers are as active, if not more so, as storytellers as any other identifiable group within society. The problem for the folklorists is that teenagers are usually very private about their storytelling. There is a common mistrust and suspicion amongst adolescents of adults in general and folklorists in particular (for reasons previously outlined, folklore has a bad name amongst teenagers), and this makes the collector's job a difficult one. However, if a level of trust can be built up with a teenage group, then a very rich and wide vein of folk tradition will inevitably be unearthed.

The teenage repertoire

Where the existence of teenage storytelling traditions has been recognised (Ellis, Samuelson et al), this has usually been limited to the study of contemporary-legend telling in semi-formal 'camp-fire' ghost storytelling sessions. However, my own researches would seem to indicate that the teenage repertoire covers a much wider range of material than previously assumed.

The contemporary legend and the ghost story clearly have a very important and pivotal rôle in teenage storytelling traditions, and the use of violent and supernatural motifs and images is apparent throughout the whole repertoire. However, there is also strong evidence to show that teenagers include a large number of personal and family narratives, riddles, local legends, superstition-based stories and jocular tales in their personal bank of material. In fact, there are even occasional instances of fairy tales continuing to be told by teenagers, for example, in the case of Eva Shannon who tells a full version of 'Tom-Tit-Tot' (Wilson 93) as learned from her grandmother. Eva's own exceptional skills as a storyteller and her rapport with a teenage audience enable her to hold a group of her contemporaries spellbound with a story which many teenagers would reject as being too 'baby-ish'.

The widespread use of images from ghostlore reflects the adolescent obsession with such things, but this will not simply manifest itself in the form of a straightforward ghost story, but spreads throughout the whole repertoire and across many different genres. In fact, if a ghost story is specifically requested, the collector is just as likely to get a personal narrative or even a joke, as anything else. In the teenage understanding of it, it would seem that a ghost story is simply a story where something unusual or out-of-the-ordinary happens, or even in some cases that a 'ghost story' is synonymous with any story, that it carries a sub-text that this is 'one of our stories', a teenage narrative.

We must, therefore, exercise extreme caution when classifying ghost stories in the teenage repertoire. Although a large percentage of stories have supernatural content, it is not always helpful to classify them as ghost stories.

Another defining feature of the teenage oral narrative would seem to be the question of length. With a few notable exceptions, all stories are relatively short. In the past (and sometimes in the present too) there has been a tendency to hold in greater esteem those storytellers who tell the longest stories, implying that the length of a story is proportional to the skill that a particular storyteller has. Whilst it is indeed true that it requires a high degree of skill to tell a long narrative in a competent fashion, recent contextual studies have shown that length is often determined by situation; paraperformative influences, more than the inherent skill of the performer. Of course, a storyteller will be careful not to overstretch themselves and run the risk of turning out a poor performance, which may influence narrative length, but I would suggest that the short nature of most teenage stories may well be due to other factors.

It must be remembered that many of the stories in the accompanying archive were collected when time itself was very pressured, often in a school situation, at the end of a lesson before making off somewhere else, or even within a lesson where pressure of time was equally great. In other words, many of the stories were told when there was very little time to tell a large number of narratives, and this context necessitated that each performance was short to allow the greatest possible number of stories to be told. In this sense the brevity of many texts in the collection suggests a certain level of skill amongst the storytellers in that they were able to adjust the length of their performances according to the available time.

Of course, there were also many occasions where the pressure of time was not as great, for example, when collecting stories in youth clubs. However, even here, stories were short by necessity, because there was often a large number of storytellers waiting to take their turn. It is one of the ground rules of storytelling events (cf. Bauman, 1977, p.28) that where there is a queue of storytellers waiting to perform, no single person will hog the floor for too long. Therefore, once again the length of the narratives is to some degree governed by contextual considerations. In this case, the shortness of many stories points to a full and thriving repertoire as much as anything else.

Finally, it is important to note that the teenage oral narrative repertoire draws upon and is influenced by material that is conveyed through a whole range of other media such as published sources, television, radio, cinema, etc., and this is, of course, a two-way relationship. Far from oral storytelling declining and the repertoire being narrowed amongst what we see as a technology-obsessed generation of adolescents, instead it continues to thrive, incorporating all forms of popular culture into its processes of circulation.

We can thus conclude that the teenage oral narrative repertoire is a wide and varied one, covering the whole spectrum of narrative genres, and that many of the stories in that repertoire are short in length due, at least in part, to the contexts in which they are generally told.

The performance of teenage narratives

Teenage storytelling is no different from other instances of narrative discourse in that it is best understood as communication through performative action. It readily conforms to models of storytelling performance, in that it is metacommunicative signals which announce both the beginning and ending of the performative frame and the rules and conventions that govern it. However, teenage storytelling always seems to operate along the lower half of the performance continuum at more informal and low-intensity levels and so the 'rules' that govern storytelling events are likely to be less rigorously applied. For teenagers storytelling is an essential and integral part of the process of social interaction and as such is absorbed into everyday communicative practices rather than set up as 'cultural performance events'. In this sense, much teenage storytelling is sub-conscious, the most formal storytelling event at which teenagers participate being the camp-fire or slumber party session. Here the rules of performance are more in evidence and the storytelling is conscious and structured, but it still operates primarily on a social level. As with all storytelling performances, teenage storytelling is influenced, indeed determined, by context and aspects of paraperformance.

Teenage storytelling can happen at any time, although it is normally restricted to times of social activity. There are exceptions to this, for example, when storytelling may take place during the course of an English lesson at school, but here the event tends to be adult(teacher)-controlled. Moreover, most storytelling, at least the semi-formal kind, takes place at times when more physical activity is restricted due to bad weather or light. Thus, teenagers recognise that most of their 'conscious' storytelling happens at night time and during bad weather.

Interviews with teenagers about their storytelling habits also reveal a number of other interesting facts. Firstly, there is some evidence to suggest that storytelling events are sometimes calendar-influenced. Many adolescents will quote Hallowe'en, Christmas, Midsummer's Eve and Friday 13th as popular times for telling stories, and ghost stories in particular. These are, of course, traditional times for storytelling exchanges.

Secondly, it would appear that place is an important consideration in these events. Bill Ellis firmly links place to story (Ellis, 1982) and teenagers themselves will make use of sites associated with stories or types of stories as venues for storytelling. However, the most common place for storytelling would seem to be small, confined spaces, in particular tents and bedrooms, although other places quoted to me include attics, garden sheds, cellars, the cupboard under the stairs, under the kitchen table, and even the toilet! The restricted performance space presumably provides the intimacy and sense of security required for storytelling.

Thirdly, teenage storytelling events are by and large restricted to small groups of around half a dozen or so. Of course, there are exceptions to this, but adolescents are singularly private about their storytelling, and events normally take place amongst a small group of friends and associates. The trust that exists between friends provides the safety needed for an audience to enjoy the experience of being scared, if that is the purpose of the storytelling session. Narratives then circulate as members of a particular circle of friends intermingle with other such groups.

Teenage storytelling performances also serve a number of purposes. They are always used as items of currency within structures of social exchange, but sometimes their function is to amuse, sometimes to scare, sometimes to warn, sometimes to shock and very often to subvert, or indeed any combination of these. Teenagers tell stories in order to address the concerns of their own cultural agenda and in doing so will use a wide variety of techniques and devices to serve the specific functions of the performance.

It is very difficult to isolate any precise differences between male and female storytellers at the teenage level. Whatever hypothesis is assembled, there are always plenty of exceptions to undermine it and prove otherwise, since so much is determined by the audience as well as the performer. It would be an interesting object for further study to examine the differences between male and female storytellers telling to single sex and mixed gender audiences, although this would still fail to eliminate the influence of the presence of the collector.

However, we might draw a tentative conclusion that, on the evidence so far, there may appear to be a tendency for female storytellers to lean towards a cautionary presentation of their narratives, whereas male storytellers are more prone to employ the grotesque in pursuit of shocking the audience or raising a laugh. Furthermore, this has implications for our understanding of the representation of truth in teenage storytelling. Female storytellers are, thus, more likely to tell their stories as true and males will more readily sacrifice believability in pursuit of immediate dramatic effect.

What is clear, in any case, is that teenage storytelling performances incorporate a complex relationship of social and cultural factors, operating in a range of situations and thus conveying a variety of meanings.

Traditional factors in teenage storytelling

We have already concluded that teenage storytelling corresponds to other traditional models of storytelling performance in its choice of time and place for events and in the way it fits into the performance continuum for traditional storytelling exchanges. However, there is further evidence that teenage storytelling does not occur in isolation but has a continuing dialogue with the wider oral narrative tradition.

Of course, much depends on how we define tradition in terms of storytelling, but if we turn our attention to the process of storytelling, we might define traditional storytelling processes as follows:

> the creation, re-creation, dissemination and circulation of a wide range of narratives through oral and other means between groups and sub-groups within society, resulting in the maintenance and development of those stories in increasing variants, so that they become independent items of

verbal social currency available to all members of that group or sub-group, anonymous (or semi-anonymous) in authorship.

It follows, therefore, that teenage storytelling can be said to be traditional or at the very least to display aspects of tradition in the processes by which it is circulated.

In terms of the collected texts we can also see tradition operating in two ways. Firstly we can see that 'new' stories will adopt structures and devices common to many older traditional narratives. Moreover, many of these stories can be seen to have been passed down through generations for a considerable time and so to have become traditional. We can also see that folk and fairy tales lend much of their imagery and motifs to stories within the teenage repertoire and indeed often continue to be told in their entirety, albeit in modernised forms, as in 'The Singing Bone' or 'The Golden Arm'.

Teenage storytelling, therefore, displays aspects of tradition in its performance, processes of circulation and texts, and whilst creating and maintaining its own traditions within these areas, it also remains part of a wider oral narrative tradition, reaching out to other storytelling practices and the traditions of the pre-industrial folk tale.

Closing remarks

The conclusions that I have been able to draw from the present study are very much those based on work in progress and as such have their limitations. Future research may well prove some to be ill-founded and others in need of modification, as they are formed upon a small, but representative sample of texts and performances, but I hope they will open up the debate. What is clear from the research I have done is that there is so much more to do. It is an area that has received scant attention from folklore scholars in the past and my hope is that this study has in its own small way done something to reverse this.

Teenagers, it would seem, have a rich and vibrant folklore that deserves our attention and our respect, and it is a potentially fruitful area for folklore, popular culture and performance research. It is perhaps somewhat ironic that, as many bemoan the advent of the technological age and see the modern teenager as the epitome of a consumerist post-modernist society, spoon-fed its over-processed culture through populist mass-media, it is at the slumber parties, around the camp-fires, on the school buses and around the bike sheds that the modern adolescent maintains and cherishes an active and vital oral narrative tradition.

Appendix 1

Selection of fieldwork texts

Introduction

Since embarking on this study of teenage oral narratives I have accumulated a collection consisting of approximately five hundred texts. This appendix contains a selection of one hundred and thirty-eight of those texts. It should, of course, be remembered that it is only a selection and not the complete collection, which was considered too unwieldy for this purpose. Amongst those five hundred texts there are transcriptions, summaries and fragments, some, of course, of greater value and interest to the scholar than others. There are also some stories of which more than twenty variants have been collected. It was felt, therefore, that there was a danger of obscuring the wood with the trees. Hence, this selection aims to give a greater clarity to the type of material currently in oral circulation amongst adolescents than the full archive would give. There is undoubtedly a use and a need for the full archive, and anyone interested in studying it in greater detail would be very welcome to make use of the copy currently lodged at the Department of Drama, University of Exeter.

It should also be remembered that this study has only been a beginning, an initial investigation into a field that requires much more work. Likewise, the archive of stories, although substantial, has its limitations. It is the work of only one person over a few years and as such is merely the tip of the iceberg, albeit a large enough sample to be a representative tip. There are many, many stories still to be collected and, therefore, the whole five hundred stories would not necessarily provide us with a more accurate overview than a carefully selected sample of texts.

The texts in this appendix have been selected for inclusion on three basic criteria.

191

Firstly, it is hoped that all the individual texts together constitute a body of material that accurately represents the wide range of material currently in circulation, and to this end texts have been chosen so that the following selection to some degree is simply a scaled-down version of the larger archive.

Secondly, texts have been selected on their importance to the central argument of the main study. This is not to say that the excluded texts are unimportant to the study, but one of the purposes of the selection is as an appendix to the preceding analysis, and so preference has been given to those texts which are either directly referred to in the analysis (marked with an asterisk*) or contribute to an understanding of the arguments contained therein.

Thirdly, also included in the selection are those stories which, as individual texts, are worth commenting on in some detail, even if they do not feature to any great extent in the general argument of this book. For this reason the accompanying annotations are intended to supply the reader with additional information and cross-referencing which add and contribute to the central arguments but have not been able to be easily incorporated into the general flow of the analysis. It is hoped, therefore, that the accompanying selection is a clear, accurate and helpful supplement.

No.1*

There was this man and he lived with his wife and he was very rich and one day his wife had her arm cut off in a car accident, it was crushed and had to be amputated. He thought, 'I can't live with someone who's had their arm amputated.'

So he was incredibly rich, so he went down and he bought her a gold arm.

So she had this gold arm and a couple of years later she died of cancer and she was buried and she had this great big tombstone - it was all decorated and ornate, it was beautiful. He was really depressed and he took to drinking and gambling and eventually he gambled all his money away and he just had no money left. He used to have a Ferrari and now he just had a Skoda, he lived in a little cottage and he used to live in a mansion. So he thought, 'I can't live like this, I've got about 5p left to last me the rest of my life, I'm never going to make it.'

So he thought, 'Right, I'm going to have to go and get my wife's arm. I'm going to have to melt it down and sell it.'

So he went into the graveyard and he was digging up the grave, and he got halfway down when he saw a hooded figure walking towards him. So he quickly buried her up and ran away.

And the second night he went in and he starts to dig her up and he got two-thirds of the way down and the hooded figure, and he ran off.

The third night he dug all the way down and opened the coffin and got hold of the arm and he saw the hooded figure again. So he grabs the arm off, buried her down and ran off.

He melted the arm down and one day, he's driving along in his Skoda through this wood and his car breaks down. He sees a light in the distance, so he goes off to this cottage and he knocks on the door. And a woman opens the door and says, 'Ah, I've been expecting you.'

He thinks, 'That's rather odd. Maybe she's just a bit senile. She says that to everybody she meets.' So she offers him a bowl of soup and he thinks, 'This soup tastes just like the soup my wife used to make. It's delicious.'

So, anyway, he drinks the soup and he can't help noticing that, on one arm, the sleeves of her jacket and her hood come right down and the other just hangs limply.

Eventually, he summoned up the courage and he asked her: 'What happened to your arm?'

And she turned round and pulled off the hood and there's a skull and she went, 'YOU DID IT!'

Natasha Tillbrook, aged thirteen, Gillingham School, Dorset, 11.11.92.

Notes

See Jacobs, 1967, pp.138-9.
What is particularly interesting about this telling is the storyteller's use of contemporary symbols to convey meaning. For example, at the beginning of the story the protagonist drives a Ferrari, symbolising his wealth, and later he owns a Skoda, which has a specific rôle in popular joke culture as the cheapest and most unreliable of cars, to symbolise his downfall and ruin.

No.2*

There's this man, about thirty years old, his mum and dad live in London and his gran, she's died. She's very, very rich and her leg is golden, because it's a false one and it's twenty-four carat gold - that was how rich she was. She could just afford to throw money away. And in her will everything went to him.

He was very rich and he started to gamble, just a little bit of money, but it grew and grew until he had a massive problem and he couldn't stop and he gambled away all the money and then he dug up the grave and dug up the leg and sold it, and then he gambled away all that money.

So he decided to dig up all her rings, she had about five on each finger and that was every finger she had it and even on her toes, bracelets around her leg and neck and everything, she was so rich. And he dug her up and sat her in the chair, and her eyes they're all rotting out, there weren't any eyes, just the sockets, and her leg, and her hair is all rotting and he goes: 'What's happened to your eyes, Grandma?'

The ghost said: 'All rotted with time.'
And he goes: 'What's happened to your hair?'
'It's rotted with time.'
'What's happened to your face and skin?'
'It's rotted with time.'
'What's happened to your leg?'
'YOU'VE GOT IT!'

Allan, aged c.12, Pyworthy Youth Club, Devon, 31.10.92.

Notes

The telling of the story is quite expert, especially in the way that Allan builds the pace and the tension of the narrative as it heads towards the climax. In this version, the ghost does not simply return to haunt the thief, but the body of the deceased is taken from the grave along with the jewellery and then comes alive. The image of the rotting corpse in the chair is, of course, reminiscent of the famous scene in Alfred Hitchcock's *Psycho*, where the character of Norman Bates does exactly the same thing with his own mother.

Allan's version of the story is a fascinating mix of traditional and modern influences and his highly structured and formulaic conclusion to the telling is almost identical to that of Jacobs a century previously. Additionally, in his notes to 'The Golden Arm', Jacobs commented that, 'I also have traces of it as "The Golden Leg"' (Jacobs, 1967, p.310).

No.3*

Well, there's this couple lived, like, in the olden days, and were quite a wealthy couple, had their own business and that. This man he only had one leg and he just had, like, an old bit of wood on there. What he wanted more than anything in the world was a golden leg, so he thought, 'I'm going to have to save up for one before I die.' Going to do his business and that.

So he saved up, he saved up, saved up for years and years, and then finally he's got enough. So he gets the golden leg.

He gets the golden leg and they're quite old now. And he starts to getting really ill. His wife doesn't know what to do or anything and eventually he dies.

And the business starts going downhill and everything. And his wife got all these bills and she doesn't know what to do. And she thought, 'I'm going to have to dig my husband up and get his golden leg.' Everything's all right.

She goes out one night, starts digging him up, finds him, and the golden leg's still there all nice and shiny. She unscrews it, takes it off and takes it home.

And after a while she's feeling really guilty about it.

She needed the money to pay off all her debts, and one night she's lying in bed and she hears the back door go.

'What's that?'

She don't take no notice of it, she just thinks it's the wind. And she hears it open and she's started to get a bit worried now. The door shuts. She can hear it walking through the kitchen. It starts coming up the stairs, walking up the stairs. It's coming up the stairs now and she's under the covers now. The door shuts, can hear it coming up the stairs, across the landing. And she can hear this murmuring. And he's getting closer, she can hear it.

'Who's got my golden leg? Who's got my golden leg?'

He's getting closer and closer. He gets up to the door, opens the bedroom door.

'Who's got my golden leg?'

'YOU'VE GOT MY GOLDEN LEG!'

Dave, aged c.16, Sheerness Youth Club, Isle of Sheppey, Kent, 6.7.94.

pp.6, 112

Notes

This was very much a story that was associated with Dave by his contemporaries and he was encouraged to tell it as 'his' story. Certainly, the telling displays clear evidence that he is extremely conversant with the material and employs a range of techniques to maximum effect. Note particularly the extensive use of repetition and rhythm. During the course of the story he also became progressively quieter, so building up the tension to the final shout. Interestingly and unusually, in Dave's story it is the ghost that is male and the graverobber who is female.

No.4

(Summary)

A man is upstairs in bed when he hears, 'I am the man with the bleeding finger. I'm getting closer.' This continues as the man gets closer and closer. Everything in the story suggests a 'jump' and, indeed, that is exactly what the audience expects. However, at the climax of the story, the man says, 'I am the man with the bleeding finger.....Have you got a plaster?'

Unidentified Male, aged c.12, King Edward VI School, Totnes, 7.12.93.

Notes

This is a well-known joke story in the teenage repertoire that can also be found much in evidence in the repertoires of younger children. It relies, of course, on the audience being aware of the 'jump' story format and is often told as a follow-on from a 'jump' story. It works by undermining the audience's expectations.

No.5

There was this girl and she'd been left alone by her parents, they'd gone out for the evening and she was sitting watching the television and she heard, 'I'm Bloody Fingers and I'm coming to get you.'

So she thought, 'Oh it must be just on the television.'

So she turned it off and went upstairs. And she heard, 'I'm Bloody Fingers and I'm coming to get you.'

So she hid under the bed and she heard, 'I'm Bloody Fingers and I'm coming to get you.'

So she climbed up into the attic and put all the stuff on top of the attic door and it said, 'I'm Bloody Fingers and I'm coming to get you.' And she was really scared and she saw the attic door being pushed up and she heard, 'I'm Bloody Fingers.. .....have you got any elastoplasts?'

Natasha Tillbrook, aged 13, Gillingham School, Dorset, 11.11.92.

Notes

This is a variant of No.4 but, interestingly, it is more reminiscent of (and a parody of) 'The Babysitter' story, a well-known contemporary legend (see Nos 42-4), than 'The Golden Arm'.

No.6

There's this girl and her mum went out and the phone rang and the voice said, 'I'm Bloody Fingers and I'm coming to get you.'

So she slammed the phone down and run upstairs. They had a phone upstairs and the phone rang. She answered the phone and it said, 'I'm Bloody Fingers, I'm coming.'

She ran up into the attic, hid behind a box and she could hear a voice at the door and it said, 'I'm Bloody Fingers and I'm here.'

He smashed down the door, walked up the stairs into the attic, slammed down the box which she was hiding behind and said, 'Has anyone got a plaster wrap?'

Clinton Laurie, aged c.13, Brannel School, St. Austell, Cornwall, 30.4.93.

Notes

Again, this particular variant uses the telephone motif, a vital constituent in 'The Babysitter' story. The storyteller is using his knowledge of the genre to maximum effect.

No.7*

One day there was this man and this woman, married, and driving down the road in their car and they seen this girl on the side of the pavement and she looked like she needed help, so they picked her up and asked her where she wanted to go and she said, 'Can I go home?' So they asked her where her home was and she told them, so they took her there. They didn't actually go in, but the girl knocked at the door and she walked indoors.

But that night they wondered what had happened to her, so they decided to go back the next morning and they went back, knocked on the door and this old lady came out and said, 'Come in.' And the man and the woman go, 'We sent a girl in here last night, we picked her up off the side of the road.' And she showed them this photo and it's a picture of the girl and she said, 'She's been dead for thirteen years!'

Alex Cossley, aged 12, Gillingham School, Dorset, 11.11.92

pp.32-9, 71

No.8*

There was this man and he was going out in his car and there was this really pretty girl, blonde hair and everything, y'know - all the works! And she's hitchhiking, and so he decides to give her a lift.

And they were talking and he dropped her off and she must have left her wallet or something.

Anyway, he was going along again and he gave this man a lift.

So he handed it in to the police - the wallet - and said, 'Oh, I gave this young lady a hitch-hike and she left her wallet.' And he goes, 'Oh, thanks,' or something like that.

And so they phoned the parents and they said, 'Our daughter's been dead for seven years!'

Catherine Wriggle, aged c.14, Falmouth Youth Club, Cornwall, 9.3.93.

pp.32-9, 71

No.9

It were a dark and misty, rainy night. Twelve o' clock midnight. It were belting it down. And this man were walking down the road with this yellow raincoat and yellow hat.

This woman came down the road with a red Escort convertible and said, 'Pop in, love, you're going to get soaked out there.'

She said, 'Where do you want to go?' and he just pointed and said, 'Down there.'

So she took him down to this pub. It's called The Bedford Arms. And he got out and went in.

This woman said, 'He looks a bit mysterious,' to herself. So she went in and looked for him and she couldn't find him anywhere.

She asked the barman. She said, 'Have you seen that man that came in with the yellow coat and yellow hat?'

He goes, 'Yeah, he went in the taproom. Every night he comes in, but he disappears. He got knocked over on that road and he always comes down every night.'

Jason, aged c.12, Priestman Middle School, Bradford, 24.11.93.

Notes

This is a very interesting variant of 'The Vanishing Hitchhiker' in that it employs many of the standard motifs and yet the usual genders of driver and passenger are reversed. Jason spends some time and effort creating the atmosphere for his ghost story with his description of the weather, which might suggest that the story is a fiction, and yet he counters this by providing us with the name of the pub where the hitchhiker is heading, so giving his tale some authentication.

It is also worth noting that he uses the car (red Escort convertible) as a symbol of wealth to contrast with the fact that the man has no transport and is, by implication, poor.

Presumably, the man is dressed in a distinctive yellow coat and hat not only to make him visible to the driver on such a dark night, but also to provide a clear description later on in the story to allow his identification as a ghost. As is common in variants of this story, the character who confirms the ghost's identity shows no surprise at the driver's story.

No.10*

A bloke is driving home late one stormy night. Suddenly he sees a young woman in the headlights. He tries to brake, but it is too late and he knocks her down. He gets out of the car in a panic and looks around, but can't see her anywhere. He drives to the Police Station to report the incident.

'Where did this happen?' asked the officer on duty.

'On Blueberry Hill,' replied the driver.

'Oh,' said the policeman, 'in that case that will be the Ghost of Blueberry Hill!'

Louise, aged c.12, Gillingham School, Dorset, 12.11.92.

pp.71, 98-100

Notes

Presumably, the storyteller here has heard the story of 'The Ghost of Bluebell Hill' and it has been transformed, probably subconsciously, during transmission, due to the famous pop song 'Blueberry Hill'!

No.11*

1st: He (Telly Savalas) was, like you said, just driving along and he picked up this young girl. Actually it was a blonde he picked up and he got to the house and he left his hat in the back and he went in, you know.
The woman said, 'Oh, that's my son, he died so many years ago.'
2nd: Yeah.
1st: There's meant to be one up Bluebell Hill, up Maidstone.
MW: Bluebell Hill?
2nd: Yeah.
MW: What ghost is that? Is it the same thing?
2nd: A young girl innit?
3rd: Yeah.
1st: We walk up there every year on our camp.
2nd: Like one part of the hill they always see her and run her over. And when they stop and get out, she's not there under the car.
MW: I see.
2nd: It was in the news recently. A coach.
1st: Yeah.
2nd: Yeah.
1st: A band of people and it screeched to a halt. And when they came out, there's no one there.
3rd: Urrgh!

Group of Unidentified Males, aged c.15-17, Sheerness Youth Club, Isle of Sheppey, Kent, 6.7.94.

pp.71, 98-100

Notes

Here the story of 'The Ghost of Bluebell Hill' leads on quite naturally from a discussion of 'The Vanishing Hitchhiker', indicating that the two stories are seen, in terms of the teenage repertoire, as emanating from the same tradition, although, strictly speaking, one is a local legend and the other is a more widespread contemporary legend. Interestingly, the linking of 'The Vanishing Hitchhiker' with Telly Savalas goes back to the film star's telling of the story as a personal experience narrative on an American chat show, illustrating the influence of the mass media on the oral repertoire.

No.12*

This boy and girl were out somewhere and they were listening to the radio and there was an urgent newsflash come on. It said, 'This man has just escaped from this loony bin,' and he had a hook instead of a hand and they said, 'Be careful!' 'cos he's very near where they were.

So the girl got a bit worried and said, 'Take me home.' So the boy sort of said, 'Yes, OK.' and when they got home, he got out of the car, he went to open her door and the hook was on the door.

Karen Young, aged 13, Gillingham School, Dorset, 11.11.92.

pp.42, 94

No.13*

A man and a woman were driving over Dartmoor and they had the radio on in the car. They heard a news bulletin which said, 'Don't stop outside Dartmoor Prison, because an axe murderer has escaped from prison.' The car broke down just outside Dartmoor Prison and the man got out and found the petrol tank was empty, so he went back to ask somebody if he could use the phone. The woman turned on the radio and a voice came on saying, 'Remember, don't stop outside Dartmoor Prison.' She turned it off and shut all the windows and locked the doors. The next thing she knew the police pulled up and told her to get out of the car. They said, 'Whatever you do, don't look up.' She looked up and there was this man with an axe and her husband's head on a stick, banging it on the roof.

Tanya Boon, aged c.12, Ernesettle Library, Plymouth, 10.1.92.

pp.12, 43-4, 76

No.14*

One day this family of two children and two adults, they went on a trip to Dartmoor. They had just passed Dartmoor Prison and the petrol ran out.

So the husband went to get some petrol from the garage and the woman heard on the car radio - the woman and two children were left in the car while the husband went down, so the wife turned on the radio - and they heard this:

'Be careful, there's a headless mad axeman running around Dartmoor, just escaped from the prison, watch out, all right!'

So the next moment she heard a police car pull up behind her and a tapping on the roof as well and the policeman goes, 'Lady, don't look behind you.'

So she walks on and she looks behind her and she sees her husband's head on a stick, on the axe were her two children. And then the headless axeman chopped off the lady's head.

And that's all, really.

David, aged 12, Sparks Youth Club, Okehampton, Devon, 23.10.92.

pp.6, 43-4, 52, 53, 76

No.15*

Right.

There's these two people, they be going for a drive in the countryside and the boyfriend purposefully leaves the petrol at home and he says - they're in the middle of the countryside - 'Right, I'm going to have to go back for some petrol, right, I think I've left some at home.'

So off he trots and he goes, 'Oh by the way, lock the doors, lock the windows and don't let anyone in until I get back. Not even if they're the police.'

And she's quite happily sat there, but two hours later there's this bloke, right, jumping on the top of the car, going, 'Hoowah! Hoowah! Hoowah!', right.

Then she wonders what it is and she stays there and all of a sudden all these lights come around flashing and that and this bloke comes up to her. 'Get out of the car, don't look back whatever you do.'

So she goes, 'No, my boyfriend'll be back in a minute, it'll be all right.'

He goes, 'Look, I'm the police, get out of the car.' She winds down the window and sees the badge, opens the door and runs, but she turns round and there's this mad bloke, right, and he's got this neck thing and the boyfriend's head and he's jumping and going, 'Hoowah!' Like that.

Barrie Griffiths, aged c.13, Lipson Community College, Plymouth, 5.11.92.

pp.6, 43-4, 52, 76

No.16*

The Exmoor Beast.

There was this man and this lady and they were driving along and they stopped at this bridge 'cos they ran out of fuel and he said, 'There's a fuel station only a few miles from here.'

So he said, 'Lock your windows and doors and I'll walk on up.'

And it's about twenty minutes and she thought, 'He should have been there by now.'

And forty minutes, she said, 'Oh he should have been back by now. Perhaps he's stopped for a drink.' She began to get worried when it was an hour later and then another hour passed, then another hour until she heard thumps on the roof. She didn't think anything of it, but the farmer - there's a farmer in his truck and he stopped right at the other end of the bridge and he got out and he saw it and he drove off again.

And about twenty minutes later the police arrived and the farmer coming behind them and a policeman came up and said, 'Get out of the car, but don't look behind.'

So she got out of the car carefully and walked on and when she was about to get into the police car, she looked on the roof and there was a funny black ram-type thing with her husband's head on the end of a stick and banging it on the end of the roof.

Simon Harris, aged 13, Lipson Community College, Plymouth, 5.11.92.

pp.6, 43-4, 52, 76

Notes

The most interesting element of this particular story is that Simon titles it 'The Exmoor Beast'. Rumours that wild cats have been living on Exmoor and Dartmoor have not been uncommon over the years, and The Exmoor Beast achieved greatest prominence during the early 1980s. More recently, there have been recorded sightings of a similar creature on Bodmin Moor. None of the 'evidence' has to date been authenticated, although the Beast of Bodmin was recently the subject of an inconclusive enquiry by the Ministry of Agriculture.

Black dog stories are an important part of folklore tradition in the South West and particularly on Dartmoor. It is quite possible that large cats are living in small numbers on the moors - theories have been advanced that they were once pets that were released into the wild following legislation to make them illegal - but it is another example of how the public imagination can be fired when reality seems to echo a folkloric truth. Here Simon seems to be unwittingly linking 'The Mad Axeman' with the same black dog traditions.

No.17*

I heard this one off one of my mates in the primary school.

There's just been a newsflash that some mad man had escaped from the Dartmoor Prison and so everyone was told to lock their windows and doors and everything.

There was a couple driving along in the car and they stopped at a petrol station 'cos they needed some oil, and it was about twelve o' clock at night and - 'cos they'd heard the newsflash - the husband said, 'Right, lock all the windows and doors and when I come back I'll give three knocks and then you let me in, like that.'

So he went away and she waited five minutes, ten minutes and about an hour later she started getting really worried.

Then she heard three knocks coming on the roof. So she was just about to open the door and the knocks carried on, the knocks didn't stop and she was getting really scared. She saw a dent of like two feet in the roof and the police pulled up and they said, they told her to get out of the car and come quietly and don't look back. She went along, she looked back and there was a madman, the mad bloke from Dartmoor Prison, on the roof with an axe in one hand and the bloke's hair in the other, his head as well, banging it up and down on the roof.

Mark Duff, aged 13, Lipson Community College, Plymouth, 5.11.92.

pp.6, 43-4, 76

Notes

This variant contains all elements of the most commonly-told versions of the story, including the folkloric 'three knocks' on the roof of the car!

No.18*

My dad told me this story that this man and woman were courting in the
woods and that and the man went outside to do his business.

He didn't come back and suddenly there was this rain coming down and it
wasn't raining outside and she called the police on the mobile car phone and
the police came and told her not to look back and all that and it was this
man's body hanging from its toes from a tree with his head cut off, and the
blood was dripping from his neck all over the windows for the rain and his
fingernails were scraping, and the police told her not to look back, and she
looked back and aaagh!

Christian Waterhouse, aged 13, Gillingham School, Dorset, 11.11.92.

pp.6, 43-4, 76

Notes

This version combines the elements of 'The Mad Axeman' (British) with the
'The Boyfriend's Death' (American). The victim is indeed decapitated, as is
usual in British versions of the story, but here he is also left hanging from a
tree with his nails scraping on the car roof. This is consistent with most
variants from the United States. The two versions are also broadly in line with
the two types of the story identified by Mark Glazer (1987) in his study of the
legend in South Texas.

No.19*

There's this woman and a man ages from a petrol station and they run out of
petrol.

And, anyway, the man goes, 'Well, I'll go and get it. You stay in the car.'

And about an hour later there's sirens all around them and there's lights.
And she got out of the car and the policeman said, 'Whatever you do, don't
look....' And of course she turned around and looked and there was a joker
with a poker and her husband's head on a stick and he was going, 'Ha, ha,
killed him!'

Emma Grimshaw, aged 14, Falmouth Youth Club, Cornwall, 9.3.93.

pp.6, 43-4, 76

Notes

Here the killer is not a mad axeman, but is poetically described as 'a joker with a poker'. Presumably, the poker refers to the stick on which the severed head is impaled and the reference to the killer as a joker merely served to heighten the sinister nature of the story, as is emphasised by the murderer's laughter. It is certainly an effective use of language and reminiscent of other traditional rhyming constructs.

No.20*

Right, there was these newly-weds and they'd just been married and they said, 'Mmm, let's go up to Dartmoor,' and they were driving along and the lady gets really bored, so she goes, 'Let's play some music,' so the bloke (imitates turning on radio and music).

And they're driving along (more music imitation).

And they're still driving and they come to this place and..., but there's some fog and there's this river and he goes (sound of car and bursting tyres) and he looks down the car and he's got one puncture there and one back there. And he goes (look of disappointment).

And the lady's next door (more music sounds) and the bloke goes, 'Have you noticed something?' and the lady goes (more music sounds). And he goes, 'Look I've got punctures!' And the lady goes, 'The jack's in the boot,' and the bloke goes, 'Aren't you going to help me?' And she goes (more music sounds), and the bloke goes, 'Great!'

And then suddenly there appears this (grunting noise) and what's happened is there's Mad Max, right, and he came along and he just grabbed Nigel and put him against the car and out comes the axe and Tracey looks out the window and she goes (screams), like that, opens the door, comes out and she sees the blue flashing lights (siren noise) and it comes along (screeching brakes) and the policeman goes, 'Keep moving, keep moving.' (more screaming sounds)

She's like that all the way up the hill and you can see Mad Max (more grunting) and then suddenly this man, he comes out of the boot of the car, and he's like a gorilla with this tommy-gun (grunting sounds) and Mad Max looks and he grabs him and slings him over his shoulder and carries him by the arm and he's dragging him down the hill and then the bloke, the gorilla (grunting) and then there's (gun noises) and then you see Mad Max dragging him and there's this trail of blood going up the hill and everything.

And then the policeman comes along, walking up, and then suddenly the blood stops and it's never seen again.

Unidentified Male, aged c.14, Pyworthy Youth Club, Devon, 31.10.92.

pp.6, 43-4, 52, 76, 102-3

No.21*

This man was going to take his kid away, right, for a holiday or something like that and so they were in the car and they stopped in a lane near a mental institute and the guy said, 'Right, you've got to get some sleep now. See you in the morning.'

And the little kid was woked up by a banging noise and his dad had gone. And all he could hear was sirens and stuff and the police goes, 'Get out of your car and keep running and don't turn away, o.k.?'

And he says, 'All right then.' And as he was running, he....he had to turn and look around and he saw a mental man with his dad's head going bang, bang, bang on the roof of the car.

Catherine Wriggle, aged c.14, Falmouth Youth Club, Cornwall, 9.3.93.

pp.6, 43-4, 53, 76

No.22*

(Summary)
A man and a woman, out driving, run out of petrol, whilst on honeymoon. The man goes off to fetch petrol, but gets the feeling that he is being followed by a large animal. He gets increasingly nervous as he walks along.

Suddenly he hears a heavy panting noise from behind a hedge. He drops the petrol can in fright and runs back to the car as fast as possible, still being followed. It is only when he safely reaches the car that he notices, in the car headlights, that he has been followed by a horse!

Unidentified male, aged c.12, Mullion School, Cornwall, 3.11.93.

pp.6, 43-4, 76

Notes

This is a jocular tale which uses the device of many such traditional jocular narratives. It uses the audience's knowledge of narrative (or, in this case, a particular narrative) to lead the audience along a specific and familiar path, only to then undermine its expectations. The comic effect is achieved by the very juxtaposition of the horse with the expectation of the supernatural threat that has been implied and developed up to that point. Again it relies on the audience's familiarity with 'The Mad Axeman' to achieve its maximum effect.

<h3 style="text-align:center">No.23*</h3>

Rachel: There was this person and she had a dog and every night when she went to bed, it licked her hand.
Katie: And then this night she couldn't sleep.
Rachel: So she put her hand out and the dog licked it and then she heard a dripping noise. It went drip, drip, drip, drip. So she went to find it and she couldn't.
Katie: And then she went back to sleep and the dog licked her hand. Then she woke up again and she heard drip, drip, drip, drip...
Rachel: Drip, drip, drip, drip, drip.
Katie: Yeh, that as well. And then...
Rachel: So she went in the bathroom and there was her dog and it was...
Katie: It was lying over the shower door with its throat cut and the noise was all its blood dripping and she thought, 'Well, how can that be? It couldn't be my dog....
Both: 'My dog just licked my hand.'
Rachel: So she went back in the room...
Katie: And turned the light on....
Rachel: And there was a man there that was licking her hand!
(laughter)

Rachel and Katie, aged 12, Fitzharrys School, Abingdon, Oxford, 21.11.91.

pp.58, 59-61, 64, 76

No.24*

Right, it's dark and this lonesome old granny lives up on Dartmoor and it's about half past nine at night and she hears about during the day that people have escaped from Dartmoor Prison and she left her window open during the night because it's hot and she always hangs her hand over the bed for her dog to lick it.

And then outside her bedroom there's a woodpile and there's an axe in the stump of wood the person that comes and takes the axe.

He goes under and kills the dog and licks her hand and she wakes up in the morning and all the dog's splattered everywhere, blood everywhere, and on the wall it says, 'Guess who licked your hand last night?'

Allan, aged c.13, Plymstock Comprehensive School, Plymouth, 3.11.92.

pp.58, 61-3, 64, 76

Notes

In setting this popular and widespread story on Dartmoor, Allan is demonstrating an awareness of local folklore traditions which portrays the Moor as a mysterious, threatening and ghostly place. Note also the traditional axe motif.

No.25*

There was a lady who lives up on Dartmoor in a little cottage up on the top of a hill and about half past nine she goes up to bed and every night, when she goes to bed, she hangs her hand over the bed and the dog would lick her hand to sleep.

So she goes to bed, she puts her hand down and she goes to sleep.

She wakes up in the morning and the dog is just all splattered around the room. There's blood all up the walls, his head's on the end of the bed and his legs are hanging off and on the wall it's got in blood, 'Guess who licked your hand last night?!'

Neil, aged 13, Plymstock Comprehensive School, Plymouth, 3.11.92.

pp.58, 76

210

Notes

Again the setting is Dartmoor, which could be a kind of authentication. However, more likely is that, as in No.24, the storyteller is simply recognising the role of the Moor in traditional narrative. The rest of the story is told with exaggerated grotesque descriptions, which would suggest that the story is not first and foremost being told as true.

No.26*

There's this woman in Dartmoor in a tumbledown cottage. It's announced on the news, there's a warning - close all your windows and doors.

So she goes to bed and she feels the dog licking her hand and she hears a dripping and she knows she's turned off all the taps and everything.

So she goes down and it's just the tap and next night she feels the dog licking and she hears the drip and she goes, 'Oh God, not again.'

So she goes into a room. There's blood, there's a sawn-off pipe, you know, and there's blood running all down the wall and dripping onto the floor. She goes up, but she's felt her dog lick her, so it's alive. She goes up and there's this dog with a knife through her and she's stuck to the ceiling and the knife's stuck right through her with blood pouring down, and written in the window panes, a letter a pane, it says, 'Men can lick too!'

Allan, aged c.12, Pyworthy Youth Club, Devon, 31.10.92.

pp.58, 76

Notes

Another Dartmoor setting, but this time the descriptions, though horrific, are much less grotesque. Particularly effective is the melodramatic ending with the added detail that the message is written 'a letter a pane'.

No.27*

I heard one as well, but it was with a cat, and this old lady was best friends with this cat and the cat followed her everywhere, and it slept by her bed. And she sleeps with her hand over the bed and the cat's always licking it and in the morning she hears this drip, drip.

So she gets out of bed and follows it and it takes her all the way down to the kitchen and on the kitchen fridge there's her cat - I think it was diced up - and it said, 'The Devil can lick as well!'

Jamie Carmichael, aged 13, Lipson Community College, Plymouth, 5.11.92.

pp.58, 76

Notes

Jamie's story is far more a summary than the others. He makes it clear at the beginning that it is not his story, but one that he has heard from somebody else. It is not until the end that he makes a half-hearted attempt to introduce some detail with, 'I think it was diced up'. Unusually, the mutilated animal is a cat, rather than a dog.

No.28*

There was an old lady who had a bulldog. And she lived in a flat by herself with her dog and every night, whenever she was scared, she put her hand under the bed, where the dog slept, and it licked her fingers.

And one day in the newspapers, the police said that there was a murderer on the loose and you had to be in bed by six o' clock and have all your doors and windows locked.

So at six o' clock that night she went to bed and locked all her doors and windows and put her hand under the bed and the dog licked her fingers. Then she went to sleep.

But later on in the night she heard a drip, drip, drip, and she woke up. And she went down to the kitchen and the tap was dripping, so she switched it off and she went back to bed, and she put her hand under the bed and the dog licked her fingers, so she went to sleep.

And later on she woke up again and she could still hear a drip, drip, drip. So she went outside and the tap was still on, so she turned it off and went back to bed, put her hand under the bed and the bulldog licked her fingers.

Then later on she woke up again and she could still hear a dripping noise, so she put her hand under the bed, the bulldog licked her fingers, and she went into the bathroom, and her bulldog was hanging upside down, dripping blood, and on the mirror it said in blood, 'Humans can lick too!'

Ellen Raynor, aged 12, Gillingham School, Dorset, 11.11.92.

pp.58, 76

Notes

In contrast this is a much fuller version of the story. Ellen includes a good degree of detail, including the breed of dog and the time at which the old woman retires to bed. The narrative is also very tightly structured into her being wakened by the dripping noise three times.

No.29*

There's this woman and every night before she goes to bed she puts her feet underneath the bed so this dog can lick her feet. One night she puts her feet under and it licks everything. She goes to bed and hears this dripping noise.

So she goes into the bathroom to make sure the taps are off and everything, but it carries on, so she goes downstairs and hanging from the window is her dog and somebody had written on the window, 'Humans can lick too!'

Amy Prestwick, aged 14, Lydford Youth Club, Devon, 16.11.92.

pp.58, 76

No.30*

There was this lady, she was watching the telly, the news, and they said, 'Watch out, there's a madman about, so check your windows.'

So she turned it off and went to bed and usually the dog licks her hand. He was licking her hand, then she hears this dripping in the bathroom, so she just ignores it and it comes on and she goes into the bathroom and the dog's hanging up in the shower and on the wall it's written, 'You forgot to shut the windows!' - in blood.

That's it.

213

Ben, aged 13, St. Stephen's Youth Club, St. Stephen-in-Brannel, Cornwall, 26.4.93.

pp.58, 76

Notes

Although this is a short version of the story, it is satisfyingly neat. The main difference between this and other versions is the message that is written on the wall. In this version, the message is perhaps less threatening, but all the more effective because it refers directly back to the warning issued in the very first sentence of the story. Here, the woman is not a powerless victim. In other variants of the story, the woman is the victim in spite of her locking all the doors and windows; in Ben's story, she becomes a victim precisely because she has not been vigilant and has failed to heed the warning.

This is, of course, the traditional motif of the violation of the interdiction, whereby a character disobeys instructions often to disastrous consequences. Another such example is when the girlfriend/wife turns to look back in 'The Mad Axeman'.

No.31*

One day a man was driving along the road and these hairy hands came through the window and grabbed onto his wheel and threw him off the road.

And this was reported to the police when a man was walking along the road.

And then a couple of weeks later, a motorcyclist was driving along and the hairy hands grabbed onto his steering wheel and swerved him off the road.

And that was reported to the police.

And then a month later, a car was driving along the road and he saw these hairy hands thumbing a lift to go to the M1.

Nathan Shaw, aged 11, Gillingham School, Dorset, 11.11.92.

p.71

Notes

'The Hairy Hands' is a well-known local legend from Dartmoor and, although Nathan is from Gillingham, it transpired that the school organises residential trips to Dartmoor for many of its students. Such trips often involve the telling of local stories. Interestingly, although much of the narrative lacks detail, the story is organised into three encounters with the ghostly hands. The final encounter is primarily comic, but has echoes of 'The Vanishing Hitchhiker'.

No.32*

His mum wanted this boy to get her some liver, but the boy went to get him some sweets.

So he dug up a dead body, then he got the liver out and he took it home and he bought some sweets and then they ate the liver and that night his mum and dad went out without him knowing.

And well, he was upstairs in his bed, doing homework, and then he heard this:

Johnny, I want my liver back,
Johnny, I'm outside your bedroom,
Johnny, I'm in your bedroom,
Johnny, I want my liver back,
Johnny, I'm on your bed,
Johnny, - YOU'RE DEAD!!

Tony Martin, aged 12, Fitzharrys School, Abingdon, Oxon, 21.11.91

pp.51, 110

No.33*

There was this lad and his mum and dad asked him to go down the shops to buy some liver and the mum gave him the money and he set off down the road. He kept on down the road and he passed a sweet shop and he goes in and buys some sweets instead of a liver.

So he walks past the church, so he goes, 'I've got an idea,' or something. He goes into the churchyard and digs up his gran. Then he gets hold of a little penknife, cuts his nan's liver out and runs home.

He gives the liver to his mum, she cooks it for tea and....'Mmm, nice dinner' and all that.

So a couple of hours later his mum and dad went out to a meal, see, and Johnny was up doing his homework and downstairs her could heard:

Johnny, I want my liver back,
Johnny, I'm on the first step,
Johnny, I'm on the landing,
Johnny, I want my liver back,
Johnny, I'm in your bedroom,
Johnny, I want my liver back,
Johnny, I'm on the pillow-case,
Johnny, I want my liver back,
Johnny, I'm on your he-ad,
Johnny....BOO!!

Jamie, aged c.13, Sparks Youth Club, Okehampton, Devon, 23.10.92

pp.51, 110-11

No.34*

There was this boy and he was given some money by his mother to go down to the butcher's and buy some liver.

So he went down and he saw a funeral procession on the way, and he thought, 'Well, if I just buy some magazines, I can collect the liver on the way back from the body.' So he goes down and buys lots of magazines with the money.

He comes back and he goes into the graveyard and luckily everyone had gone into church cos it had started raining and they hadn't covered it over - the coffin was just there. So he opened the coffin and cut the liver out and put it in a plastic bag and took it home to his mum.

Anyway, his mum made it into a liver and bacon casserole and the family had it for tea that evening, but he said he wasn't feeling very hungry, so he had a boiled egg.

Later that evening he was in bed and he heard:

'Johnny, I want my liver, I'm in the graveyard.'

And he thought, 'Oh I must be dreaming.' And a bit later he heard:

'Johnny, I want my liver, I'm on your doorstep.'

And he was frightened then. He hid under the covers. Then he heard:

'Johnny, I want my liver, I'm on your staircase.'

216

And he was really frightened and he was hiding under his sheets and he was hoping that he was just dreaming it. Then he heard:

'Johnny, I want my liver, I'm by your door now.'

He was really frightened, hiding. Then he heard:

'Johnny, I want my liver, I'm by your bed.'

Then he heard:

'Eerrgh. Johnny, I love you, I've got my liver.'

And in the morning his parents found the boy dead with his liver cut out.

Natasha Tillbrook, aged 13, Gillingham School, Dorset, 11.11.93

p.51

Notes

This is a very detailed telling of the story, with descriptions of the funeral procession, the open grave and even what they ate for tea! Most interesting, however, is that this variant offers an alternative ending to the 'jump'. Here the ghost's revenge is to take the boy's liver in return, and although the 'jump' ending is the more common, this alternative from Natasha is certainly not unusual and confirms that the dramatic intention of stories is no more fixed than the text itself.

No.35

There was this boy and his nanny, and he killed his nanny and shredded her skin.

And he was starving, and he had her holed up in the wardrobe and there was no money at all in the house, he had no money.

And he went into the wardrobe and opened her up and took out her liver. And he ate it. And all he could hear was, when he was asleep, 'Johnny, I'm in the garden.'

So he goes out into the garden to see if there was anybody there and there was nobody there.

So he goes back to bed and he hears, 'Johnny, I'm in the hall. I'm coming to get you.'

So he goes out into the hall and there's nobody there.

So he goes back to bed and he hears, 'Johnny, I'm up the stairs, I'm coming to get you.'

So he goes over to the stairs and there's nobody there.

So he goes back to bed and he hears, 'Johnny, I'm in the room..(quickly).I'M GOING TO GET YOU!'

Darren O'Connor, aged 12, Scoilmhuire, Dublin, 29.3.94.

Notes

This is an unusual variant of the story in that it begins with Johnny murdering and flaying his grandmother rather than simply stealing the liver from the corpse. There is no mention of Johnny's parents (perhaps he has killed them too?), but it is only when he is faced with starvation that he resorts to cannibalism, something of which he is not guilty in other versions of the story. From this point on the story progresses as might be expected, ending with a 'jump'.

Although this story was collected in Dublin, it would be wrong to draw the ethnocentric conclusion that this was the normal Irish variation of the tale. The usual version of 'Johnny' is still prevalent throughout all of Ireland and I would suspect that the variations in Darren's story owe more to the publicity given in recent years to cannibalistic serial killers, such as the fictional Hannibal Lecter in the film *The Silence of the Lambs* and the non-fictional Geoffrey Dahmer in the United States.

No.36*

There was a young girl called Mary and she was about to go to bed and she says, 'G'night mum,' and she started walking up the stairs, and she had this doll and she could hear kids' voices going, 'Mary on the first step, Mary on the second step...' up to, like, the fifth step.

And she was going, 'Oh no!' and she ran back and says, 'Mum, mum, I can hear these voices,' and she says, 'Oh it's just your imagination, go back to sleep. Go on, go back upstairs.'

So she started walking and she could hear these voices going, 'Mary on the sixth step, Mary on the seventh step..' right up to the ninth step.

She said, 'Oh mum, I can still hear these voices, it's really scaring me.' She said, 'Well, don't worry about it, dear. Go on, go on upstairs.'

And she walked to the bottom step and started walking to see what happens, and she started walking up and got to the landing and she could hear, 'Mary on the landing. Mary in the bedroom, Mary in her bed.'

So she'd gone to bed and went to sleep.

And the next morning her mum went up to get her and she'd got a pierrot doll and the little girl had been killed. Mary had been killed and the pierrot doll was smiling and the tear had gone.......There was a knife in her back.

Catherine Wriggle, aged c.14, Falmouth Youth Club, Cornwall, 9.3.93.

pp.79-80

Notes

'Mary on the First Step', as the story is often known by teenagers is clearly a variant of 'Johnny', although it is often seen as quite separate by teenage tellers. It is certainly a widespread story and uses the traditional motif of the killer doll which has been so favoured by twentieth century writers and film makers in the horror genre. Although the formula used to develop the story towards its conclusion is the same as in 'Johnny', it seems that the 'jump' or, in this case, the death of the child, is, in fact, motiveless. In 'Johnny' the ghost is the ghost of a human and, therefore, acts through motivation (revenge), but here the doll is inanimate and has no reason, which implies a greater threat.

No.37*

There was this girl and she's got a boyfriend called Davey and one night he came over 'cos it was her birthday or something and he gave her some pearls and she said, 'Oh, thanks a lot.'

Next morning he came around and he goes, 'Oh I need the pearls back, I need the money.' And she goes, 'No, no, it was a present from you.'

And he got the pearls, he ripped them off her neck and he killed her and made a piano out of her bones.

And anyway, he gave the piano to the girl's parents and they put it up in the attic.

And one day, they brought it down, after a year, and the mother pressed one of the keys on it and it goes:

'Mother, Mother, you're playing on my bones,
Someone killed me and stole my precious stones.'

And then the mother called the father and he pressed one of the keys and it goes:

219

'Father, father, you're playing on my bones,
Someone killed me and stole my precious stones.'
And then Davey came round, who was the girl's boyfriend, and he goes to
it, and it says:
'Davey, Davey, you're playing on my bones,
Someone killed me.. YOU KILLED ME!'

Emma Grimshaw, aged 14, Falmouth Youth Club, 9.3.93.

pp. 122-6, 127-8, 129-30, 130-1, 133

No.38*

(Summary)
There was this man and woman and two children, a boy and a girl. The boy
was called David. One day they were walking in the woods and the father
picked a rose for the girl. The boy wanted the rose and he killed her and stole
it and then made a piano out of her bones.
    When the dad played it, it sang:
    (rhythmically spoken)
'Father, Father, someone killed me and stole my great rose.'
    When the mum played it, it sang:
'Mother, Mother, someone killed me and stole my great rose.'
    When David played it, it sang:
'David, David, someone killed me and stole my great rose. YOU DID!'

Lee, aged 12, Redruth School, 21.3.95.

pp. 130-1, 133

No.39*

(Summary)
There was a husband and wife and he suspected her of having an affair. So he
removed a string from the piano and strangled her. He then made a string out
of some of her skin and used it to replace the missing string in the piano.
However, when the piano was played, it sang the story of the murder. The
story ended with a jump.

Unidentified Female, aged 12, Cheyne Middle School, Sheerness, Isle of Sheppey, 8.11.94.

pp.81-2, 131-3

No.40*

It's about a story I was told.

There was this lady who lived near this school. She lived up the road, there's this pub that had been boarded up and things like that and she told me a story.

The landlord that lived in it about ten years ago, killed his wife and two children in the front room and took them down into the cellar and buried them in the corner. Then he killed himself and when the police came out they only found his body and blood all over the wall.

So they got rid of all their possessions and things and the next tenants moved in, the landlord. And when they went in they found all this blood and like thing on the wallpaper.

So they stripped it all off and put on their own expensive wallpaper and they didn't know why, but red patches kept on showing where the blood was on the walls.

So they stripped it down again, thinking there was something wrong with the paste, and it was a different paste and the same thing happened again.

So they ended up getting some professional decorators to come in and then decorate it. And they decorated it and the blood was coming through as well.

And then at nights things started moving around, around the pub, bottles and things.

So the landlord and tenant was a bit scared of this and they called in their cousin or auntie who was a ...what d'you call them?...and she stayed in the room where the blood kept on seeping through onto the wallpaper and she was asleep and she imagined herself getting up and walking out of the door and down to the cellar and she was looking at this hump of earth in the corner of the cellar, 'cos it was an old pub and the cellar floor was still out of mud. And she saw this lump and she woke up and ran and got the landlord or whatever and took them down to see and showed them this lump she'd seen in her dream.

So they called the police and the police came down with spades and dug up the lump and found the decayed bodies of the landlord's wife and child.

John, aged 13, Lipson Community College, Plymouth, 13.11.92.

221

No.41

(Summary)
There were two twins and their mother wanted to send them to boarding school. One was keen to go and the other wasn't. But off they were packed and on the first night at school, one of them heard a tapping on the door. She ignored it and in the morning she opened the door to find her sister dead on the landing, her body gorily mutilated.

Unidentified Female, aged c.12, Combeshead College, Newton Abbot, 9.11.94.

Notes

This is a variant of the well-documented contemporary legend 'The Roommate's Death' (see especially Brunvand, 1981, pp.57-62). The story is widespread in the United States where it is often related as happening to two new students at a college or university. In Great Britain, where it is less usual for students to share dormitories, the story is less common, but here the setting is transferred to the one context where communal sleeping arrangements are still the norm - the private boarding school. This seems to give the story a particularly British flavour.

Of course, the story would seem to concern itself with the dangers and uncertainties that face young people when they step out into the world and leave the security of home. In this sense it may be seen as a cautionary tale. It is certainly the case that both this version and other American variants are consistent in that the events always happen away from home to people who have recently left home.

No.42*

There was this teenage girl babysitting and she had a dream about this man, Freddie Kruger face, and she was babysitting and she had this phone call - the kids were upstairs - she had the phone call which said, 'I'm outside in the car.'

She just put the phone down and then she had another call saying, 'Chinese Take-Away.'

So she says, 'Sorry, you've got the wrong number.' So she put the phone down and she had another call saying, 'I'm outside, you'd better have a look.'

So she ran upstairs and had a look out of the window and the kids are in the back of the car.

Kay, aged 13, Lipson Community College, Plymouth, 5.11.92.

p.101

Notes

'The Babysitter' is a well-documented contemporary legend (see, for example, Brunvand, 1981, pp.53-7) and one that is very widespread, in many variant forms, amongst teenagers today. It retains many of the motifs and structures that are found in the most popular teenage oral narratives, namely, a teenage protagonist, violence (threatened or actual) and a steady increase in tension (again the 'phone rings three times). In Kay's version, the ending is not as violent as is often the case, which suggests that she may be telling the tale as a warning to other teenagers who may be considering earning some money by babysitting!

No.43

There was these two people, Mr and Mrs Jones, with their two children and they all had to go out for the evening. So they got a babysitter to babysit and so, when about....when they went out for an hour and the babysitter was there, she sent the children up to bed and then she got a phone call saying, 'Come upstairs.' And she totally ignored it.

And so about five minutes later, it was going, 'Come upstairs.'

And she got this phone call about three or four times, and so then she heard these screams.

And so she went upstairs and she opened the door and she saw these two bodies lying in front of her, their faces totally chopped off. And she looked up in the ceiling and the babies were dangling with string.

Carla, aged c.13, Budmouth School, Weymouth, Dorset, 12.11.93.

223

Notes

The violent ending to Carla's story is not unusual in this story and is often received as comically grotesque by teenage audiences, but as distasteful and horrific by adults. It is usual for the babysitter to be looking after two children, who are occasionally twins.

No.44

O.K. It's about this woman who goes out, 'cos she's got a boyfriend. She goes out 'cos she's split up with her mum......sorry, split up with her husband, so she needs a babysitter, and goes out with her boyfriend in a flashy car.

Later on the....woman who's looking after the baby gets a weird phone call from this weird-sounding man, who says, 'Don't look up the stairs.'

So, out of curiosity, she looks up the stairs and sees this man, this awesome-looking man, with sharp, long fingernails, holding this baby, sort of cracking his nails down on the baby and scraping along, scratching the baby and then dripping all the blood off.

So later on, as soon as she sees that, she runs out and screams out and leaves everything as it was.

Christian, aged 12, St. Luke's Secondary School, Portsmouth, 9.11.93.

Notes

Although Christian's telling is full of mistakes and contradictions, it is interesting in a number of respects. Unusually there is only one child being looked after and the killer, although never named, would be instantly recognisable to most teenagers from the description of his fingernails as Freddy Kruger. In No.42 the killer is also likened to the same fictional character. It is also interesting that there is an implied criticism of the child's mother in that she submits to the temptations of her boyfriend and his 'flashy car', abandoning her child to a terrible fate.

No.45

Right, there's this lady, sitting down watching telly, it's all blank going, (rhythmically) 'Bits and Pieces, Bits and Pieces.'

Then she was listening to this radio and it stopped and it goes, 'Bits and Pieces, Bits and Pieces.'

Then the phone rang and it was there, going, 'Bits and Pieces, Bits and Pieces.'

And then the phone rang again and it goes, 'Bits and Pieces, Bits and Pieces.'

So she went upstairs, checked on the kids and they were all in Bits and Pieces, Bits and Pieces.

(General laughter)

Kelly Hodges, aged c.14, Cinderford Youth Club, Gloucestershire, 3.95.

Notes

This jocular tale uses the structure and plot of 'The Babysitter' for its effect. It relies for its humour on the rhythmic repetition of 'Bits and Pieces, Bits and Pieces', rather than by undermining our expectations. In fact, it is precisely because it conforms to our expectations that the violent ending is not shocking, or even grotesque. The audience knows exactly how the story will end and the humour lies in the fact that the chant never really makes sense until the very end, when everything becomes comically clear.

No.46

There's this lady and she's coming home from work quite late and she's on the motorway and there's this little dog and it's in agony, like it's broken its leg or something. So she's pulled over and she's helped it and it's all right again and it starts walking again.

And she went on in her car. And there's this car right up behind her, really behind her car and the lights are all right on her and she's really scared and this car is following her and it's followed her right up to her house. She got out of her car and ran into her house and she's really scared. And there's a knock at the door, so she opens the door and there's this man and he goes, 'I was following you because there was this man who got into your car when you were helping the dog.'

He'd got into the back of the car.

Catherine Wriggle, aged c.14, Falmouth Youth Club, Cornwall, 9.3.93.

Notes

Brunvand names this contemporary legend 'The Killer in the Back Seat' (see Brunvand, 1981, pp.52-3). Although the story is quite widespread, it is more usually told in adult circles rather than being part of the teenage repertoire. This may be because (at least in Britain) driving is beyond the experience of most under 17s, although many aspire to it and cars are important motifs in many other stories in the teenage repertoire.

No.47

There was this woman driving her car down the motorway going to Belfast and she seen like a box by the side of the road that she thought was a baby inside it.

So she pulled over and found it wasn't a baby inside, but like a plastic doll. So she got back in the car and started to drive on.

She's about half an hour away from her home and all of a sudden this other car starts hitting her in the back, starts pushing her and kept doing it till the whole way she was getting home and she ran out of quick and went to her dad, and her dad came running out with a baseball bat and told the man in the car, why was he doing it. And he was about to hit him.

And then he just shouted over, 'Look in the car, look in the car. There's a man in the back of your car.'

They pretended he was hitting the car, he was hitting it because a man was coming up behind her to grab her neck and try and kill her.

Thomas, aged c.14, Oakgrove Integrated College, Derry, N. Ireland, 2.3.94

Notes

Another variant of 'The Killer in the Back Seat'. Here the story is given a local setting, as is often the case in the telling of contemporary legends as an authentication device. Interestingly, the day after this story was told to me, the exact same story was told me by an adult colleague from N. Ireland. In spite of the authentication of the local setting, Thomas, unlike the adult, did not try to claim that the story was true.

'The Killer Motorbike'
In the country there lived a husband and wife, who were very happy. They had a son, who loved motorbikes.

So, coming up was their son's eighteenth birthday and his parents loved him so much that they bought him a magnificent motorbike. They didn't really want to buy it because they were so dangerous, but they knew how much he loved them.

So when the son came down on the morning of his eighteenth birthday, his parents showed him the magnificent motorbike. He was so pleased that he drove it straight away. He drove it everywhere, but then he was in a fatal accident. He crashed and he died.

His mum and dad were so upset. His dad tried to get on with life and lived things to the full, but his mum just wouldn't forget. She kept on moaning and crying. She was getting so ill with it and one day there was a knock at the door. (knocking sound). She opened it and there was a man dressed in a long dark cloak. He said, 'You want to buy a monkey-paw? It'll give you three wishes.'

She thought for a moment. Three wishes. Three wishes. Three wishes. She said yes. She said she hadn't any money. So the man at the door said, 'I will trade it with you for your lovely silk coat.' So she did.

The lady held the monkey's paw to her heart and thought, 'Three wishes. Three wishes.'

Her husband knew what she wanted to say, but he wouldn't let her have it, until one day she was almost on her death bed, he said, 'You may have your wish.'

So the lady opened the box, took out the monkey's paw and rubbed it three times...(some text missing here as tape ran out)...the son would come back from his grave. Her husband then said, 'Oh no, please, you shouldn't have said that.' But the lady was determined.

They was waiting for a couple of hours for something to happen and then they suddenly heard, down by the garden path, footsteps. But they weren't child's footsteps, they were the footsteps of an old person. They drew closer until they were right outside the room of the husband and wife. They heard a creak of the door (creaking) and slowly he walked in.

But before he could do so, the husband grabbed the box from the lady, rubbed it three times and said, 'Oh, I wish my son to go back to his grave.'

And the son went back to his grave and he said, 'You did this to me, father. You! I shall pay you back!'

Then the man said the third wish, 'I wish this monkey-paw was gone forever.' And it was.

The lady was upset to start with, but she soon started to learn she couldn't weep forever. The husband and wife soon lived happily ever after.

Kerry, aged 12, Mullion School, Cornwall, April 1993.

pp.6, 91-4

No.49

I heard this in Dartmoor. It's called 'The Monkey's Paw'.

In winter on a farm in Dartmoor, there was a family - there's a mum, a dad and a boy, aged fourteen - and one night they were sitting in the front room and they heard a knock at the door and it was ten o' clock. And the dad said, 'I wonder who that could be at this time of night.'

So he went to the door, opened the door, and it was an old man at the door, and he says, 'Could you give me shelter for the night?'

So they let him in and they gave him shelter.

And then in the morning, when they all wake up, the old man came downstairs and said, 'I don't know how to repay you for letting me stay the night.'

He took out of his pocket a monkey's paw and said, 'This will grant you three wishes, evil and good.'

So, then, the old man went and then the farmer was really in debt a couple of months later, and he was really thinking about the monkey's paw. He couldn't get it out of his mind.

And one night, all he could hear was, 'Monkey's paw, monkey's paw, monkey's paw.'

And then he went downstairs, went to the front room and there was the monkey's paw on the fireplace tapping. And he picked up the monkey's paw and said, 'I wish I had....I wish I had five thousand pounds.' So then he put the monkey's paw down and ran back upstairs.

Then in the morning he got a letter through the post saying that his relative in Australia had died and his will was to him and was five thousand pounds.

And then he didn't know what to spend it on.

First he bought his son a motorbike, a Harley Davidson, 'cos his son was mad about motorbikes and then they all went out.

One day the son was riding down a narrow road on his motorbike and there was a great big army truck at the bottom of it and he was riding down and he couldn't stop in time or get round it and he slid right underneath it.

And his arm got caught behind him and snapped his arm off. His leg got caught...his leg got caught in the wheel and got ripped off. His chest....the chain of the motorbike got congested through his chest. And when he went into the motorbike, his head got caught on the bumper and ripped his head off.

Then, when...at his funeral....then, they were really.....then the parents were really upset about the death of their child and the lady kept thinking about the 'monkey's paw, monkey's paw, monkey's paw.'

And then one night, all she could think about was the monkey's paw, so she went downstairs into the front room and seen the monkey's paw in the fireplace and it was tapping. So she picked up the monkey's paw and she said, 'I wish I had my son back.' And she put the monkey's paw back down and went back.

And all she could hear was slither, clunk, slither, clunk. And it was getting louder and louder, and getting closer and closer, and at the door there was a knock. And then she opened the door and it was her son, but it weren't the same as it was, because he had the chain congested through his chest, his leg was dragging along and so was his arm and he was holding his head.

And then suddenly he grabbed hold of her neck and started shaking her around. And then dropped her and she was dead on the floor.

And the father heard it from down....upstairs and he came downstairs and seen the boy. And then the boy came towards him and he, the father, went into the front room to get the monkey's paw and the monkey's paw's climbing up the wall.

And then he was jumping up and down to get it and it was getting high. And he got it and he said, 'I wish my son would go away.' And then he put the monkey's paw back down.

And then his son was so close to strangling him. Then he started to walk away out of the door. And that's it.

Donna, aged c.13, Budmouth School, Weymouth, Dorset, 12.11.93.

Notes

This is another full version of 'The Monkey's Paw', which, interestingly, uses the motorbike motif once more. It is also significant that Donna sets the story on Dartmoor with its traditional associations with ghosts. It is unclear whether Donna first heard the story as being set on Dartmoor or whether she simply heard it whilst on school camp on Dartmoor, but either way she firmly associates the story with this particular setting.

No.50

(Summary)

There was a girl named Rebecca whose father worked on the railway.

One night he went out to work and she went out to play with her ball. She strayed onto the railway line and was playing on the track, bouncing her ball, when she was killed by a train.

Now, at midnight, you can still hear the sound of a ball being bounced along the track.

Unidentified Female, aged c.12, Priestman Middle School, Bradford, 15.9.92.

Notes

After I had been told this story, I was also informed that there were a number of stories about Rebecca, that she was a well-known local ghost. This seemed to be borne out when I spoke to other teenagers from the school, although few were able or willing to tell me the other stories in the cycle. The Rebecca Cycle was completely unknown to the teachers and other adults I spoke to from the area and I have likewise never come across the same stories in other parts of the country, even though many of the motifs contained within the story above (the railway, the midnight hour, haunting by sound) are highly traditional in ghostlore.

No.51

It's a Rebecca story. Just a short one.

Right, Rebecca's going to visit her Auntie, right, and she has to go on a train to get there. And she's at the train station playing with her ball and she's bouncing it about. And it goes along the tracks, right. She climbs down onto the tracks, where she makes sure there's no trains coming, climbs down onto the tracks and gets the ball.

And she hears a train coming, right. She tries to get up from the tracks, but it's too deep down and the train runs her over. And whenever you go to that train station on that day that she got killed, you'll hear a ball bouncing and you might hear Rebecca.

Tammy, aged c.12, Priestman Middle School, Bradford, 12.11.93.

Notes

This story was collected the year following the first Rebecca story and, although it differs in some respects, it is largely a variant of the first story, the central motifs of the railway and the bouncing ball being the same. However, the opening to the story seems to suggest that there is indeed a cycle consisting of a number of such stories and that many others are much longer than this. If this is true it may well explain why I was unable to collect those other stories at the end of lessons when time was very short.

No.52*

When my grandad was alive, well, when he died, he had this clock that he gave my dad when he was younger. It had always been working and it stopped on exactly the time he died, and it started again the same time the next day exactly.

Yeh, it started going again and it's been going ever since.

Neil Hardy, aged 14, Lipson Community College, Plymouth, 5.11.92.

p.71

Notes

The motif of a timepiece stopping on the death of its owner is one that is epitomised in the popular nineteenth century music-hall song 'Grandfather's Clock', which tells of a long case clock which kept perfect time during the owner's lifetime, but 'stopped short, never to go again / When the old man died'. The song was apparently based on a true incident in the house where the songwriter was lodging and it is due to that song that long case clocks became known as Grandfather clocks. It is also a very common motif in memorates.

No.53*

My gran had three watches, and when she died every single watch stopped at the same time and none of them have ever worked since.

And the other day, the clock on the fridge stopped at ten to twelve. Also my mum's watch.

Jolene Lanyon, aged c.14, Falmouth Youth Club, Cornwall, 9.3.93.

p.71

Notes

This is actually two fragments in one. The first is another 'Grandfather's Clock' story, whilst the second is just the reporting of a recent coincidence, although the second is given added weight and significance by the first.

No.54

It's not a story, it's just they're pictures. And my mate out there, his ex-girlfriend used to have them hanging up in her house, in the living room.

And she went out with her mum in the kitchen, doing some dinner or something, and they got the two pictures on the wall, side by side, and in the middle there's a calendar. And they were sitting there, you know, just waiting for them to come up with some food, and it started, like, flapping, really off the wall.

(The calendar?)

Yeh, the calendar.

And Haley, her name, said to her mum, 'They're back again.'

And they're pictures, they're meant to....called crying pictures...I'd never heard of them till he said. And they're meant to cry or something if they're unhappy. They reckon it's the oil from the painting or something.

They say if you burn them, they come back in ashes. Even in an ash tray, or something like that. Whatever you do, you can't get rid of them. Throw them away and they come back.

My mate'll tell you all about it.

Unidentified Male, aged c.17, Sheerness Youth Club, Isle of Sheppey, Kent, 6.7.94.

Notes

Georgina Boyes (Boyes, 1989) offers an analysis of a rumour legend which she claims first appeared in the press in 1985. The story concerns a picture called 'The Crying Boy' which causes inexplicable fires in the houses in which it hangs and yet the picture itself always survives the fire completely undamaged. Here we have the same story being told, although here it seems the picture also possesses other qualities such as the ability to cause poltergeist-type disturbance as well as a supernatural homing instinct.

Here the teller is telling a story which he perceives is not his own, but actually his friend's story. Because of this his handling of the information is sometimes confusing and inconsistent. However, he also makes it clear that his incomplete telling of the story is not because he cannot tell stories, but rather because it is not really his story to tell. If we want the complete version, he tells us, 'My mate'll tell you all about it.'

No.55

We've got this picture of a little boy crying and nobody in our family likes it except for me.

And there's been stories that other people in the country's had them and bad things have happened, like their houses have burned down, but the picture's always survived.

And they reckon that the picture is the Devil inside it and they call me 'Devil-worshipper', 'cos I like it.

Kelly Hodges, aged c.14, Cinderford Youth Club, Gloucestershire, 3.95.

Notes

Another variant of 'The Crying Boy' story. Kelly's story limits the picture's activities to causing and surviving fires, although she is also aware that these stories are widespread. However, she uses this to authenticate her story. Both of these variants are told as true stories.

No.56

I got two about my Auntie, right.

My Auntie Tracey, who you all know, yeh? (murmurs of agreement from rest of group) Right, she had these two pictures, one of a girl, one of a boy.

And one night she was watching telly and in the room she saw this little boy go past and this little girl go past. She looked at the pictures and realized there was nobody in there.

So she broke the pictures and they're gone.

Unidentified Female, aged c.14, Brockworth Youth Club, Gloucester, 21.2.94.

Notes

Stories of personal encounters with the supernatural, or memorates, are very common within the teenage repertoire and many of those stories originate in a family's repertoire. This is a typical example and, although the theme of ghostly pictures is common within ghostlore, the storyteller uses the family connection to add credibility to the story - this story not only happened to a close relative, but she also emphasises that the audience know the person she is talking about. Thus the storyteller also raises her own status through her relationship to her Auntie and through the fact that she is privy to these personal stories.

No.57

I know something, you know, the old workhouse, on Hallowe'en Night you see a big donkey's head rising from the grave, hanging from the lamppost, and whenever you walk down and turn the street, you hear a banshee and all, laughing and all.

Unidentified Male, aged c.12, Fountain Youth Club, Derry, N. Ireland, 2.3.94.

Notes

Here we have an example of a local ghost story. The storyteller is very confused about the content of the story and the result is a rather fragmentary performance. He seems, however, to make up for his lack of knowledge by weaving two strong traditional images into his narrative to give it added weight. The first, of course, is that he makes the story calendar-related, setting it on Hallowe'en Night, which is not only a traditional time for ghost activity according to British folklore, but also a traditional time for telling ghost stories.

In Irish folklore, it should be noted, Hallowe'en is more a time for fairy activity and it is interesting that the storyteller concludes his story with a reference to the banshee. The banshee is one of the most enduring images of Irish fairylore and is an anglicised version of the Irish 'Bean Si', meaning fairy woman. Traditionally, the banshee is a harbinger of death, continually wailing outside the house of a person who is about to die. There are many people in Ireland today who claim to have heard the banshee's chilling cry, for the banshee is a lamenting fairy, rather than a mocking one as is suggested by this story. See Briggs, 1976, pp.14-16.

No.58

There was a story in Derry...a ghost. That was down our road, there's like an abandoned warehouse, hospital. In the 1900s it was working and there was dead people there.

And these kids were playing around there on a football field and this nurse, a ghost nurse, just went up to them and touched them and they just ran and all.

It's meant to be really abandoned.

Andrew, aged c.14, Oakgrove Integrated College, Derry, N. Ireland, 2.3.94.

Notes

I suspect that this story is a variant of No.57. Although Andrew intially calls the haunted site a warehouse, he corrects himself and calls it a hospital. This suggests that he had indeed intended to describe it as a workhouse. Although workhouses were not hospitals by any stretch of the imagination, they were often inhabited by the poorest people who may have been made destitute through illness. This was certainly the case during the Irish Famine of 1845 when the workhouses became breeding grounds for disease amongst the starving peasantry.

Otherwise this story is quite different in content from No.57. I suspect that a number of different stories have grown up around this place and possibly a number of stories have been relocated to what seems to be a traditional ghost site.

No.59

They say in the graveyard there's this baby's grave and that, 'I'm not dead, I'm just sleeping.' And if you walk up it's supposed to say.....well, you know the two wee graves beside it? Well, I don't know what they say, but the lettering's supposed to change on Hallowe'en Night.

They say there's a Green Lady on Hallowe'en Night, there's a Green Lady and the two gravestones change.

Unidentified Male, aged c.12, Fountain Youth Club, Derry, N. Ireland, 2.3.94.

Notes

Another local ghost story, the graveyard in question being that of St. Columba's Cathedral in the centre of Derry. The Fountain is a working class loyalist enclave in the very heart of the republican part of the city and edges on to the cathedral grounds. Many of the stories told to me by the teenagers of the Fountain were centred around the cathedral. Interestingly, the storyteller hangs the story on the exact two same traditional images as in No.57. The story is said to take place on Hallowe'en Night and, although there is no mention of a banshee, the story is concluded with the appearance of a Green Lady. Green is traditonally the colour most associated with fairy dress in Ireland.

No.60

There used to be a chap on the top of Roche Rock and there was a hermit lived there, and one day the chap fell down and the Devil came along and pushed him off the edge - something like that.

If you stand on the edge you can see a witch on the bottom and the Devil on the side. You can see the faces in the rock.

Unidentified Male, aged c.13, Brannel School, St.Austell, Cornwall, 26.4.93.

Notes

Roche Rock is an imposing granite outcrop in the middle of the china clay villages of Mid-Cornwall. In Cornish folklore it is the place to which Jan Tregeagle (or Tregargle) was pursued by the Devil's hounds and so it is not surprising that it should feature prominently in the stories told today. Its association with the Devil seems to be as strong as it always was. On the summit of Roche Rock are the ruins of an early chapel.

No.61

It is said that an old hermit used to live up at the Devil's Edge.
One night his daughter brought his food up and they sat on the edge eating.
Suddenly there was a tremor and the old hermit fell off the edge. His daughter was so distraught that she jumped off and killed herself.
If you go up about one a.m., it is said that you can hear her screaming.

Unidentified Male, aged c.13, Brannel School, St.Austell, Cornwall, 26.4.93.

Notes

Another variant of the same story, this time without the presence of the Devil himself, but with a coda that brings the story into the present.

No.62

You know that hill in Sticklepath with all the rocks? That's haunted with the Devil, his hands. If you go and tread in his footsteps, his hands come and kill you, his hands come up the hill.

Elliot Stallion, aged c.12, Sparks Youth Club, Okehampton, Devon, 23.10.92.

The hill in question, just on the edge of the village of Sticklepath on the old A30 and about four miles east of Okehampton, is crowned with a flagpole and is said to be the site from where John Wesley preached a sermon when he visited the area. As with Roche Rock, here we have a site that has associations with both a holy mortal and the Devil.

No.63

One day these trekkers were trekking through Dartmoor with all their bags and stuff, one man and one lady, and they thought it was too late to set up their tent, so they went into one of those bunkers that the army used to use.

And in the middle of the night they heard these footsteps over the roof and then they heard it jump off and they actually heard a big thud on the floor. Then they looked out one of the windows and saw this big black dog about as big as a donkey roaming round outside the hut, and then when it saw them it came and took a big chunk out of the window and kept slashing away at it until it made a little tiny hole, and then it ran off.

And no one has ever seen it since.

Simon O'Dell, aged 13, Gillingham School, Dorset, 11.11.92.

Notes

Once more, this may well have been a story heard on school camp, but it presents a perfect blend of a contemporary context and traditional imagery. These days Dartmoor is a favourite place for hikers and army huts are to be found in many places inside the three military firing ranges. Black dogs, however, feature largely in local folklore and provided the inspiration for Conan Doyle's famous novel *The Hound of the Baskervilles*.

No.64

There used to be a railway line running past at the top and this man was meant to have got run over when he was working and a train rolled over him.

And people reckon they saw his ghost and a train going by it, really late at night.

We all went up there one night and he's meant to have one leg and three arms.

Jodie, aged c.14, Bugle Youth Club, Cornwall, 27.4.93.

Notes

In spite of being very short, this story is yet another example of a railway ghost, a common motif in ghostlore in general and teenage narrative in particular. The exaggeration in the last line unfortunately undermines the gravity of the rest of the story and renders it less credible.

No.65*

I've got this ghost book and I think it was during the building of the Queen Elizabeth, well the building of a boat, whatever boat it is, it showed a picture of the bow during the building of it and the air between the inside of it and the outside of it is like a tunnel going down and up.

There was actually someone stuck in there, someone got built into it and there was like an x-ray of the ship, like a cut-out of it. There's a little skeleton there in the corner like that. A tiny skeleton and every night thay say that they can hear the screaming of him, like the echoes down in the tunnels.

Mark Duff, aged 13, Lipson Community College, Plymouth, 5.11.92.

p.148

Notes

Here is a good example of how a story that has originated in printed form has captured the imagination of the storyteller, who has adopted it into his own oral repertoire. If anything, Mark is surprisingly honest about the story's origins.

No.66

(Summary)
There were these people building a boat and one of the builders disappeared. Then when the ship set sail on its maiden voyage, people kept hearing this hammering and tapping. Then the funnel blew up.

When they got back they took the ship apart and they found a skeleton inside.

There's a photograph of it; a tiny skeleton inside this huge ship.

Luke, aged c.12, Combe Dean School, Plymouth, 18.10.93.

Notes

Another variant of the same story, which shows that this particular narrative has captured the communal, as well as the individual imagination. The existence of more than one variant of the same story in different schools would suggest that this tale is now alive in the wider teenage repertoire.

No.67*

My friend, she's called Samantha Tucker, she doesn't live around here, she lives at Southway.

She was in the toilet and she looked in the mirror and she saw this lady, like a ghost, and she turned round and there was no one there, and she looked in the mirror again and there was still no one there, and she reported it to the teacher and the teacher didn't do nothing about it, 'cos she didn't believe her.

Unidentified female, age unknown, Ernesettle Library, Plymouth, 2.12.91.

p.71

Notes

Traditional elements in this otherwise modern memorate include the visibility of the supernatural in the mirror, that being a window to the supernatural world. In the teenage repertoire in general bathrooms and toilets are the site of many ghostly encounters.

No.68*

We went to Dartmoor for the weekend with the school.

We had this dormitory and it was the Devil's number, 666. And we had like a glass mirror and we were all brushing our hair and it wouldn't open. We were trying really hard to open the mirror and it wouldn't open.

So the week went by and we couldn't open it and on the way out the mirror opened.

Amy, aged 14, Lipson Community College, Plymouth, 5.11.92.

p.71

Notes

Another contemporary memorate with traditional elements contained therein. School camps are popular places for the telling of ghost stories and supernatural experiences, the more so, it would seem, when the camp takes place at locations such as Dartmoor with its traditional associations with such matter. Amy also incorporates the folklore surrounding the number 666 into her story. Once again we have the recurring motif of the mirror.

No.69*

This is a true story.

My dad, he used to work for the Council and there was this series of complaints from this house. The couple had moved in sort of five months before with this little boy. And this little boy kept saying that he had seen this boy in the house, in the loft, and this boy, he could hear talking in the loft. And every time his mum and dad went up to see their child, their boy was talking to somebody and they couldn't find who it was.

So they called my dad to see if there was a tape recorder or something, because they obviously didn't believe in ghosts. My dad checked all over the place, under the beds and stuff 'cos they thought it was a practical joke.

And one day their boy says, 'Can I invite David for tea?', and they said, 'Who's David?'

And the little boy goes, 'Oh, my best friend.'

And they go, 'Where does he live?'

Then the boy says, 'In the roof.'

So they started getting a bit suspicious.

So they called up my dad in the end to have a look in the roof and they looked in the roof and there's all these old books, ghost stories, all piled up. And this little boy had been getting ideas from all these ghost stories and making it all up.

And so, sort of a year or so later, he got some more of these phone calls, my dad did, and so he's getting really annoyed this time 'cos he knew it was this boy.

So he went up there and there was a shadow of this boy reading a book in the loft. Just a shadow. There was nobody, just a shadow on the wall.

Robert Morton, aged 12, Gillingham School, Dorset, 11.11.92.

p.158

Notes

This is a story full of detail and Robert stakes everything on the credibility of the tale. He begins with the statement that the story is true and indeed if we were to doubt the story, then we doubt Robert's own father. If, however, we believe the story, then Robert gains status via his relationship with his father. Robert is, therefore, playing a high-risk strategy with his status in terms of his performance.

No.70*

I was with my mum and dad 'cos they were seeing some friends and I went out with them 'cos my sister was out and - I was about eleven, so I couldn't look after myself, but it was getting late and my mum and dad and their friends and they were all drunk and telling ghost stories and I thought of all the stories and stuff and there's one where one of their friends said that he was reading in bed when a lady walked across the room a couple of feet off the ground and I thought nothing much but I had to sleep in their bed and that 'cos it was late and I fell asleep and just woke straight up and a lady walked across the room and she was a couple of feet off the ground and she, like, came from the wardrobe and she went right through the window, and that's it.

And I reckon it was true. It was up Mount Gould Road.

Dillon, aged 13, Lipson Community College, Plymouth, 13.11.92.

p.158

Notes

In this story Dillon's position is less high-risk. Although he tells the story as true and wants us to believe it, he also seems to admit to his own fallibility. He only believes it to be true, but of course he may have been dreaming all along. Therefore, he risks very little by adopting this neutral stance and leaves the question of credibility entirely to the audience.

No.71*

Now, this is a hundred per cent true and I'm not lying you.

It was in Liskeard and they had a park. I can't remember ...... I was walking along the park with some friends saying, 'I'm the champion', and we got off the swing - we went onto the swings and we started swinging, got bored and just left.

We were half-way across the field and we always looked back and we looked back and there was a little girl on the swings and we thought, 'Oh, we haven't seen her before.'

And so we carried on walking and when we looked back again - it was about.... quite a long walk or even a long run to get to any, like, bush or anything, it was sort of put in the middle of a big field - and when we looked behind again, there was no one there and the swing just, like, began to stop swinging and we don't know where she could have gone to, it was all flat, like.

Simon Harris, aged 13, Lipson Community College, Plymouth, 13.11.92.

p.158

Notes

Here we have a personal memorate and Simon adopts a high-risk strategy. He lets us know from the outset, in no uncertain terms, that the story is absolutely true, and since the story is about himself, then the narrative's credibility is inextricably linked with his own.

No.72*

One day when my step-mum was about ten or eleven, she went on this ouija board and spirits said that she would die on 30 December, on her birthday. Instead of her dying, her gran did.

Daniel, aged 13, St. Stephen's Youth Club, St. Austell, 26.4.93.

pp.152-3, 154

No.73

Well, my grandad was going across this graveyard and we know he saw something, something out of the ordinary, 'cos he suddenly went to a phone box and called the police.
　　The police went there, but they didn't find out what it was and he said he'd do an interview in the morning. But an hour before the interview, he died.

Paul Harding, aged c.13, Sir James Smith's School, Camelford, 25.1.95.

Notes

The 'we' Paul refers to in the first sentence is the most important word in the whole story, because it refers to his family and it suggests that it is one of the most popular and oft-told tales in his family's repertoire. It is also part of Paul's personal repertoire of stories and he tells it as a true story, staking his and his family's status on the credibility of the tale. Paul later told me that his family believed that his grandfather had seen Death.

No.74

My Great Grandma, she always tells me the story of my Great Great Great Grandad. He fought in the war. When they had the first tanks out, you know the ones with the silly wheels on them and that. One, they reckoned, was haunted.

And he was going up this steep hill with his tank and it stopped dead and a figure was sat next to him, putting rivets in the side of it and I think it was for twelve days this ghost was, like, stood by the side putting rivets in it, as if he was trying to build it, but it was already built.

When they told them, the (..??..) was shot. For lies. They reckon.

Gary, aged c.13, Sir James Smith's School, Camelford, 25.1.95.

Notes

It would seem that Gary has got a little carried away with the generations in this story. It would appear that this is a story about the First World War and so we should assume that he is really refering to his great grandfather or, perhaps, his great great grandfather. It is, however, interesting that many family stories concern a grandparent's wartime adventures and that these sit easily within the teenage repertoire.

No.75

There was this woman, right, and she used to live in Pakistan and she had this child named Natala.

And one day, at night time, she forgot that she didn't have any milk and she told the child to get milk. So on the way there, right, he went through the snicket and he didn't know there was a right long wooden stick, right, and behind it there was a ghost. And he didn't know, but when he was walking through the snicket, he could feel that something quite hard touching him and squeezing him and he could feel it and he could just remember that his mum had said that if anyone's behind you, just run it.

So he was running, but he could see that someone was picking him up and hurting him and squeezing him really hard, and like he's doing piggy-back to someone and he went to….eventually he got to the shop and he told the man that, 'Oh, there's somebody behind me and it's a ghost. I think it's a ghost. It's really hurting me right a lot.'

And then he found out that it's that ghost and he got sort of a bottle and in the bottle, right, there was this medicine that he could spray and it disappears for a minute or so.

So he did that and then he told the child that, 'Where do you live?'

And, 'Sir, I live in a street just round the corner.'

And so he took him there, but the ghost eventually found out that he was down there. And the ghost went down there. And the ghost went down there and touched the boy again. And he could feel it really hard, stinging him and he was doing a piggy-back to him, right. And then he stinged him again and the spray all over his back and he disappeared.

So the boy went over to somebody...something else, right, and his dad was there and people were there. So they killed the ghost and the ghost killed...and he wrote a story about it and told my cousin's brother and my cousin's brother told us.

Nadia, aged c.12, Priestman Middle School, Bradford, 24.11.93.

Notes

Nadia's school has a very large multicultural mix and Nadia's first language is not English, which would explain a lack of clarity in parts of the story. However, Nadia told the story with confidence and with a very clear sense of the whole narrative. Although the story is part of a non-Western tradition, this story demonstrates that ghost stories also play an important rôle in the teenage repertoire in Pakistan and that those stories are also circulated by friends. In Nadia's case the extended family of which she is part also enables the trading of stories between family members of the same generation.

No.76*

Right, once there was this man and (he) had an argument with his wife and he ran off. And he went to this bridge and jumped off into the water and he tried swimming and that but he couldn't keep up 'cos of the current and he went under and he died.

And then the police were searching for him for three days, then they couldn't find him and then after three days he turned up on one of the river banks and he was all wrinkly and everything. And then that's it.

Gary Moore, aged 13, Lipson Community College, Plymouth, 13.11.92.

p.70

246

No.77

(Summary)
There was a tinker in the thirteenth century who went around selling bone-handled cutlery, which he made from rabbit bones. (The storyteller actually said he was a tailor, but I presume he meant tinker.)

At one village, at Christmas time, he sold all his cutlery and, in fact, is a set short.

(There is some suggestion that he always visits this village at this time of year to sell his cutlery.)

He promises to make a new set for this old woman, but he is unable to get any more rabbit bones. In the end he resorts to digging up a body from the local graveyard and using the bones to make the knives and forks. He delivers the cutlery and the old woman is very pleased.

However, it transpires that the body he has used to make the cutlery is the body of the woman's dead husband. When the woman sits down to her meal, she sees the ghost of her husband sitting at the table.

(At this point the storyteller lost his thread and the narrative became very confused, but the storyteller did explain that the story ended with a 'jump'.)

Unidentified Male, aged c.12, King Edward VI School, Totnes, 7.12.93.

Notes

Although the storyteller was unable to complete the story, up till that point the narrative was told in great detail. It is highly traditional in its motifs and has strong echoes of 'The Golden Arm' whereby a ghost returns to avenge the theft of a part of the body, ending with a 'jump', and also of 'The Singing Bone', which tells of the bones of a corpse being fashioned into a practical utensil. I have not come across any other knowledge of this story.

No.78

He raped some woman, I think. The King, he sent him into exile or something.

And he rode out into the sea - when the King was going from somewhere - into the sea and begged for his pardon, got the pardon, and away back with the horse.

And when he got back on the shore, this old woman was saying that, 'The horse will be the death of you.' There and then he chopped the horsehead off.

A year later he's going along the beach and he tripped over and cut himself on the bone.

And he died of blood poisoning.

Smiley, aged c.16, Sheerness Youth Club, Isle of Sheppey, Kent, 6.7.94.

Notes

There are some communities where a particular local legend is still known and told by everybody who has been brought up in that community. These stories often find expression in the teenage context. In Okehampton, the story of Lady Howard who haunts the castle and the road between Okehampton and Tavistock is universally known. In fact, I was told by one group of teenagers that there was a man in the village of Bridestowe who had Lady Howard on video, although nobody was able to say who this man was! The story of Robert de Shurland, above, is likewise known by all who have been brought up on the Isle of Sheppey. In fact, the ruins of Shurland Hall can still be seen today.

No.79*

I read it in this magazine and it had this separate thing about these children doing and saying things that they didn't know anything about, and it had one where there was this little boy and he was in this car and they went past this graveyard and he pointed out the window and said, 'Look, Mummy, there's that place you buried me the first time!'

Tammy, age unknown, Ernesettle Library, Plymouth, 2.12.91.

p.94

Notes

An example of a story that has entered the repertoire from a written source, this time a magazine. Although strictly speaking it is a reincarnation story rather than a ghost story, teenagers themselves would certainly describe it as a ghost story.

No.80*

Right, this is what my friend told me. He said that if you've got a post and you've got your partner the other side and you just link on to them and you just turn round and you say 'Black Jack' forty times, they say after you come home from school you've got a spirit called Black Jack following you and they say that he goes like that (storyteller squeezes shoulder), and then they say you look back and there's nothing there.

Nicola Allen, aged c.12, Ernesettle Library, Plymouth, 2.12.91.

p.9

Notes

This is a variant of a commonly-held superstition amongst teenagers. Sometimes they are carried out as a dare, very much like the legend trip, as described by Bill Ellis (see Ellis, 1982) and involve a large amount of ritual participation. Although most teenagers, I have found, will view such beliefs with disdain, many will show a marked reluctance to tempt fate.

No.81

You crack a mirror, turn the lights out and say 'Bloody Mary' a hundred times, turn them back on and you see the future in the actual mirror.

Unidentified Male, aged c.12, Sparks Youth Club, Okehampton, Devon, 23.10.92.

Notes

A similar superstition to No.80, except that Bloody Mary is a character who appears in a number of guises throughout folklore. As well as Bloody Mary, she is sometimes known as Mary Worth, Mary Whales, Mary Jane, Mary

Worthington, etc. and she is also probably related to Typhoid Mary and Aids Mary, characters who knowingly and deliberately pass on the disease as an act of revenge on the world. In particular see Brunvand, 1986, pp.80-2, Brunvand, 1989, pp.195-202, Langlois, 1980 and McCoy Ray, 1976.

No.82

You all hold hands with your little fingers and go round in a circle saying, 'Bloody Mary, I killed your child,' three times and look at a curtain. You should see a figure of somebody.

Dave, aged 11, Dyron's Leisure Centre, Newton Abbot, Devon, 3.8.93.

Notes

Another variant of the Bloody Mary superstition.

No.83*

My Auntie Jan put the poodle in the microwave and cooked it.

Anne-Marie Emond, aged 10, Ernesettle Library, Plymouth, 11.11.91.

pp.101, 142-3, 146-7, 157-8

No.84*

My uncle's friend, his cat usually sleeps in the washing, so he picked up the washing and the cat was in it, and the cat was going round in the washing machine and died.

Lee Woodward, aged 11, Ernesettle Library, Plymouth, 11.11.91.

p.101

Notes

This story is most likely a variant of 'The Poodle in the Microwave', although putting the cat in the washing machine is more believable and so this story could be a personal story.

No.85*

When I was about two, my sister put one of my cats in the washing machine and, after it came out, it was all fluffed up and bubbles coming out of its mouth.

Sean Parry, aged 11, Plymstock Comprehensive School, Plymouth, 3.11.92.

p.101

Notes

This variant is perhaps slightly less believable. It is told as a comic tale and it is hard to imagine a cat surviving in a washing machine, never mind it having bubbles coming out of its mouth!

No.86

This woman went on holiday, she got bitten on the arm and it came up in a massive boil and when she went in the bath, it popped and this large spider and its babies crawled out.

Amy Prestwick, aged 14, Lydford Youth Club, Devon, 16.11.92.

Notes

A well-documented contemporary legend. See especially Brunvand, 1986, p.76.

No.87

There was this man and underneath his eye it kept itching and itching, it was really itching. Just before he itched it raw, he went to the doctor's and just as he was about to lift the skin off, a cockroach crawled out of his nose.

Amy Prestwick, aged 14, Lydford Youth Club, Devon, 16.11.92.

Notes

This story, told by the same storyteller as No.86, is probably a variant of the same story, although it also has echoes of another well-documented contemporary legend which tells of an animal infestation of a woman's beehive hair-do. Certainly the telling of the first story reminded the teller of the second.

No.88

There's this woman and she goes to Marks and Spencers and buys this tropical plant that's been imported. She takes it back to her house and it dies.

So she takes it back to the shop and they find a half-eaten spider on there and it's a black widow, and wherever you find a half-eaten black widow spider, it means there's another one.

So she had to have her house evacuated, searched, and they looked everywhere for it, and they found it in her bed covers with all its babies.

Amy Prestwick, aged 14, Lydford Youth Club, Devon, 16.11.92.

Notes

Amy did in fact name the person in her village to whom this is supposed to have happened. It is, however, another contemporary legend usually known as 'The Spider in the Yucca' (see Brunvand, 1986, pp.83-4).

No.89

It's all about this woman and she has a tea party and she has fifty people and she has this massive casserole to make and she goes upstairs to get dressed and she comes downstairs and she finds this cat and it's got its head and paws and that and it's eating it.

So she just picks up the cat and puts him down and she just stirs round the casserole cos she doesn't have time and she puts it down.

And all her guests come and they all eat it and she goes outside to get a breath of air and in her drive there's the cat, and he's dead. And she realizes that the casserole must be poisoned.

So she goes to her dinner party guests and says, 'I'm sorry, but I've poisoned you all.'

So they all went down to the hospital and they all had their stomachs pumped like that.

And the next morning there was a knock at the door and these two people came and said, 'We're sorry, but we ran over your cat last night.'

Dean Stanley, aged c.13, Gillingham School, Dorset, 11.11.92.

Notes

Another contemporary legend documented in Brunvand, 1981. pp.111-12. This is a particularly full and well-told version of the story.

No.90

There was this woman and she got home from work and she had a dog, a doberman, and when she got home it was choking.

So she was a bit concerned, so she took the dog to the vet.

Well, the vet said, 'You'll have to leave the dog here for a couple of days for observations.'

So she left the dog there and went home.

When she got home the phone was ringing. So she answered it and the vet said, 'Get out of the house immediately.'

The police came round and were searching the house and in her wardrobe was this man with his three fingers missing. The dog had bitten the fingers off the man and was choking on the fingers.

Karen Young, aged 13, Gillingham School, Dorset, 11.11.92.

Notes

'The Choking Doberman' is the title of the contemporary legend which lend its name to Brunvand, 1984. It is probably a story that is related to a much older folktale (see Simpson, 1981). Karen's version of the story conforms to most other collected variants from both teenage and non-teenage sources.

No.91

This is about my cousin.

My cousin went with his friends into Kentucky and had a two-piece meal each and everyone was o.k. apart from this girl and her last bit, the biggest bit, and she bit into it and a load of pus went onto my cousin's face.

That's it.

Jodie, aged c.13, Lipson Community College, Plymouth, 5.11.92.

Notes

Bizarre food contaminations are a common subject matter in contemporary legends and is also a recurrent motif in a variety of other traditional narratives. Other variants of this story often refer to a 'Kentucky Fried Rat' and stories of this kind seem to reflect our distrust of fast food. It might be seen as a cautionary tale. See Brunvand, 1981, pp.81-4.

No.92

She heard that when someone bit into a Big Mac, there was a mouse in there and he bit half the mouse off. Or something. And there was another half in there. Oh God!

Unidentified Female, aged c.14, Cinderford Youth Club, Gloucestershire, 3.95.

Notes

Another variant of the 'Kentucky Fried Rat', this time refering to another well-known fast-food chain. The storyteller here seems a little unsure of the facts, but she certainly believes the story to be true and sums up her own horror with the words 'Oh God'. In this sense it becomes unimportant whether or not she is able to furnish the story with lots of detail, as long as the right effect is achieved. Her lack of knowledge of the details gives the story an air of reportage and so increases its credibility.

No.93*

It's called Tom Tit Tot.

Once upon a time there was a girl and she lived in the north woodlands and she lived with her dad. Her dad was a poor farmworker and one day the king was riding past the cottage. He was looking for a prospective girlfriend at that minute and he was riding past their cottage. The old man came out of the cottage and bowed to the king touching his forelock and that kind of thing and the king said, 'Have you got a daughter?'

The man said, 'Yes, I've got a daughter.'

And he said, 'Ah, well bring her to me then.'

The man brought out his daughter, he said, 'Come on, come on, Elsie, come out. The king's here.' She came out and she curtsied, fluttered her eyelashes, and the king said, 'Well, what are your assets then, girl?'

And before the girl could speak, the old man said, 'Well, she can spin gold.'

And the king said, 'Well, o.k. then, if you say so.'

And the man said, 'No, really she can.' But she couldn't really.

But the king took her anyway to his castles, put her into a room where there was just a little stool and a spinning wheel and some wool. The old man - the old king - said, 'Right, you spin some gold for me and I'll marry you.'

And the girl said, 'But, but...'

And the king said, 'Oh, get on with it, girl,' and left.

Now the girl was that bad she began to cry. 'Oh dear, what shall I do? What shall I do? He said if I don't spin all this gold, he'll cut my head off.'

A few minutes later a little dwarf appears, more like a green imp kind of thing and he said, 'I'll help you.'

The girl said, 'Oh will you? What can you do then?'

He said, 'Well, I'll turn it into gold, but...'

She said, 'What?'

255

And he said, 'Oh, don't worry about it.' He sits down and spins all the cotton into gold.

Next day, the king came in and said, 'I've brought you some breakfast and another piece of cotton wool, so you can spin me some more gold.'

'Oh dear, what shall I do now?'

And later on the little nymph thing appeared again and he said, 'I'll spin that gold for you, but only this time, when you're married to the king, your first-born child you shall give to me.'

The girl thought, 'Oh well, I'll just say yes now and cross that bridge when we come to it.' Well, the little nymph spins the gold and the king marries the girl.

A year later the girl's had her baby, her first baby, and she's a little girl. She's sat in a room with her little baby and the little nymph appears and says, 'Aye, that child's mine that is,' and takes it out of the cot and runs.

And the girl thinks, 'Oh, what shall I do? What shall I do?' He keeps running, the little animal runs away and the girl's stuck there.

She thinks, 'What shall I do? What shall I say to the king?'

Now the king doesn't know anything about what really happened, but a few weeks later the little nymph appears again after the girl had been crying bitterly for weeks and weeks and he says, 'Now, I'll give you back your child, but only if you can guess my name.'

And she says, 'Well, is it Bathuzalum?'

And he says, 'No, that's not my name.'

And the girl says, 'Well, is it Paul?'

And he says, 'No, it ain't.'

She says, 'Right, is it Phillip?'

'No, it ain't.'

He says, 'Well, you've had your three guesses today and I'll come back for another week and mind you've guessed my name by then else I'll keep the child, but if you get it right, then you'll have the child back.'

And the girl thinks, 'Oh, there can't be that many names.'

He says, 'Well, mind you, you've only got three guesses each day.'

The next day the man came along again, the little nymph, and said, 'Well, have you got my name?'

She says, 'Well, is it Bandon?'

He says, 'No, it ain't.'

'Is it Phillip? No! I've had that one before! Is it Andrew?'

'No, it ain't.'

'Is it Carl?'

'No, it ain't. That's your three guesses today.'

Now this carried on for five days and on the fifth day the girl decides she can't think of any more names so she sends out a little messenger and the messenger is roaming the countryside looking for strange names. When he's found three names and he sits in a tree resting for a while and down below the tree he sees a strange sight - a little green nymph dancing about, saying:

'Nimmy, nimmy, not,
My name's Tom Tit Tot.
Nimmy, nimmy, not,
My name's Tom Tit Tot.'

Now the messenger boy thinks, 'Ah! That's a strange name. I must remember that one and tell the queen when I see her.'

So he goes back to the castle and tells the queen. He tells her the story of what happened. Now from the description the queen guesses that that must be the name of the little animal who's taken her child away.

So when he came that day, he says, 'Have you got my name?'

'Oh, I don't know. Is it Paul?'

He says, 'No, it ain't.'

'Is it Mark?'

'No, it ain't. You've only got one guess left and you're not going to get it.'

She says:

'Nimmy, nimmy, not,
Your name's Tom Tit Tot.'

He says, 'Aaagh,' and stamps his little feet and jumps up and down and he says, 'Well you've guessed my name, so you can have your child back.'

And she took the child back and the king came and they lived happily ever after. The little nymph ran away jumping up and down.

That's a nice one!

Eva Shannon, aged 13, Lipson Community College, Plymouth, 13.11.92.

pp.6, 184

Notes

This is a highly skilled performance of a traditional tale, which is listed as 'Tale Type 500 - the name of the helper' (Aarne and Thompson, 1961). Other well-known variants include 'Rumpelstilzchen' (Grimm, 1992, pp.209-11) and 'Whuppity Stoorie' (Briggs, 1970, A.I. pp.567-9).

Eva told me that she had heard the story from her grandmother in Liverpool and it is probable that she was imitating the way that her grandmother had told the story. Certainly her grandmother's influence was obvious in her telling, as she adopted a 'northern' accent for those parts of the story in direct speech. Her metacommunicative indicator that announces the ending of the story ('That's a nice one!') not only concludes the story very neatly, but it is also a device that effectively lowers her own status at the end of the performance. She is in fact diverting any praise for her performance onto the story itself.

No.94*

There was a king who, when he got old, had no children to leave his kingdom to. He went to the wizard and said that he wanted to have a baby. He told the wizard that he was going to adopt a baby. The wizard told him that wouldn't work because it won't be your child. 'In which case,' the king said, 'you must make me younger so I can marry and have children.'

The wizard then told him, 'You must find the dragon with the red horn and bring back a hair from his head. This I will make into a potion, which will make you young again.'

Off the king went, looking for the dragon. Along the way he came to a village. All the villagers were standing around a huge tree which was looking very ill. 'What's the matter?' asked the king and the villagers told him that all the food they needed came from this tree, but for some reason it was dying. The king told them that he would find out what was doing this when he found the dragon.

The king travelled on and came across a dragon lair. It was dark by this time, but the king decided that if it was the wrong dragon, he would just have to ride out again. Inside the cave he found a dragon's maid who looked after the dragon. 'Don't come in here or the dragon will eat you,' she said.

The king then explained that he needed a hair from the dragon's head to make him young again. The maid smiled and said that she knew the wizard that had sent him and that she would help. She would get a hair for the king that evening. The king had to go down the road to an old deserted mine and find a lump of gold to give the maid for her help.

When the king returned from the mine, the dragon heard his footsteps and ran out of the cave. The king hid and managed to speak again to the maid. 'Please ask the dragon why the tree in the village is dying.'

When the dragon returned, the maid started to comb his hair. 'Dragon, why has the tree in the village started to die?'

'As it gnaws at the roots, so the tree dies. Kill the rat and the tree will grow again.'

When the dragon had fallen asleep, the maid came out and gave the hair to the king. She also told him about the rat in the tree. The king went on his way, but stopped when he came to the village and told them about the rat. They were so grateful they gave the king a huge load of gold.

When the king got home, the wizard said that the hair came from the wrong dragon.

Away the king went and came to another village. All the villagers were standing on the banks of the river, which was frozen solid.

'What's the matter?' asked the king. They told him that all they ate came from the pond and river and now that it was frozen, they would starve.

'Never mind,' said the king, 'I will find out the answer from the dragon when I find him.'

The king travelled on and came across another dragon's lair. This time he waited until morning to see what colour the dragon was. When the dragon left, the king entered the lair, but was caught by the dragon's maid. The king explained why he was there and this maid also said that, as she knew the wizard, she would help. This would also cost him a lump of gold, which he found in an abandoned mine. The king also asked the maid to ask the dragon why the river had frozen in the village.

That evening when the dragon returned, the maid waited until she was brushing his hair to ask about the river in the village.

'Oh, that!' said the dragon. 'That is because the ice frog is sitting on a lily pad in the middle of the pond and has frozen the pond and the river.'

When he was asleep the maid brought the hair to the king and told him about the ice frog. The king thanked her and left.

When he reached the village, he told the villagers about the ice frog. They also thanked him with a gift of gold.

As he left the village the king came across a detour, so down he went. At the end of the road he found a river, and on the river a raft with a very sad-looking riverman standing on it.

'What is wrong?' asked the king.

'I have been here for fifty years and will stay here, not dying, until someone takes my pole from me.' When the king heard this he thought he knew just the man for the job.

When the king got home he found the man called Flag; he knew that Flag would try to kill any child he might have by asking the matron to strangle it at birth. The king told him, 'Look, I found loads of gold.'

'Where did you find it?' demanded Flag.

'I found it on the other side of the river, but when you go, ask the river boatman for his pole, because he is so slow, and it will take ages to get across. He has been known to fall asleep.'

Flag ran off and when he got to the river, he snatched the pole from the riverman. The riverman jumped for joy and ran away and Flag began his long stay on the raft.

The king was young again by the wizard and married a beautiful princess and they had a beautiful baby. The end.

Alan, aged 13, Brannel School, St. Austell, 29.4.93.

p.6

Notes

A version of this well-known folktale appears in Grimm as 'The Devil with the Three Golden Hairs' (Grimm, 1992, pp.109-117) and can be found in many other folktale collections. Alan's telling of the story was a monumental effort and earned him a spontaneous round of applause upon completion.

No.95*

O.K. My name is Dean Taylor, Sir, and I've come from up Northlands. The story I told was about being up North and all the streets were dirty and all that 'cos of all the pits, all the coal dust. It would get all the washing dirty and all that. We couldn't go swimming on the beaches 'cos of all the coal making it dirty and all that.

The strike up there....we had no money. My dad works down the pit and when the strike was on we had no money and we had to eat tomato ketchup soup. 'Cos nobody had no money.

So that's all I've got to say.

Dean Taylor, aged 14, Audley Park Secondary School, Torquay, 4.2.92.

pp.138-9, 142, 145-6, 158

No.96*

It's the first day of school camp and we were all picked to go in our tents and it was me, Anthony and three other boys; Shane, Craig and Jamie.

260

I was sitting on my bed eating our packed lunches and I put my drink beside my bed. My bed was beside Shane's, we had about a foot gap between us. I put my drink down, I saw this rat - it was under my bed and it had blood coming out of its eye and it had a cut down at the side and I said, 'There's a rat under your bed', and Shane goes, 'Yeh, I believe you.'

I go, 'Go on, have a look', so he looks round.

He goes, 'Ugh, rat', and Jamie goes, 'Let's have a look', and he runs out, saying we've got a dead rat in our tent. Everyone was coming round looking in our tent. When I came out with the rat, Shane was going, 'I killed it!' When I brought it out, they all run away because they were afraid of it. I brought it out in some loo roll and chucked it over the hedge.

The last night we were there, we had all been to Padstow and Jamie had bought a big lolly and he left it in his bag because he was going to take it home for a present for someone.

I was in bed and I couldn't sleep and everybody else was asleep and I was just looking at the end of the tent and there was this little bit of light come in the tent and I was watching it. There was a half circle in black with a little tail sticking out and it came straight for me, so I picked up a welly and threw it at it.

I go, 'Jamie, Jamie, wake up, there's a rat here.' I was looking under my bed to see if it was there, and we had plastic groundsheets to keep our clothes dry and it was going under one of them.

In the end I think it ran away or something because we didn't know where it was. We went back to sleep and in the morning Jamie got up and all his clothes were wet and the lolly was wet as well.

Unidentified Male, aged c.13, Brannel School, St. Austell, 30.4.93.

pp.144, 147-8, 148-9, 152

No.97*

I bought this giant bag of gobstoppers and I was giving them all around. Everybody was having one. Then it was time for us to go to sleep.

I woke everybody up at about one o' clock in the morning and handed out more gobstoppers in our tent and Jamie says, 'What?'

I said, 'Have a gobstopper.' So he puts it in his mouth and goes to sleep, then I give one to everybody.

When they're all asleep and about three o' clock or so I give out more and there's Craig still asleep, snoring with his mouth open, so I drop one in.

By the third time everyone was getting pissed off. Jamie said, 'Get lost', Shane was swearing his head off, Craig was still sleeping. Then I go back to sleep.

Just before it was morning, I was just about to give out the next lot and Shane gets out and says, 'If you give me another gobstopper, I'm going to kick your head in.'

Unidentified Male, aged c.13, Brannel School, St. Austell, 30.4.93.

pp.144, 147-8, 149-51, 152

No.98*

We were in a tent and we were all talking about stuff and we were doing wrestling and I picked up a welly and threw it at Anthony (Copper) and it fell on Shane's bed cover and it had all clothes laid out on it and they all went everywhere and Copper fell off and he picks up the welly boot and throws it back to me. I duck and it hits Jamie smack on the gob.

Craig, aged c.13, Brannel School, St. Austell, 30.4.93.

pp.144, 147-8, 151, 152

No.99*

I call this one 'The Legend of Copper'. This was why we named him Copper.

Simple reason was, when we was on school camp, we all had our beds a foot apart and we had our sheets, but Anthony was laid on his bed. His leg was a bit funny, so we kept racking it up and collapsing the bed and he started to cry a little bit because we kept scatting up his bed. Someone broke the spring by jumping on it. He sat on the bed and he went straight to the ground. We had scat up his bed completely.

So then he goes out and says, 'I'm going to go and play with an electric fence.' He conducts electricity, so we call him Copper.

Unidentified Male, aged c.13, Brannel School, St. Austell, 30.4.93.

pp.144, 147-8, 151-2

No.100

There was this boy and his mum asked him what he would like for his first birthday and he said, 'A little yellow ping-pong ball.'

And then on his second birthday, she asked him what he wanted for his birthday and he said, 'A little yellow ping-pong ball.'

And it went all along the way like that and each year she asked him and he said, 'A little yellow ping-pong ball.'

And she kept buying them, all the little yellow ping-pong balls.

Then when he was a hundred, he was in hospital, and she said, 'What do you want for your birthday?' And he said, 'A little yellow ping-pong ball.' So she bought him one.

Then she said to him, 'Why do you keep wanting all these little yellow ping-pong balls?' And he went, 'Urrgh!', and he was dead.

Katie, aged 12, Fitzharrys School, Abingdon, Oxon, 21.11.91.

Notes

This is an example of what is commonly known as a shaggy-dog story. Shaggy-dog stories are usually defined as jocular tales that go on for a long time, with much use of repetition, and with a punchline that is so weak as to produce a groan from the audience or an ending, such as this one, which renders the whole build-up quite pointless. Such stories are widely evident in the teenage repertoire, although I have been unable to collect many, since most collecting has been done under a pressure of time that has made the telling of shaggy-dog stories impossible. Katie's story is clearly a shortened version of what could be a much, much longer performance.

Clearly there is much satisfaction to be had by the performer in duping the audience into listening for so long to a pointless story and, although the audience rarely laughs at the punchline, they will usually join in the laughter at their own expense. The storyteller is, in effect, playing a practical joke on his/her audience.

No.101*

Two legs sat upon three legs,
With four legs standing by,
Four then drawn by five,

263

Read me a riddle you can't,
However hard you try.
Somebody sat on a milking stool, milking a cow.

Andrew Norris, aged 11, Braunton School, N. Devon, 6.7.91.

pp.164, 171, 175

See Taylor, 1977, Nos 55, 976-9, Bryant, 1994, No. 94 and Opie & Opie, 1959, p.76.

Note: References to Taylor and Bryant in the riddles section of this archive refer not to page numbers but to the archival numbers assigned to particular riddles in those collections. For example, Bryant's variant on Andrew's riddle above will not be found on p.94, but is No.94 in Bryant's collection. References to Opie & Opie, however, are to page numbers.

No.102*

One day there was this two legs sat on a three legs and [with] the two legs was a one leg. In came a four legs and took the one leg and the one leg was taken away. The two legs went after the four legs and the two legs and the four legs and the one leg was never seen again. What were they?
A butcher, sitting on a stool with a leg of lamb, when in comes a dog.

Clare Wise, aged 12, Fitzharrys School, Abingdon, 21.11.91.

p.164

Notes

A variant of No.101, but this time told as a straight narrative.

No.103

Two Legs sat on Three Legs eating One Leg, when Four Legs took it away.

264

A person sat on a stool eating a leg of meat when it was stolen by a dog.

Keiran, aged c.12, Sir James Smith's School, Camelford, 15.2.95.

Notes

This variant seems to be incomplete and yet still works as a riddle in its own right. This illustrates that even short pieces of verbal expression such as riddles are not learned as fixed, but fluid text with significant variation.

No.104*

What has four legs, then two legs, then three legs?
A person.

Unidentified male, aged c.12, King Edward VI School, Totnes, 7.12.93.

p.176

Notes

This is a well-known riddle, a variant of which was asked by the Sphinx according to Greek Mythology. It was Oedipus who was able to give the correct answer. See Taylor, 1977, No. 46, Bryant, 1994, No. 1135 and Opie & Opie, 1959, p.76.

No.105*

It comes and comes, but never comes.
Tomorrow

Unidentified female, aged c.14, Estover School, Plymouth, 5.3.91.

p.171

Notes

See also Taylor, 1977, No. 97 and Bryant, 1994, No. 69.

No.106*

Ninny nanny netticoat,
In a white petticoat,
The longer I stand,
The shorter I get.
A candle

Unidentified male, aged c.13, Gillingham School, Dorset, 11.11.92.

pp.177-8

Notes

See also Taylor, 1977, Nos 607-31, Bryant, 1994, No. 950 and Opie & Opie, 1959, p.77

No.107

The more you feed it, the bigger it gets.
Fire

Unidentified Female, aged c.12, Paignton Community College, Devon, 10.11.94.

Notes

This has the sense of being a half-remembered fragment of a longer, possibly rhyming riddle and Bryant gives two fuller versions. See Bryant, 1994, Nos 34, 87.

No.108

What has a back, a spine and contains the world?
An atlas

Unidentified Female, aged c.12, St. Martin de Porres National School, Tallaght, Dublin, 23.11.94.

Notes

Bryant, 1994, Nos 101 and 524 are not dissimilar to this descriptive riddle, although they give the answer less specifically as 'a book'.

No.109

When you take off my skin, I make you cry.
An onion

Unidentified Female, aged c.11, Scoilmhuire, Ballyboden, Dublin, 24.11.94.

Notes

Bryant, 1994, Nos 541 and 887 provide fuller, more lyrical riddles which incorporate the same imagery of crying whilst harming the onion.

No.110

What's full of holes and holds water?
A sponge

Unidentified Male, aged c.12, St. Brecan's Secondary School, Derry, N. Ireland, 9.6.95.

Notes

This the kind of riddle that the Opies described as 'true riddles' in that the question consists of two parts, the second seemingly contradicting the first. The two parts are then reconciled by the answer. See Opie & Opie, 195, p.74 for a variant of this riddle and pp.74-6 for a wider discussion and further examples of 'true riddles'. Also see Bryant, 1994, No. 137.

No.111

It can be false, but can't be true.
It can be filled, but never emptied.
A tooth

Unidentified Male, aged c.12, Scoil Oilbhear, Ballyvolane, Cork, 2.6.95.

Notes

The references here to filled and false teeth seem to suggest that this is a modern riddle, although the contradictory structures are highly traditional.

No.112

When it's open, it's closed.
When it's closed, it's open.
A level crossing

Unidentified Male, aged c.13, Faughan Valley Secondary School, Derry, N. Ireland, 6.6.95.

Notes

This is another riddle that would seem to be relatively modern because of its subject matter, but again the structure and contradictory devices are traditional.

No.113

What has roots that nobody sees,
Is taller than trees,
Up, up it goes,
And yet never grows?
A mountain

Unidentified Male, aged c.14, Sir James Smith's School, Camelford,
1.3.95.

Notes

I have heard variations on this riddle many times, although this rhyming
variant is certainly the most satisfying. It appears in Bryant, 1994, No.1350,
where it is attributed to J.R.R. Tolkein who included many riddles in his novel
The Hobbit (1937). It is unclear whether Tolkein invented the riddles himself
or drew on existing oral tradition. Other riddles from *The Hobbit* which have
found their way into the teenage repertoire include the following riddle
collected from an eleven year old boy from Upottery Primary School in
Devon (4.10.93):

A box without hinges, key nor lid
Inside which golden treasure is hid.
An egg

Bryant attributes the riddle to Tolkein (Bryant, 1994, No.1354), although
similar riddles can be found in Taylor, 1977, Nos 1132-9 and Opie & Opie,
1959, p.77.

No.114*

Patches and patches,
Without any stitches.
Answer my riddle,
And I'll give you my breeches.
Cabbage patch

Unidentified female, aged c.12, Audley Park Secondary School, Torquay, 14.5.92.

p.170

Notes

See Taylor, 1977, No.1438, Bryant, 1994, No.111 and Opie & Opie, 1959, p.77.

No.115*

There was a girl in our town,
Silk an' satin was her gown,
Silk an' satin, gold an' velvet,
Guess her name, three times I've told it.
Anne

Andrew Smith, aged 10, Glusburn C P School, W. Yorkshire, 10.10.91.

p.171

Notes

Riddles such as these whereby the answer lies within the riddle are relatively common. Nos 119 and 128 are further examples.

No.116

A riddle, a riddle, as I suppose
A hundred eyes, but never a nose.
A potato

Unidentified Female, aged c.12, Priestman Middle School, Bradford, 21.9.94.

Notes

See Bryant, 1994, No.1398.

No.117

Thirty white horses on a red hill
First they champ, then they stamp,
Then they stand still.
Teeth

Unidentified Male, aged c.14, Sir James Smith's School, Camelford,
1.3.95.

Notes

Another riddle which I have heard many times from teenagers. Taylor cites a
number of variants (1977, Nos 502-10).

No.118

Alive without breath,
As cold as death,
Never thirsty, ever drinking,
All in mail, never clinking.
A fish

Unidentified Male, aged c.14, Sir James Smith's School, Camelford,
1.3.95.

Notes

See Bryant, 1977, No.1355. Bryant attributes this riddle to Tolkein and
quotes an identical text to the one above. However, I have heard variants of
the riddle on a number of occasions, from both teenage and non-teenage
riddlers, including the following from a colleague:

Always drinking, never thirsty,
Cold in life, colder in death.

No.119*

Two twins were born in March, but had birthdays in May. One was twenty
and the other was twenty-two, and then they married each other.
*The twins were born in the town of March in the month of May. One was
twenty and the other was twenty too, and they both married each other
because they were both vicars officiating at each other's wedding.*

Unidentified male, aged 12, Falmouth Community School, Cornwall, 14.7.93.

p.171

Notes

An example of a riddle which contains the answer within the question. See
also Opie & Opie, 1959, p.85 for a distant variant.

No.120*

If you have two haystacks at the front and thirteen haystacks at the back and
you put them together, how many do you get?
One big haystack

Unidentified male, aged c.12, Audley Park Secondary School, Torquay,
14.5.92.

p.171-2

No.121

An electric train is driving along at seventy miles per hour. The wind is
blowing at the same speed in the opposite direction. Which way does the
smoke blow?
It doesn't. There's no smoke, because it's an electric train.

Unidentified male, aged c.12, Gillingham School, Dorset, 12.11.92.

Notes

The presence of the electric train at the centre of the riddle suggests it is of a modern pedigree. Catch riddles themselves are, of course, highly traditional and very popular amongst teenagers. This particular one is very widespread.

No.122*

One train leaves Dublin for Galway at 100 m.p.h. Another leaves Galway for Dublin at 50 m.p.h. When they meet, which one is nearer Dublin?
They are both in the same place when they meet.

Unidentified male, aged c.12, St. Martin de Porres National School, Tallaght, Dublin, 23.11.94.

pp.178-9

No.123*

An electric train leaves Dublin for Cork and a steam train leaves Cork for Dublin. When they meet, which one is nearer Dublin?
They are both in the same place when they meet.

Unidentified male, aged c.11, Scoilmhuire, Ballyboden, Dublin, 24.11.94.

pp.178-9

No.124

A peacock sits on top of a gabled roof and lays an egg. Which way does it fall?
Peacocks don't lay eggs.

Unidentified Male, St. Martin de Porres National School, Tallaght, Dublin, 23.11.94.

Notes

Another catch riddle that is popular throughout Britain as well as Ireland.

No.125

There's an elephant, and it lays an egg on the top of a mountain. Which way will the egg roll?
Elephants don't lay eggs.

James, aged c.13, Coombe Dean Comprehensive School, Plymouth, 18.10.93.

Notes

A variant of No.124, but one that is much easier to spot as a catch riddle. The peacock (or another male bird) is, in my experience, the most common variant.

No.126

There's a blue house and a green house and a white house. What colour's the green house?
No colour. Greenhouses are made out of glass.

Christian, aged 14, Sir James Smith's School, Camelford, 1.3.95.

Notes

Another commonly told catch riddle that exists in many variant forms. Sometimes the audience is told that the stairs in the blue house are blue, and then asked what colour the stairs in the green house are, or some other such variation.

No.127

There's a hole one metre wide and one metre deep. How much mud in it?
None. Holes are empty.

Christian, aged 14, Sir James Smith's School, Camelford, 1.3.95.

Notes

Holes seem to feature quite regularly in riddles, especially catch riddles. The following, from a young riddler, is not strictly a variant of the above riddle, but certainly of the same tradition:

> If one man digs one hole in an hour, how long will it take three
> men to dig three holes?
> *It depends on the size of the hole.*

John Peters, aged 10, Okehampton College Playscheme, 27/28.8.92.

No.128

If there are ninety (nine tea) cups and one gets broken, how many are left?
Eight tea cups

Unidentified Male, aged c.13, Sir James Smith's School, Camelford, 15.2.95.

Notes

This riddle is another punning catch riddle where the answer lies within the question. Another riddle that works in a similar way, and which is well-known with teenage and non-teenage audiences alike, is the following:

> If there are fifty-six sheep in a field and one dies, how many are left?
> *Forty-nine sick sheep*

No.129*

What do you brush your teeth with, sit in and sleep on?
A toothbrush, a chair and a bed

Joanne Simons, aged 10, Glusburn C P School, W. Yorkshire, 10.10.91.

pp.166, 171

No.130*

There's this man and he's travelling towards this field and when he hit the field, he knew he was going to die and he had a pack on his back. What do you think that is?
It was a parachute and the parachute hadn't opened.

David Price, aged 11, Gillingham School, Dorset, 11.11.92.

p.165

No.131*

A man in the desert. Around him is a solid concrete box and around that, a hedge. All he has is a plank of wood. How does he escape?
He rubs his hands until they are sore. He uses the saw to saw the wood in half. Two halves make a whole, so he climbs through the hole. Then he shouts until he is hoarse, then jumps on the horse and rides away over the hedge.
Unidentified male, aged 12, Ivybridge Community College, 22.3.94.

pp.170-1

Notes

A very widespread punning riddle amongst teenage audiences. Other solutions include the man singing a note until he finds the right key, then using the key to unlock a door. The man also sometimes escape over a ditch by sitting around until he gets bored and then using the board to bridge the ditch!

No.132

There's a man in this room with no door, just one window, all bars, just one big whole room and he saw a table in the corner and a chair.

So he saw the table in half, two halves make a whole and out he escaped.

And he shouted until his voice was hoarse, and you get on the horse and ride away.

Unidentified male, aged c.11, Okehampton College Playscheme, Devon, 27/28.8.92.

Notes

A common variant of No.131, but this time the riddle is told as a story rather than a question being posed.

No.133*

A man lives at the top of a block of flats and gets the lift down to work in the morning. When he returns home, he only goes to the top when it is raining. Why?
He's a dwarf and only uses his umbrella to reach the button on a rainy day.

Unidentified male, aged c.12, Ivybridge Community College, 22.3.94.

pp.173-4

Notes

Of all the logic ridles so popular with teenagers, this one is probably the one most widely known, although the variant above is incomplete. I would normally expect around fifty per cent of any teenage group to be familiar with this particular riddle.

No.134*

A man goes into his house, climbs the stairs and turns off the light. In the morning he shoots himself. Why?
He is a lighthouse keeper.

Unidentified male, aged c.12, Eggbuckland Community College, Plymouth, 15-17.3.94.

p.174

No.135*

A man is walking along the road when he comes across a puddle of water with a carrot and two lumps of coal in it. The sun is shining. What has happened?
A snowman has melted.

Unidentified male, aged c.12, King Edward VI School, Totnes, 7.12.93.

pp.174-5

No.136

These three boys went to get a meal and they paid for it. The waiter gave them the bill - £10 each, £30 all together. And they complained it was cold, so the waiter told the manager. The manager said, 'Give them £5 off', so the waiter went back in and said, 'There's three of them and there's £5.' So he put £2 in his pocket and give each of them £1 back, so they've each paid £9. £27 plus the £2 in his pocket, £29.

Richard, aged c.14, Oakgrove Integrated College, Derry, N. Ireland, 2.3.94.

Notes

The purpose of this riddle is for the audience to try and find out what happened to the missing pound. There is a very simple maths error in the story which is disguised in the telling to make it very difficult to identify. At the end of the story, the £2 should be taken off the £27, rather than added on to make £25, which is the amount in the till and the actual cost of the meal - a figure that is deliberately never mentioned.

Richard told this story as a result of my telling his class a variant which involved three travelling salesmen staying in a hotel. I had set the story in my home village. At the end of the story, Richard announced that the story had actually happened to three lads in a restaurant in Omagh and proceeded to tell his story!

No.137*

As I was going to St. Ives
I met a man with seven wives
Each wife had seven sacks
Each sack had seven cats
Each cat had seven kittens.
How many were going to St. Ives?
One

Unidentified Female, aged c.14, Audley Park Secondary School, Torquay, 4.2.92.

p.178

Notes

A very well-known rhyming riddle, that is popular throughout Britain and Ireland and not just in South-West England.

No.138*

There once was a man who'd gone to St. Ives
He passed a man with seven wives
Seven wives had seven bags
In the seven bags were seven children
The seven children had seven cats
The seven cats had seven kittens.

So how many people were going to St. Ives?
One

Ian Gillard, aged 11, Plymstock Comprehensive School, Plymouth, 3.11.92.

p.178

Further Appendices

Appendix 2: Interview with Jayne Tucker, South Zeal, re 'Mad Axeman', 25.8.94

MW: Just tell me what you told me before.

JT: Which was what?

MW: About Mitchell. What you knew about him.

JT: Well, the only thing I can remember was when he escaped from Dartmoor, the day he escaped we were coming back from Exeter on the bus and they were searching all the buses, you know, searching all the traffic rather around Exeter and they searched our bus. That's a vague memory I've got. I couldn't have been very old. And then there was always this folklore about the Mad Axeman thing on Dartmoor that I can remember from being a kid, a teenager. And you saying about the Axeman story reminded me of the Axeman on Dartmoor, but that was actually based on fact rather than anything else. It was based on the fact that this guy escaped from prison on Dartmoor.

MW: So you're referring to a story that Frank Mitchell, the Mad Axeman was supposed to be still around on Dartmoor?

JT: Not necessarily that he was still around, not necessarily that he was still around, but if - when you heard stories about the Mad Axeman you tended to believe them, you knew this man had escaped from Dartmoor Prison and, I suppose, the implication was that it could be him. And it was just made all the more believable because of that, but not necessarily that it was him.

MW: When you say a Mad Axeman story, were there more than one, do you remember, or are you remembering specifically...?

JT: I only remember the.....When you were telling me the Mad Axeman story in the pub, I just remembered hearing a similar story, and I suppose it's now I'm confusing it with stories, I don't know. But I do vaguely remember a story about a woman being in a car on Dartmoor near Princetown and somebody banging the head on the car. That story.

MW: And that was the Mad Axeman story that you remember?

JT: Yeah. And I believed the story because of Frank Mitchell.

MW: So, when the story was told you were a teenager...?

JT: Well, I was young - I can't remember how old I was...

MW: You associated that story with Frank Mitchell?

JT: Yeah. And therefore, I believed it as being a true story.

MW: And can you remember that as being something that everybody said? I mean do you remember that as being a popular story at that time and being specifically related to Frank Mitchell? Did the storytellers explain that link?

JT: Yes, I suppose. I don't remember how old I was, but I must have been in the early years of my secondary school, so I suppose it was popular with my peer group. Especially 'cos at that age I didn't mix with boys, you know, it was a peer group of girls and there was all this sort of giggly, girly talk about a Mad Axeman up on the Moor and I suppose there were undertones of sexuality developing - this man up on the Moor as this threat to good clean girls. But, I mean, I don't remember specifics, I can't remember the exact story - it's just a vague recollection of a period. It's like a period of jokes that go round, like knock-knock jokes would be trendy for a while and then they fade off, and I suppose this story at that time was going around. And then there was all this stuff in the paper about him, about before he escaped he used to drink in this pub on the Moor and there became like a whole sort of thing about Frank Mitchell, you know, being given a free rein up at Dartmoor Prison to do as he pleased, and I suppose that just added to the mystery of this Mad Axeman up on Dartmoor.

MW: And were you aware of this story before?

JT: No.

MW: But that may have been to do with your age? You were only nine when he escaped.

JT: Yeah.

MW: Can you remember anything else about the time he escaped? Were people worried? Was it a big talking point? When you say the bus was searched on the way back from Exeter...

JT: Yes, I think it was. I remember saying, joking to my mum, because Marilyn (Jayne's sister) was going out with Peter at that time and they used to drive back from Plymouth. They used to go back to Plymouth at weekends - it was when she was working in Plymouth or something - anyway, she used to drive back from Plymouth or drive down to Plymouth at nights sometimes with Peter and I used to say about the Axeman on the Moor and stuff. And my mum used to get quite wound up about that. And so, yeah, people did....it was a concern, I suppose, but, as I say, I was quite young and I don't really remember all the details. I suppose it must have been quite a big thing for the things to have stuck in my mind really. OK, the bus being searched would obviously stick in my mind. Whether it was just my peer group it was quite important to, because that's when you're getting in to all the horror stories and stuff and maybe that's what....it just happened when I was at an age when it would hold some fascination for me. But as far as I can remember, yes, it was a fairly big thing and certainly my peer group would have had concerns about it.

MW: But certainly specifically in your mind now, and as you remember as a young adolescent, when that particular story was told of the head banging on the roof and all that, that was a story told about the Mad Axeman and that was specifically linked to Frank Mitchell?

JT: Yeah, I think so. Certainly in my mind it was and I think it was in general. In my peer group I'm sure it was. I'm sure it wasn't just me who made that association and I'd like to remember if it was totally, 'Oh, you know that Frank Mitchell, the Mad Axeman,' but I can't remember. It might well have been, but also might not have been. It could just have been me thinking....

MW: But you do remember that it was told as a Mad Axeman? This wasn't just a story about a lunatic on the Moor....?

JT: Oh no! It was definitely 'Mad Axeman'. Because all the newspapers called him a Mad Axeman, anyway. I couldn't even remember his name, it was always the Mad Axeman. You never talked about Frank Mitchell, you talked about the Mad Axeman. So the Mad Axeman 'joke' would, therefore, stick in my mind as about Frank Mitchell. I think.

MW: Yeah, that's OK.

Note

For purposes of this interview when it is not clear whether it is Frank Mitchell, the Mad Axe-Man, or the Mad Axeman character in the story that is being referred to, I have resorted to using the non-hyphenated 'Mad Axeman' in all cases to avoid confusion.

Appendix 3: The Story of Grandmother

There was a woman who had made some bread. She said to her daughter: 'Go carry this hot loaf and a bottle of milk to your granny.'

So the little girl departed. At the crossway she met *bzou*, the werewolf, who said to her:

'Where are you going?'

'I'm taking this hot loaf and a bottle of milk to my granny.'

'What path are you taking,' said the werewolf, 'the path of needles or the path of pins?'

'The path of needles,' the little girl said.

'All right, then I'll take the path of pins.'

The little girl entertained herself by gathering needles. Meanwhile the werewolf arrived at the grandmother's house, killed her, put some of her meat in the cupboard and a bottle of her blood on the shelf. The little girl arrived and knocked at the door.

'Push the door,' said the werewolf, 'it's barred by a piece of wet straw.'

'Good day, Granny. I've brought you a hot loaf of bread and a bottle of milk.'

'Put it in the cupboard, my child. Take some of the meat which is inside and the bottle of wine on the shelf.'

After she had eaten, there was a little cat which said: 'Phooey!....A slut is she who eats the flesh and drinks the blood of her granny.'

'Undress yourself, my child,' the werewolf said, 'and come and lie down beside me.'

'Where should I put my apron?'

'Throw it into the fire, my child, you won't be needing it any more.'

And each time she asked where she should put all her clothes, the bodice, the dress, the petticoat, and the long stockings, the wolf responded:

'Throw them into the fire, my child, you won't be needing them any more.'
When she laid herself down in the bed, the little girl said:
'Oh, Granny, how hairy you are!'
'The better to keep myself warm, my child!'
'Oh, Granny, what big nails you have!'
'The better to scratch me with, my child!'
'Oh, Granny, what big shoulders you have!'
'The better to carry the firewood, my child!'
'Oh, Granny, what big ears you have!'
'The better to hear you with, my child!'
'Oh, Granny, what big nostrils you have!'
'The better to snuff my tobacco with, my child!'
'Oh, Granny, what a big mouth you have!'
'The better to eat you with, my child!'
'Oh, Granny, I've got to go badly. Let me go outside.'
'Do it in the bed, my child!'
'Oh no, Granny, I want to go outside.'
'All right, but make it quick.'
The werewolf attached a woollen rope to her foot and let her go outside.

When the little girl was outside, she tied the end of the rope to a plum tree in the courtyard. The werewolf became impatient and said: 'Are you making a load out there? Are you making a load?'

When he realised that nobody was answering him, he jumped out of bed and saw that the little girl had escaped. He followed her but arrived at her house just at the moment she entered.
(Zipes, 1993, pp.21-3)

Appendix 4: List of schools, libraries and youth clubs where fieldwork was conducted

Avon

Ashton Park Secondary School, Bristol

Bedfordshire

Hastingsbury Upper School, Bedford
Mill Vale Middle School, Dunstable
Youth House, Bedford

Berkshire

Trevelyan Middle School, Windsor

Cornwall

Brannel School, St. Austell
Bugle Youth Club
Callington Community College
Camborne School
Falmouth Community School
Falmouth Youth Club
Looe School
Mullion School, The Lizard
Penrice School, St. Austell
Poltair School, St. Austell

Redruth School
St. Dennis Youth Club
St. Stephen's Youth Club
Sir James Smith's Community School, Camelford
Treverbyn Youth Club, Stenalees, St. Austell
Young People Cornwall, Penzance

Devon

Audley Park Secondary School, Torquay
Austin Park Primary School, Plymouth
Bideford Community College
Braunton School
Chulmleigh Community College
Clyst Vale Community College
Combeshead College, Newton Abbot
Coombe Dean Comprehensive School, Plymstock, Plymouth
Dyron's Leisure Centre, Newton Abbot
Eggbuckland Community College, Plymouth
Ernesettle Library, Plymouth
Estover Community College, Plymouth
Exmouth Community College
Hele's School, Plympton
Hyde Park Primary School, Plymouth
Ivybridge Community College
John Kitto Community College, Plymouth
King Edward VI School, Totnes
Lipson Community College, Plymouth
Lydford Youth Club
Okehampton College
Okehampton College Playscheme
Paignton Community College
Peverell Library, Plymouth
Plymstock Comprehensive School, Plymouth
Preston Primary School, Torquay
Pyworthy Youth Club
Sidmouth Community College
South Molton Community College
South Tawton Primary School, Okehampton
South Zeal Youth Club, Okehampton
Southway Comprehensive School, Plymouth

Sparks Youth Club, Okehampton
Tamarside School, Plymouth
Teignmouth Community College
Upottery Primary School

Dorset

Budmouth School, Weymouth
Gillingham School
Wey Valley School, Weymouth

Gloucestershire

Brockworth Youth Club, Gloucester
Cinderford Youth Club
Cleeve School, Cheltenham
Heywood School, Cinderford
Wooton-under-Edge Youth Centre

Hampshire

St. Luke's Secondary School, Portsmouth

Kent

Archbishop Secondary School, Canterbury
Channel High School, Folkestone
Cheyne Middle School, Sheerness, Isle of Sheppey
Danley Middle School, Sheerness, Isle of Sheppey
Minster College, Isle of Sheppey
St. George's Middle School, Sheerness, Isle of Sheppey
St. George's Secondary School, Broadstairs
Sheerness Youth Club, Isle of Sheppey
Simon Langton Girls' School, Canterbury

Lincolnshire

Chapel St. Leonard's Primary School
Tetney Primary School

London

Queen's Gate School, Kensington

North Yorkshire

Austwick C.E. Primary School

Oxfordshire

Fitzharrys School, Abingdon

Somerset

Wells Cathedral School

South Yorkshire

Hatfield High School, Doncaster

Sussex

Patcham High School, Brighton

West Yorkshire

Glusburn Primary School, Keighley
Priestman Middle School, Bradford

Northern Ireland

Claudy Secondary School, Co. Derry
Faughan Valley Secondary School, Derry
Fountain Youth Club, Derry
Oakgrove Integrated College, Derry
St. Brecan's Secondary School, Derry
St. Cecilia's Secondary School, Derry
St. Mary's Secondary School, Derry

Republic of Ireland

Bishop Galvin National School, Willington, Dublin
Bray School Project National School, Co. Wicklow
Dalkey School Project National School, Glenageary, Dublin
Douglas Girls' National School, Cork
Eglantine Girls' National School, Cork
Gael Scoil Inse Chor, Inchicore, Dublin
St. Joseph's Boys' National School, Terenure, Dublin
St. Martin de Porres National School, Tallaght, Dublin
St. Patrick's Senior National School, Corduff, Dublin
St. Peter's Boys' National School, Greenhills, Dublin
Scoil Olibhear, Ballyvolane, Cork
Scoilmhuire, Ballyboden, Dublin

Bibliography

Books and articles directly cited or referred to

Aarne, A. A. and Thompson, Stith (1961), *The Types of the Folk-Tale: a Classification and Bibliography*, 2nd rev. ed., Folklore Fellows Communications 75: Helsinki.

Abrahams, Roger and Dundes, Alan (1972), 'Riddles', in Dorson, Richard (ed.), *Folklore and Folklife*, University of Chicago Press: Chicago, pp.129-43.

Baker, Ronald L. (1976), 'The Influence of Mass Culture on Modern Legends', *Southern Folklore Quarterly*, vol. 40, pp.367-76.

Bakhtin, Mikhail (1984), *Rabelais and his World*, Indiana University Press: Bloomington.

Barnes, Daniel R. (1984), 'Interpreting Urban Legends', *ARV*, vol. 40, pp.67-78.

Bascom, William R. (1965), 'Folklore and Anthropology', in Dundes, Alan (ed.), *The Study of Folklore*, Prentice-Hall: New Jersey.

Bauman, Richard (1972), 'The La Have Island General Store: Sociability and Verbal Art in a Nova Scotia Community', *Journal of American Folklore*, vol. 85, pp.330-41

(1977), *Verbal Art as Performance*, Waveland Press: Illinois.

(1986), *Story, Performance and Event: Contextual Studies of Oral Narrative*, Cambridge University Press: Cambridge.

Bauman, Richard and Paredes, Americo (eds.) (1972), *Towards New Perspectives in Folklore*, University of Texas Press: Austin.

Bausinger, Hermann (1990), *Folk Culture in a World of Technology*, Dettmer, Elke (trans.), Indiana University Press: Bloomington and Indianapolis.

Ben-Amos, Dan (1990), 'Foreword', in Bausinger, Hermann, *Folk Culture in a World of Technology*, Indiana University Press: Bloomington and Indianapolis.

Ben-Amos, Dan (ed.) (1976), *Folklore Genres*, University of Texas Press: Austin.

Ben-Amos, Dan and Golstein, Kenneth S. (eds.) (1975), *Folklore: Performance and Communication*, Mouton: The Hague.

Bennett, Gillian (1984), 'The Phantom Hitchhiker: Neither Modern, Urban nor Legend?', in Smith, Paul (ed.), *Perspectives on Contemporary Legend*, CECTAL: Sheffield, pp.45-63.

(1988), 'Legend: Performance and Truth', in Bennett, Gillian and Smith Paul (eds.), *Monsters with Iron Teeth: Perspectives on Contemporary Legend*, vol.III, Sheffield Academic Press: Sheffield, pp.13-36.

Bennett, Gillian and Smith, Paul (eds.) (1988), *Monsters with Iron Teeth: Perspectives on Contemporary Legend*, vol.III, Sheffield Academic Press: Sheffield.

(1989), *The Questing Beast: Perspectives on Contemporary Legend*, vol.IV, Sheffield Academic Press: Sheffield.

(1990a), *A Nest of Vipers: Perspectives on Contemporary Legend*, vol.V, Sheffield Academic Press: Sheffield.

(1990b), *Contemporary Legend - The First Five Years: Abstracts and Bibliographies from the Sheffield Conferences on Contemporary Legend 1982-1986*, Sheffield Academic Press: Sheffield.

Bennett, Gillian, Smith, Paul and Widdowson, J. D. A (eds.) (1987), *Perspectives on Contemporary Legend*, vol.II, Sheffield Academic Press: Sheffield.

Bolte, Johannes and Polivka, Georg (1913), *Anmerkungen zu den Kinder und Hausmärchen der Brüder Grimm*, Dieterich'sche Verlagsbuchhandlung: Leipzig.

Boyes, Georgina (1984), 'Belief and Disbelief: An Examination of Reactions to the Presentation of Rumour Legends', in Smith, Paul (ed.), *Perspectives on Contemporary Legend*, CECTAL: Sheffield, pp.64-78.

(1989), 'Women's Icon, Occupational Folklore and the Media', in Bennett, Gillian and Smith, Paul (eds.), *The Questing Beast: Perspectives on Contemporary Legend*, vol.IV, Sheffield Academic Press: Sheffield, pp.117-32.

Briggs, Katherine (ed.) (1970), *A Dictionary of British Folk-Tales*, vols I-IV, Indiana University Press: Bloomington.

(1976), *A Dictionary of Fairies*, Penguin: London.

Brook, Peter (1972), *The Empty Space*, Penguin: London.

Bruner, Jerome (1990), *Acts of Meaning*, Harvard University Press.

Brunvand, Jan Harold (1981), *The Vanishing Hitchhiker: American Urban Legends and Their Meanings*, W. W. Norton: New York.

(1984), *The Choking Doberman*, (pbck ed. 1986), W. W. Norton: New York.

(1986), *The Mexican Pet*, (repr. ed. 1989, Penguin: London), W.W. Norton: New York..

(1990), *Curses! Broiled Again!*, W. W. Norton: New York.

Bryant, Mark (1994), *Dictionary of Riddles*, Cassell Publications Ltd: London.

Buchan, David (1981), 'The Modern Legend', in Green, A.E. and Widdowson, J.D.A. (eds.), *Language, Culture and Tradition*, CECTAL: Sheffield, pp.1-15.

Burns, Thomas A. (1976), 'Riddling: Occasion to Act', *Journal of American Folklore*, Vol. 89, pp.139-65.

Calvino, Italo (1980), *Italian Folktales*, Martin, George (trans.), Penguin: London.

Carroll, Michael P. (1987), '"The Castrated Boy": Another Contribution to the Psychoanalytic Study of Urban Legend', *Folklore*, Vol. 98ii, pp.216-25.

Carter, Angela (ed.) (1990), *The Virago Book of Fairy Tales*, Virago Press: London.

Child Sargent, Helen and Kittredge, George Lyman (eds.) (1904), *English and Scottish Popular Ballads from the Collection of Francis James Child*, London.

Cunningham, Keith (1990), '"I Have No Idea Whether That's True or Not": Belief and Narrative Event Enchantment', *Lore and Language*, Vol. 9ii, pp.3-14.

Dégh, Linda (1994), *American Folklore and the Mass Media*, Indiana University Press: Bloomington.

Dégh, Linda (ed.) (1980), *Indiana Folklore: A Reader*, Indiana University Press: Bloomington.

Dégh, Linda and Andrew Vàzsonyi (1974), 'The Memorate and the Proto-Memorate', *Journal of American Folklore*, Vol. 87, pp.225-39.

(1976) 'Legend and Belief', in Ben-Amos, Dan (ed.), *Folklore Genres*, University of Texas Press: Austin.

Dorson, Richard (ed.) (1972), *Folklore and Folklife*, University of Chicago Press: Chicago.

(1983), *A Handbook of American Folklore*, Indiana University Press: Bloomington.

Dundes Alan (1971), 'On the Psychology of Legend', in Hand. Wayland D. (ed.), *American Folk Legend: A Symposium*, University of California Press: Berkeley, Los Angeles and London, pp.21-36.

Dundes, Alan (ed.) (1965), *The Study of Folklore*, Prentice-Hall: New Jersey.

Dundes, Alan and Robert Georges (1963), 'Toward a Structural Definition of the Riddle', *Journal of American Folklore*, Vol. 76, pp.111-16.

Eagleton, Terry (1981), *Walter Benjamin or Towards a Revolutionary Criticism*, Verso.

Ellis, Bill (1982), 'Legend-Tripping in Ohio: A Behavioral Survey', *Papers in Comparative Studies*, Vol. 2, pp.61-73.

     (1987), 'Why Are Verbatim Texts of Legends Necessary?', in Bennett, Gillian, Smith, Paul and Widdowson, J.D.A. (eds.), *Perspectives on Contemporary Legend*, Vol.II, Sheffield Academic Press: Sheffield, pp.31-60.

     (1994), '"The Hook" Reconsidered: Problems in Classifying and Interpreting Adolescent Horror Legends', *Folklore*, Vol.105, pp.61-75.

Finnegan, Ruth (1992), *Oral Traditions and The Verbal Arts: A Guide to Research Practices*, Routledge: London and New York.

Glazer, Mark (1987), 'The Cultural Adaptation of a Rumour Legend: "The Boyfriend's Death" in South Texas', in Bennett, Gillian, Smith, Paul and Widdowson, J.D.A. (eds.), *Perspectives on Contemporary Legend*, Vol.II, Sheffield Academic Press: Sheffield, pp.93-108.

Goss, Michael (1990), 'The Halifax Slasher and Other Urban Maniac Tales', in Bennett, Gillian and Smith, Paul (eds.), *A Nest of Vipers: Perspectives on Contemporary Legend*, Vol. V, Sheffield Academic Press: Sheffield, pp.89-112.

Graves, Robert (1991), *The Greek Myths*, Cassell/Q.P.D.: London.

Green, A. E. and Widdowson, J. D. A. (eds.) (1981), *Language, Culture and Tradition*, CECTAL: Sheffield.

Green, Thomas A. and Pepicello, W. J. (1984), 'The Riddle Process', *Journal of American Folklore*, Vol. 97, pp.189-203.

Grider, Sylvia (1980), 'The Hatchet Man', in Dégh, Linda (ed.), *Indiana Folklore: A Reader*, Indiana University Press: Bloomington, pp.147-78.

     (1984) 'The Razor Blades in the Apple Syndrome', in Smith, Paul (ed.), *Perspectives on Contemporary Legend*, CECTAL: Sheffield, pp.128-40.

Grimm, Jakob and Wilhelm (1992), *The Complete Fairy Tales of the Brothers Grimm*, Zipes, Jack (trans.), Bantam: New York.

Halpert, H. (1971), 'Definition and Variation in Folk Legend', in Hand, Wayland D. (ed.), *American Folk Legend: A Symposium*, University of California Press: Berkeley, Los Angeles and London.

Hand, Wayland D. (ed.) (1971), *American Folk Legend: A Symposium*, University of California Press: Berkeley, Los Angeles and London.

Healey, Phil and Rick Glanvill (1992), *Urban Myths*, Virgin.

(1993), *The Return of Urban Myths*, Virgin.

Haring, Lee (1972), 'Performing for the Interviewer: A Study of the Structure of Context', *Southern Folklore Quarterly*, Vol. 36, pp.383-98.

(1974), 'On Knowing the Answer', *Journal of American Folklore*, Vol. 87, pp.197-207.

Hobbs, Sandy and Paul Smith (1990), 'Films Using Contemporary Legend Themes/Motifs', in Bennett, Gillian and Smith, Paul (eds.), , *Contemporary Legend - The First Five Years: Abstracts and Bibliographies from the Sheffield Conferences on Contemporary Legend 1982-1986*, Sheffield Academic Press: Sheffield, pp.138-48.

Hymes, Dell (1975), 'Breakthrough Into Performance', in Ben-Amos, Dan and Goldstein, Kenneth S. (eds.), *Folklore: Performance and Communication*, Mouton: The Hague.

Ives, Edward D. (1980), *The Tape-Recorded Interview*, University of Tennessee Press: Knoxville.

Jacobs, Joseph (1967), *English Fairy Tales*, Dover Publications.

Köngäs Maranda, Elli (1972), 'Theory and Practice of Riddle Analysis', in Bauman, Richard and Paredes, Americo (eds.), *Towards New Perspectives in Folklore*, University of Texas Press: Austin, pp.51-61.

Kotkin, Amy J. and Steven J. Zeitlin (1983), 'In the Family Tradition', in Dorson, Richard (ed.), *A Handbook of American Folklore*, Indiana University Press, Bloomington, pp.90-99.

Laba, Martin and Navàrez, Peter (eds.) (n.d.), *Media Sense: The Folklore-Popular Culture Continuum*, Bowling Green State University Popular Press: Bowling Green, Ohio

Langlois, Janet (1980), 'Mary Whales, I Believe in You', in Dégh, Linda (ed.), *Indiana Folklore: A Reader*, Indiana University Press, Bloomington, pp.196-224.

Lovelace, Martin (n.d.), 'Gossip, Rumour and Personal Malice: The Rhetoric of Radio Open-Line Shows', in Laba, Martin and Navàrez, Peter (eds.), *Media Sense: The Folklore-Popular Culture Continuum*, Bowling Green State University Popular Press: Bowling Green, Ohio.

McCoy Ray, Linda (1976), 'The Legend of Bloody Mary's Grave', *Indiana Folklore*, Vol. 9, pp.175-87

McGrath, John (1981), *A Good Night Out: Popular Theatre: Audience, Class and Form*, Methuen: London.

Mackenson, Lutz (1923), 'Der singende Knochen', FF Communications: Helsinki.

Messenger, John (1960), 'Anang Proverb-Riddles', *Journal of American Folklore*, Vol.73.

Opie, Iona (1993), *The People in the Playground*, Oxford University Press: Oxford.

Opie, Iona and Peter (1959), *The Lore and Language of Schoolchildren*, Oxford University Press: Oxford.

Pearson, John (1984), *The Profession of Violence*, Harper Collins: London.

Rosen, Betty (1988), *And None of It Was Nonsense*, Mary Glasgow Publications: London.

Rosen, Harold (1985), *Stories and Meanings*, NATE: Sheffield.

(1988) 'Stories of Stories: A Postscript', in Rosen, Betty, *And None of It Was Nonsense*, Mary Glasgow Publications: London, pp.163-72.

(1993), *Troublesome Boy*, English and Media Centre: London.

Schenda, Rudolf (1992), 'Folklore und Massenkultur' in *Tradition and Modernisation*, Nordic Institute of Folklore: Turku.

Simpson, Jacqueline (1981), 'Rationalized Motifs in Urban Legends', *Folklore*, Vol. 92.ii, pp.203-7.

Smith, Paul (ed.) (1984), *Perspectives on Contemporary Legend*, CECTAL: Sheffield.

Stahl, Sandra K.D. (1977a), 'The Personal Narrative as Folklore', *Journal of the Folklore Institute*. Vol.14, pp.9-30.

(1977b), 'The Oral Personal Narrative in Its Generic Context', *Fabula*, Vol.18, pp.18-39.

(1983), 'Personal Experience Stories', in Dorson, Richard (ed.), *A Handbook of American Folklore*, Indiana University Press: Bloomington, pp.268-76.

(1985), 'A Literary Folkloristic Methodology for the Study of Meaning in Personal Narratives', *Journal of Folklore Research*, Vol. 22, pp.45-69

Taylor, Archer (1977), *English Riddles from Oral Tradition*, Octagon Books: New York.

Thompson, Stith (1977), *The Folktale*, University of California Press: Berkeley and Los Angeles.

Utley, Francis Lee (1965), 'Folk Literature: An Operational Definition', in Dundes, Alan (ed.), *The Study of Folklore*, Prentice-Hall: New Jersey.

Zipes, Jack (1992) *Breaking the Magic Spell: Radical Theories of Folk and Fairy Tales*, (repr. ed.), Routledge: New York.

(1993), *The Trials and Tribulations of Little Red Riding Hood*, (2nd ed.), Routledge: New York.

Other books and articles consulted in the preparation of this book

Babcock, Barbara A. (1977), 'The Story in the Story: Metanarration in Folk Narrative', in Bauman, Richard, *Verbal Art as Performance*, Waveland Press: Illinois, pp.61-79.

Baker, Ronald L. (1983), 'The Folklore of Students', in Dorson, Richard (ed.), *Handbook of American Folklore*, Indiana University Press: Bloomington, pp.106-14.

Ballard, Linda M. (1984), 'Tales of the Troubles', in Smith, Paul (ed.), *Perspectives on Contemporary Legend*, CECTAL: Sheffield, pp.1-17.

Bauman, Richard (1972), 'Differential Identity and the Social Base of Folklore' in Bauman, Richard and Paredes, Americo (eds.), *Toward New Perspectives in Folklore*, University of Texas Press: Austin.

(1983), 'The Field Study of Folklore in Context', in Dorson, Richard (ed.), *Handbook of American Folklore*, Indiana University Press: Bloomington, pp.362-8.

Ben-Amos, Dan (1972), 'Toward a Definition of Folklore in Context', in Bauman, Richard and Paredes, Americo (eds.), *Toward New Perspectives in Folklore*, University of Texas Press: Austin.

Bennett, Gillian (1987), 'Problems in Collecting and Classifying Urban Legends', in Bennett, Gillian, Smith, Paul and Widdowson, J.D.A. (eds.), *Perspectives on Contemporary Legend*, Vol.II, eds., Sheffield Academic Press: Sheffield, pp.15-30.

Bennett, Gillian and Paul Smith (eds.) (1991) 'Contemporary Legend: An Insider's View', *Folklore*, Vol.102.ii, pp.187-91.

Brunvand, Jan Harold (1984), 'The Choking Doberman: A New Urban Legend', in Smith, Paul (ed.), *Perspectives on Contemporary Legend*, CECTAL: Sheffield, pp.79-98.

(1993), *The Baby Train and Other Lusty Urban Legends*, W. W. Norton: New York.

Cunningham, Keith (1981), 'Mr Hook Meets Thump-Thump', *Southwest Folklore*, Vol. 5.iv, pp.52-8.

Dégh, Linda (1969), *Folktales and Society*, Indiana University Press: Bloomington.

Dorson, Richard (1968), *The British Folklorists*, Routledge and Kegan Paul: London.

Dundes, Alan (1965), 'What is Folklore?', in Dundes, Alan (ed.), *The Study of Folklore*, Prentice-Hall: New Jersey.

Ellis, Bill (1981), 'The Camp Mock-Ordeal: Theater as Life', *Journal of American Folklore*, Vol. 94, pp.486-505.

(1983), 'De Legendis Urbis: Modern Legends in Ancient Rome', *Journal of American Folklore*, Vol. 96, pp.200-8.

(1984), 'The Vanishing American Legend: Oral Narrative and Textmaking in the 1980s', *Lore and Language*, Vol. 8.ii, pp.75-102

(1991), 'Contemporary Legend - Cracks or Breakthroughs?', *Folklore*. Vol.102.ii, pp.183-6.

Gennette, Gerard (1980), *Narrative Discourse*, Cornell University Press: Ithaca.

Georges, Robert A. (1969), 'Toward an Understanding of Storytelling Events', *Journal of American Folklore*, Vol. 82, pp.313-28.

Glazer, Mark (1985), 'The Traditionalization of the Contemporary Legend: The Mexican American Example', *Fabula*, Vol. 26, pp.288-97.

Green, Thomas A. and Pepicello, W.J. (1979), 'The Folk Riddle: A Redefinition of Terms', *Western Folklore*, Vol. 38, pp.3-20.

Halpert, Herbert and Widdowson, J. D. A. (1986), 'Folk Narrative Performance and Tape Transcription: Theory Vs Practice', *Lore and Language*, Vol. 5.1, pp.39-50.

Jason, Heda (1972), 'Concerning The "Historical" and The "Local" Legends and Their Relatives', in Bauman, Richard and Paredes, Americo (eds.), *Toward New Perspectives in Folklore*, University of Texas Press: Austin.

Kirkup, James (1984), *Modern American Myths: The Folktales of The Young Today in America*, New Currents International Co. Ltd: Tokyo.

Laba, Martin (n.d.) 'Popular Culture and Folklore: The Social Dimension' in Laba, Martin and Navàrez, Peter (eds.), *Media Sense: The Folklore-Popular Culture Continuum*, Bowling Green State University Popular Press: Bowling Green, Ohio, pp.9-18.

McDowell, John H. (1979), *Children's Riddling*, Indiana University Press: Bloomington.

Maclean, Marie (1988), *Narrative as Performance: The Baudelairean Experiment*, Routledge: London.

Ni Dhuibne, Eilis (1983), 'Dublin Modern Legends: An Intermediate Type List and Examples', *Béaloideas*, Vol. 51, pp.55-70.

Nicolaisen, W. F. H. (1984), 'Legends as Narrative Response', in Smith, Paul (ed.), *Perspectives on Contemporary Legend*, CECTAL: Sheffield, pp.167-78.

(1987), 'The Linguistic Structure of Legends' in Bennett, Gillian, Smith, Paul and Widdowson, J.D.A. (eds.), *Perspectives on Contemporary Legend*, Vol.II, Sheffield Academic Press: Sheffield, pp.61-76.

Niles, John (1989), 'The Berkeley Contemporary Legend Files', in Bennett, Gillian and Smith, Paul (eds.), *The Questing Beast: Perspectives on*

Contemporary Legend, Vol.IV, Sheffield Academic Press: Sheffield, pp.103-12.

Olrik, Axel (1965), 'Epic Laws of Folk Narrative', in Dundes, Alan (ed.), *The Study of Folklore*, Prentice-Hall: New Jersey.

Opie, Iona and Peter (1969), *Children's Games in Street and Playground*, Oxford University Press: Oxford.

(1985), *The Singing Game*, Oxford University Press: Oxford.

Peters, Nancy Kammer (1988), 'Suburban/Rural Variations in The Content of Adolescent Ghost Legends', in Bennett, Gillian and Smith, paul (eds.), *Monsters with Iron Teeth: Perspectives on Contemporary Legend*, Vol.III, Sheffield Academic Press: Sheffield, pp.221-35.

Propp, Vladimir (1968), *Morphology of The Folktale*, (2nd rev. ed.), Indiana University Press: Bloomington.

Roberts, Leonard (1983), 'A Family's Repertoire', in Dorson, Richard (ed.), *Handbook of American Folklore*, Indiana University Press: Bloomington, pp.100-5.

Samuelson, Sue (1981), 'European and American Adolescent Legends', *ARV*, Vol. 37, pp.133-9.

Smith, Georgina (1979), 'Aspects of Urban Legend as a Performance Genre', *Lore and Language*, Vol. 2.10, pp.41-4.

(1981a) 'The Social Bases of Tradition: The Limitations and Implications of "The Search for Origins"', in Green, A.E. and Widdowson, J.D.A. (eds.), *Language, Culture and Tradition*, CECTAL: Sheffield, pp.77-87.

(1981b) 'Urban Legend, Personal Experience Narrative and Oral History: Literal and Social Truth in Performance', *ARV*, Vol. 37, pp.167-73.

Smith, Paul S. (1981), 'Communication and Performance: A Model of the Development of Variant Forms of Cultural Traditions', in Green, A.E. and Widdowson, J.D.A. (eds.), *Language, Culture and Tradition*, CECTAL: Sheffield, pp.16-32.

Thoms, William (1965), 'Folklore', in Dundes, Alan (ed.), *The Study of Folklore*, Prentice-Hall: New Jersey.

Widdowson, J. D. A. (1981), 'Language, Tradition and Regional Identity: Blason Populaire and Social Control', in Green, A.E. and Widdowson, J.D.A. (eds.), *Language, Culture and Tradition*, CECTAL: Sheffield, pp.33-46.

Williams, Noel (1984), 'Problems in Defining Contemporary Legend', in Smith, Paul (ed.), *Perspectives on Contemporary Legend*, CECTAL: Sheffield, pp.216-28.

Yeats, W. B. (1993), *Writings on Irish Folklore, Legend and Myth*, Penguin: London.

Yerkovich, Sally (1983), 'Conversational Genres', in Dorson, Richard (ed.), *Handbook of American Folklore*, Indiana University Press: Bloomington, pp.278-81.

Zipes, Jack (1994), *Fairy Tale as Myth/Myth as Fairy Tale*, University Press of Kentucky: Lexington.